TOWER

PROJECT EVALUATION

Also by Arnold C. Harberger

THE DEMAND FOR DURABLE GOODS (editor)

THE TAXATION OF INCOME FROM CAPITAL (co-editor
with M. J. Bailey)

KEY PROBLEMS OF ECONOMIC POLICY IN
LATIN AMERICA (editor)

PAPERS IN ECONOMIC DEVELOPMENT

PROJECT EVALUATION

Collected Papers

ARNOLD C. HARBERGER
University of Chicago

The University of Chicago Press
Chicago

The University of Chicago Press, Chicago 60637

Published 1972 by The Macmillan Press Ltd. Midway Reprint 1976
Printed in the United States of America

International Standard Book Number: 0-226-31593-2

To my Parents

CONTENTS

PREFACE

This volume is the outgrowth of an interest in the area of social project evaluation that goes back more than a decade. Its greatest impetus was the result of a year (1961–62) spent in India collaborating with the Indian Planning Commission while serving as a staff member on the program maintained in New Delhi at that time by the MIT Center for International Studies. My work there carried me into the problems of estimating the social opportunity costs of labor and of capital and led me to worry about the interrelations between the two— interrelations that are demonstrated most explicitly in Chapter 3.

On returning from India, I gradually incorporated more and more material on project evaluation into a course on development planning and policy that I was teaching. This project-oriented material grew to the point where, within three years, it became an independent course of its own. All of the papers in this volume except Chapter 8 are on the current reading list of that course. Over the years variants of this course have been given in Argentina, Brazil, Canada, Chile, Colombia, Mexico, the Philippines, and Spain, and substantial portions have been presented annually in lectures at the Economic Development Institute of the World Bank. Chapters 1 and 2 come closest to giving a general overview of the theoretical basis of this course, while Chapters 4, 5, and 7 contain the more interesting theoretical 'innovations' in the field of project evaluation on which I have recently stumbled. In Chapter 4, I set out a measure for the social opportunity cost of capital in an economy with a reasonably well-functioning (though distorted) capital market. In Chapter 5, this contribution is briefly restated in summary mathematical form; it is also shown that the same concepts as those used in Chapter 4 to obtain a measure of the social opportunity cost of capital provide the basis for measuring the social opportunity cost of a material input or a final product on the one hand and for measuring that of foreign exchange on the other. Chapter 7 is a general analysis of the social opportunity cost of labor, but its novel contribution is a demonstration that in most cases of chronic (as distinct from cyclical) unemployment, labor's social opportunity cost, far from being zero as is often supposed, is actually likely to be in the range of observed market wages.

The remaining chapters are concerned with various applications. Both Chapter 6 and part of Chapter 8 are concerned with estimating the social yield of capital. In Chapter 6 a method is presented for obtaining such an estimate (for Colombia in this case) from national accounts data, and sensitivity tests show the resulting figure to be surprisingly robust—in the sense of being insensitive to quite substantial systematic errors in the basic data. In Chapter 8 explorations are made with several different methods to estimate the rate of return to physical capital in the modern industrial sector of India. These results are then compared with measures of the rate of return to investment in education in India, the estimation of which is the subject of the remainder of the chapter. Chapters 9 and 10 are basically expository, attempting to present the general principles underlying the analysis of electricity projects on the one hand and transportation (particularly highway) projects on the other. Special attention is given in Chapter 10 to the problem of congestion costs; it is shown that important externalities associated with congestion on other roads are likely to be present on most highway projects.

Chapter 11 is an example of project evaluation in practice, done jointly with Lucio G. Reca and Juan A. Zapata. In this evaluation of an irrigation dam, special attention is paid to the effect of the dam not only on the average volume of water likely to be available in the irrigation season, but also on the probability distribution of such water.

The final chapter consists of a report presented to the Presidential Task Force on International Development on some major issues in the field of foreign aid. Though its subject matter is not strictly comparable to that of the remaining chapters, it highlights some of the special problems associated with the international financing of projects and suggests guidelines for project lending as a form of development assistance.

Any collection of papers written over a significant span of

years probably contains some items that reflect the evolution of the author's own thinking, and probably some that he would prefer, with hindsight, to modify. In preparing the present volume, I have in general maintained the original text intact. Mainly, changes were limited to correcting typographical errors. The final section of Chapter 3 was added to bring in new material that had been covered in an earlier and somewhat overlapping paper, and the discussion of land values in Chapter 6 was completely revised, using better data than were available to me at the time of the initial writing. Section III of Chapter 9 was added in order to make the treatment more complete.

Concerning the evolution of my own thinking as it is reflected in this volume, there is just one matter on which I would like to comment. Until sometime in 1968, I firmly held the position that the marginal productivity (the social yield) of capital in the private sector was the appropriate rate of discount to use for public investment decisions in a market economy. This position is clearly reflected in Chapters 1, 2, and 3. Then, at some point in early 1968, I saw that the approach that I had been following for some time in measuring the social opportunity cost of commodities and of foreign exchange could be directly applied to measure the social opportunity cost of capital as well. The revised measure is, in its simplest form, a weighted average of the marginal productivity of capital and the marginal rate of time preference in the private sector, the weights being the elasticities of response of private investment on the one hand and of private saving on the other to changes in the rate of interest. I now believe that this weighted average is the 'correct' measure of the social opportunity cost of capital for countries such as the United States, Japan, and those of Western Europe, where a well-developed capital market exists. In these economies, the social opportunity cost of capital will be less than or equal to the social yield of private-sector capital since the marginal rate of private-sector time preference is measured by the private yield on savings, after all taxes, which generally is substantially lower than the marginal productivity of capital (measured gross of taxes). Given the fact that the responsiveness of saving to changes in the rate of interest probably will be low, if not zero, it is likely that the appropriate weighted average will be close to the marginal productivity concept to which I formerly subscribed. But be that as it may, my view as to what is the correct concept has definitely changed with respect to economies with developed capital markets.

I have not, on the other hand, changed my opinion with respect to countries without developed capital markets. For these economies, the relatively sophisticated model set out in Chapters 4 and 5 simply does not apply, and my views concerning the measurement of the social opportunity cost of capital for these cases remain essentially as set out in Chapters 1 through 3. This position is also reflected in the empirical measurements undertaken in Chapters 6 and 8.

In conclusion, I would like to express my thanks to David Wall for prodding me to get this volume into print and for helping with the initial selection and to Daniel Wisecarver for his valuable aid in the laborious task of checking the original text for errors and in the preparation of the material that was added. To Alyce Monroe my debt is unending, not just for her work in typing and preparing the copy, but also for the many ways in which, by helping ease for me the burdens of a very busy life, she contributes to my continued sanity. And finally to my wife and children, who, though they have accompanied me on many forays into the world to spread the messages contained in this volume, have waited at home on many others, my deepest gratitude for their patience and love.

CHAPTER ONE

TECHNIQUES OF PROJECT APPRAISAL

In this paper, I attempt to bring into focus what I believe to be some of the important practical issues that face development planners in the field of project appraisal. I shall try, insofar as possible, to recognize the handicaps under which planners operate, most importantly the handicaps imposed by imperfect foresight and by the virtual necessity of decentralized decision-making. To elaborate briefly on these handicaps, I think we must take it for granted that our estimates of future costs and benefits (particularly the latter) are inevitably subject to a fairly wide margin of error, in the face of which it makes little sense to focus on subtleties aimed at discriminating accurately between investments that might have an expected yield of 10½ percent and those that would yield only 10 percent per annum. As the first order of business we want to be able to distinguish the 10 percent investments from those yielding 5 or 15 percent, while looking forward hopefully to the day when we have so well solved the many problems of project evaluation that we can seriously face up to trying to distinguish 10 percent yields from those of 9 or 11 percent.

Moreover, in what follows, I shall try to bear in mind the virtual necessity of decentralized decision-making. Rules and procedures can be imposed which assure a certain rough harmony among the decisions taken in such vastly different areas as roads, irrigation projects, and educational investments, but one cannot realistically expect all investment decisions to be

Reprinted from Max F. Millikan, ed., *National Economic Planning* (New York: National Bureau of Economic Research, 1967), pp. 131–49. Reprinted by permission of National Bureau of Economic Research, New York, New York. Paper presented at the Conference on Economic Planning sponsored by the Universities–National Bureau Committee for Economic Research, November 1964.

funneled through a single office or authority that exercises more than a general supervisory power. Most of the real work connected with project appraisal must, I believe, be done 'close to the ground'; this fact alone limits the range of workable procedures to those in which a substantial amount of power can in fact be delegated to decentralized bodies.

Within this general framework the focus of the paper is mainly on the fact that the relevant prices may change through time. The first section discusses the problem of real wage changes. The second section discusses the problem of future changes in the discount rate; the third section, the choice of a time path for the discount rate; the fourth section, the choice of the level of the discount rate. The fifth section discusses shadow prices for labor and capital, again coming to rest on the problem of selecting time paths. Finally, the sixth section discusses time paths of other prices and of demand functions.

THE PROBLEM OF REAL WAGE CHANGES

Most discussions of project evaluation note that expected price changes should be taken into account, but little more than lip service is paid to this idea when working procedures are outlined. Insofar as the relative prices of commodities are concerned, this neglect of expected changes is understandable. 'On the average', our best guess is likely to be that relative prices will remain as they are; cases where we have good reason to believe they will change can probably be regarded as somewhat exceptional, and project analysts can perhaps be presumed to deal with these exceptional cases as they arise.

When, however, we come to the price of labor, the story is very different. A rise in the real wage rate is one of the essential features of economic development, and this means a rise in the price of labor relative to the general price level of the economy. If we normalize on the general price level, we can therefore say that the typical investment is likely to be one in which the price of the product to be produced is expected to remain constant while the wages paid to labor rise. If a private entrepreneur leaves out of account the expected rise in wages (relative to the general price level), he does so at his peril, for this fact can readily turn a potentially profitable project into an unprofitable one.

Consider a case in which the price and volume of the output of a project and the prices and volumes of material inputs are expected to remain constant into the indefinite future, yielding an amount of value added, gross of depreciation, that is expected to be constant at R_0 per year. Assume wages are also constant, amounting to L_0 per year. Then the present value of the income stream accruing to the capital invested in the project will be $(R_0 - L_0)/r$, where r is the rate of discount used. If we assume that the capital cost is equal to this present value, it is a barely acceptable project when evaluated at r percent. But now, suppose that the wage rate is expected to rise at λ percent per year, while the product price and materials prices are expected to remain constant. Then, in the first place, the project life ceases to be infinite, as the value of direct costs $L_0(1 + \lambda)^t$ will at some time come to exceed R_0, and the operation will not be worth continuing. Defining the life of the project, N, by $L_0(1 + \lambda)^N = R_0$, we have as the present value of the income stream accruing to the capital invested in the project

$$\left[\frac{R_0}{r} - \frac{L_0}{r - \lambda}\right] \left[1 - \frac{1}{(1 + r)^N}\right].$$

This falls short of the present value obtained in the previous case by

$$\frac{\lambda L_0}{r(r - \lambda)} + \left(\frac{R_0}{r} - \frac{L_0}{r - \lambda}\right) \left(\frac{1}{1 + r}\right)^N.$$

This can more conveniently be expressed as

$$\frac{L_0}{r} \left[\frac{\lambda}{(r - \lambda)} - \frac{r}{(r - \lambda)(1 + r)^N} + \frac{R_0}{L_0(1 + r)^N}\right].$$

To guess at the importance of this element, we must evaluate the term in square brackets for alternative plausible values of its parameters. Let us assume a rate of increase (λ) of real wages equal to 3 per cent per annum. The result then will depend only on the ratio R_0/L_0, from which N can be derived, and on the rate of discount, r. Table 1.1 presents some results that illustrate how important the 'wage-increase adjustment' is in different cases. As can be seen there, for the cases examined, the adjustment ranges from 20 percent to over 100 percent of

TABLE 1.1

Reductions in Present Value (ΔPV) Assuming a 3 Percent
Annual Increase in Wages as Against a Zero Rate of
Increase, Expressed as a Fraction of the Present
Value (L_0/r) of Wages Bill Assuming a Zero
Rate of Increase of Wages

R_0/L_0	1·159	1·344	1·558	1·806	2·094	2·427
Implied value of N (years)	5	10	15	20	25	30
$r\,\Delta PV/L_0$ assuming $r = \cdot 06$	·369	·634	·816	·941	1·021	1·074
$r\,\Delta PV/L_0$ assuming $r = \cdot 10$	·264	·384	·457	·482	·485	·484
$r\,\Delta PV/L_0$ assuming $r = \cdot 15$	·206	·272	·284	·274	·268	·261

L_0/r, the present value that would be computed for wage outlays if the wage rate were assumed not to change. For what I
consider to be the most relevant part of the table—$r = \cdot 10$ and
R_0/L_0 ranging between 1·5 and 2·5—the adjustment is consistently between 45 percent and 50 percent of the present
value of wages estimated, assuming the wage rate to be constant. Clearly this is not a negligible factor; I think the conclusion is obvious that the anticipated growth of real wages
should be built into project analyses as a matter of normal
operating procedure.[1]

FUTURE CHANGES IN THE DISCOUNT RATE

The discount rate used in cost-benefit analysis should reflect the
marginal productivity of capital in the economy as a whole.
Obviously, a fully optimal situation would require that the
marginal productivity of capital be the same in all applications
within the economy, and problems are created when, because
of capital market imperfections, differential rates of taxation
among activities, or other reasons, rates of marginal productivity vary from sector to sector. Let us waive these difficulties
for the moment, however, so as to be able to concentrate on
variations in the discount rate over time. Thus, in this section
we will be assuming a well-functioning capital market without
significant imperfections.

The key element that enables us to take account of variations
in the relative scarcity of investible funds is a discount rate that
changes as we move through time. If funds are particularly

scarce this year, but are expected to be relatively abundant in subsequent years, this fact might appropriately be reflected in, say, a 12 percent rate of discount applying to this year's flows of benefits and costs, and a more modest 8 percent rate applying to future flows. The present value of a project (*PV*) would then be found by the formula

$$PV = \sum_t \frac{N_t}{\prod_{i=1} (1 + r_i)}$$

where N_t represents the estimated excess of benefits over outlays in year t, and r_i is the rate of discount applicable to flows accruing during the year i.

This formulation also brings out clearly the method of analyzing the benefits or costs associated with the postponement of a project. Assume the project costs $1 million and yields a stream of benefits (net of current costs) of $100,000 per year in perpetuity starting in two years. Let the discount rate for all years from next year onward be 8 percent, and let the discount rate appropriate to this year be 20 percent. Then the present value of net benefits, evaluated as of next year, will be $1·25 million, and brought back to this year will be $1·04 million. Benefits thus exceed costs, if the project is undertaken this year, in the amount of $40,000.

But suppose it would also cost $1 million to do the project next year, and that in that event benefits would begin to accrue three years from now. In this case the present value of net benefits evaluated two years from now would again be $1·25 million, but brought one year from now they would be $1·16 million. From this sum we must deduct the project cost of $1 million, and discount the difference of $160,000 back to this year at 20 percent in order to obtain the present value of the project if undertaken next year. This yields a present value of $133,000—clearly higher than is obtained under the option of doing the project this year, and it thus pays to postpone the project for one year. It does not pay to postpone the project for two years, however, for in this case the net present value of the project must be discounted for an additional year at 8 percent, yielding a value of $123,000.

Actual problems of project postponement are likely to be

more complicated than that above, for postponement is likely to alter the size and time shape of the stream of net benefits, and also the capital costs of the project, rather than just displacing both benefits and costs through time. But the principle of evaluating benefits and costs under alternative assumed timing patterns remains valid when these complications are taken into account.

THE CHOICE OF A TIME PATH FOR THE RATE OF DISCOUNT

I should like to begin the discussion of this problem from a different starting point than is usually taken. What should be $r_{10}, r_{11}, r_{12}, \ldots, r_{20}$, etc.? That is, what should be the one-year discount rate applicable to flows 10, 11, 12, . . . , 20, etc., years in the future? One answer is surely clear: We have very little specific information on which to base such a judgment. But it is worthwhile to add a second statement: The limited information we have is very unlikely to lead us to judge that r_{10} should be ·08, r_{11} should be ·14, r_{12} should be ·10, etc. Even though we know that there will be cyclical and other short-term variations in the relevant rate of discount in the future, we do not know when they will occur, so our best guess as to the relevant rate for year 11 will not be very different from our best guess as to the relevant rate for year 10, etc. Thus we can conclude that the relevant rate for years in the far distant future will move, if at all, only as the result of the operation of basic secular forces.

Obviously, the marginal productivity of capital will be affected by many factors: the rate of capital formation, the rate of labor-force growth, the nature and degree of 'neutrality' or 'nonneutrality' of technical advance, the nature of changes in the pattern of demand, particularly of relative shifts toward or away from capital-intensive industries, etc. Some of these factors by themselves would work to produce a secularly rising rate of marginal productivity, others to produce a secularly declining rate. One obviously cannot be dogmatic about which set of forces will dominate in the long-term future, but I think that our past experience is relevant here. If we have had steady downward trends in series that we might take as reasonable indicators of the marginal productivity of capital, that would give us some basis for projecting a secular downward trend in the future. But I do not believe that the evidence can be read in this way. Whether one looks at interest rates, at rates of return on corporate capital, or at ratios of the rent of property to its value, no case can be made for a significant downward (or upward) secular tendency. In the face of the historic sluggishness of these series, I believe it is reasonable to project far-future rates of discount, for the purposes of cost-benefit analysis, to be constant and to be somewhere near the historical average of the most directly relevant past series.

This judgment greatly eases the burden on the project evaluator. He has basically three questions to answer: (1) What is the relevant long-term future rate of discount? (2) What is the relevant rate for the current year? (3) By what path will the relevant rate move from its current to its expected future level? We have already hinted at the answer to the first of these questions, so let us set that aside for a moment and turn to the second and third questions. A general answer is easy: When investible funds are relatively scarce this year and in the near-term future, relative to what is expected for the long-term future, the near-term rates of discount should be above the rate for the far future, and vice versa when investible funds are relatively abundant. Obviously, relative scarcity here incorporates both demand and supply factors, and I think that it should be fairly easy for project evaluators to have a good sense of whether they are in a year of glut or famine in this sense. Where really good capital markets exist, one can get a direct indication of the ease or stringency of the current relative to the expected future situation from the relationships of short-term relative to long-term interest rates. From the yield curve of loans and bonds by term to maturity, one can derive implicit expected one-year rates for each year in the future. This observed pattern can then be compared with the 'average' pattern of the past to see what 'abnormalities' exist. Where current short-term rates are relatively high, the difference $(r_t - \bar{r}_t)$, where r_t is the expected one-year rate applicable to the year t and $\bar{r}_t$ is the average of past expected rates applicable to times t years in the future, will tend to look like curve A in Figure 1.1. Where the situation is normal, the difference $(r_t - r_t)$ will tend to look like curve *B*, and when the situation is one of current glut, a curve like *C* will be likely to apply.

Although, for reasons to be indicated later, the level of interest rates on bonds and loans is likely to be a poor indicator

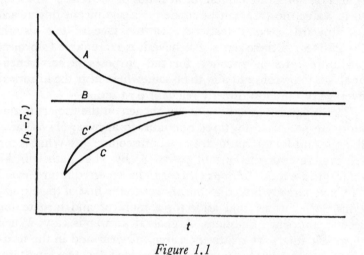

Figure 1.1

of the level of the relevant discount rate for cost-benefit analysis, the use of bond market information can give us clues as to the intensity of stringency or glut of investible funds in a given year, as to the length of time that the stringency or glut is likely to last (this being the length of time before the curve has effectively leveled out), and as to the expected pace at which the stringency or glut will be eased (compare *C* and *C'*). All of this information will be helpful to the planning authority in setting the time path of discount rates for cost-benefit work.

THE CHOICE OF THE LEVEL OF THE RATE OF DISCOUNT

We now return to question (1), above, distinguishing between the time-shape of curves representing the discount rate to be applied to flows in year *t* and their general level, perhaps best summarized by the common level of longer-term future one-year discount rates. I have already indicated that I believe this level should be set at approximately the average of the relevant rates in the past. But we do not have data on the marginal productivity of capital itself, and it certainly is not equalized across industries. I would choose here the average rate of return to capital for the economy as a whole, at least in cases in which this rate appears to have been relatively constant. In textbooks, when the average rate is constant, the marginal rate must equal the average, but we are dealing here with a considerably more complicated problem than the textbook example from which the above statement was drawn. It is not by any means necessary that the marginal rate of return from capital should have always been equal to the average, just because the average rate has been historically constant, and I must emphasize that the choice of the past average rate entails an element of judgment. What we can be dogmatic about is that one should use the marginal social rate of productivity of capital as the discount rate, that this rate includes taxes paid on the income from capital, as well as any other external effects not perceived by the individual investor, and that largely for the above reasons (principally the inclusion of taxes) the relevant rate is likely to be quite high compared with the observed rates on bonds, mortgages, etc.

One must recall that the purpose of the discount rate in cost-benefit analysis is to be a guide to decision-making. Suppose that we took some average of bond rates as the relevant one; virtually automatically, almost any corporate investment would pass the test of yielding a positive present value of benefits minus costs. This would be so because the benefits counted by corporate investors are net of tax, while the benefits relevant for social decision-making are gross of tax. Thus any corporate investment found privately acceptable at the market rate of interest, for example, would be socially an excellent investment; and many projects rejected by corporations because they fail to yield the market rate of interest net of tax would nonetheless have to be adjudged socially acceptable after including the tax component of benefits. Virtually no privately undertaken project would fail to pass the market-rate test, and many more would be added that would pass the market-rate test once taxes (let alone other social benefits) were included in the analysis. I cannot imagine that funds would be forthcoming from any source (private or public) to finance the volume of investments that would pass the market-rate test once we count social as well as private benefits.

On the other hand, if we use as the social rate of discount the rate including taxes, for example, existing private sector projects would 'on the average' pass the test, but some (with less-than-average taxes and normal post-tax yields, for example) would have negative present values while others (with higher-than-average taxes and normal post-tax yields, for example) would have positive present values. The decision rule implied by a tax-inclusive rate of discount would call for shifts in the allocation of investment from low-tax to high-tax fields—as well it should—but it would not normally call for any long-term major alteration in the propensity of the community to save.

Some writers appear to argue for a rate of discount reflecting social time-preference in some sense. Without attempting to argue the case in depth, let me note that such a procedure does not run into practical difficulties if one is able to generate a sufficient volume of savings so as to be able in fact to set in motion all the projects that pass the present-value test using such a rate. But I find it hard to support a policy that would force from the community the savings levels that would be required to do, say, all investments passing a 4 percent test, and difficult to believe that this would be possible to do even if desirable.

There is an argument for eliciting from the community more savings than it currently undertakes on the ground that, because of taxes and other possible 'externalities', the social yield of investment is higher than the private yield. But this argument would not justify extracting (perhaps by taxes) more savings from the community than it would be ready to make voluntarily if faced with a private yield equal to the social marginal productivity of capital—and the available studies of savings behavior do not show any powerful responsiveness of private savings to the private rate of return. Thus some supplementing of private savings by public savings appears to be justified, but not nearly so much as would be required to pull the typical rate of marginal productivity of capital in the economy down very substantially.

Other arguments that sometimes arise in discussions of this general point are (1) that the market mechanism fails to give a vote to future generations and therefore generates too little savings, (2) that private investors excessively discount the far future on grounds of risk, and (3) that private individuals would like to provide better for future generations than they do, if only this were done collectively, as they know that individually they can have little effect on future generations' standards of life. These arguments are discussed by Robert Strotz in a recent paper.[2] Strotz emphasizes, and I have long agreed, that the intergeneration comparison, as a normative problem, arises only if we expect future generations as a whole to be poorer than we are. There is no normative reason for making the present (poor) generation save more than it wants to in order to make future, richer generations still richer. On the risk-premium argument, Strotz notes that there are ample possibilities for risk-pooling, and that yields in industries of differential riskiness do not diverge widely from each other.[3] I would add that yield curves give us an even better way of isolating the relative discounts placed on the far-future as against near-future income, and that they provide no presumption of an excessive discount of the distant future. Consols have not gone begging for a market in this world, nor have 30- or 40-year bonds!

Argument (3), best reflected by Sen and Marglin,[4] smacks of charity. It already rests on a rather weak reed if it is assumed that future generations will in fact be better off than the present one. Such compassion as nonetheless exists for future generations is, however, dissipated because each individual's saving will presumably be reflected in negligibly small increments in the future welfare of many individuals. To avoid this a concerted effort of the present generation is needed, each individual's contribution being contingent upon those of the rest. My reaction to this is simple: Any individual who wants to help others and make sure that his contribution is not dissipated can do so by selecting one or more people of the present generation to help. By so doing he can be sure that the object of his charity is needy, and that all his charity will reach the desired object. Moreover, it is clear that by helping the youth of the present generation more fully to reach their productive potential and their human potential as individuals, one is likely to do much more for the generation of the year 2000 than by setting up a generalized trust fund in their favor.

I am thus left with recommending the observed past average social rate of return to capital as the best first approximation of the rate desirable for cost-benefit analysis. This rate should, of course, be modified whenever there are good reasons to expect that in the future the typical rate of social marginal productivity of capital will differ from that observed in the past, and for the present and near-future years should be modified whenever there is evidence of an abnormal scarcity or glut of investible funds.

SHADOW PRICES FOR LABOR AND FOR CAPITAL

It has come to be generally accepted that when prevailing prices do not reflect the true scarcity value of goods or services, one should substitute for them 'shadow prices' that in fact do so. There are many ramifications of this simple statement, and I shall not go into all of them here. For the moment let me focus on the shadow price of labor and on the shadow rate of return to capital.

The shadow price of labor should in some sense reflect the opportunity cost of such labor. When there is a substantial pool of unemployed labor, it is likely that the shadow price of that factor will be below the market price, and it is sometimes sustained that when there is really widespread unemployment in the economy, the shadow price of labor should be at or near zero.

Let me begin by attacking what is surely a straw man. Suppose an economy in which we can take it for granted that the shadow price of labor is zero. The wages bill of the nation is then, in effect, not a required payment to labor because of its scarcity-induced productivity, but rather a sort of transfer payment out of the 'true' marginal product of capital. If, for example, we have a capital stock of $30 billion and a national income of $10 billion divided equally between labor and capital, the full $10 billion should be counted as representing the social marginal product of capital, and the estimated rate of social productivity of capital should be $33\frac{1}{3}$ percent, not the $16\frac{2}{3}$ percent that we would estimate using the observed return to capital.

The point of this example is to emphasize that to the extent that we set the shadow price of labor below the market wage, we are obliged also to set the social marginal rate of productivity of capital above that which we would compute by counting all wages paid as true economic costs. As one pushes the shadow wage to zero, one simultaneously pushes the shadow rate of productivity of capital toward the ratio of national income to capital stock in the economy. With this come some rather embarrassing implications: A rate of discount as high as the income-capital ratio is virtually a kiss of death for projects with long gestation periods or long economic lives. Waiting cannot well be afforded at a 33⅓ percent rate of discount, and far-future incomes are virtually worthless when discounted back to the present at such a rate. Moreover, as one looks at the full equilibrium of an economy with a zero shadow wage, one finds that the appropriate prices for all goods are proportional to their capital-service components; that is, in such a full equilibrium, the ratio of net value added to capital would tend to be equal in all industries and sectors. I shudder at what this means for house rents, electricity prices, road charges, and the prices of the outputs of other similarly capital-intensive activities; and I doubt that any who may momentarily believe that a zero shadow price for labor is truly relevant for any given economy will continue to sustain this view after they follow through its full implications.[5]

In practice, the shadow wage for labor is, I venture to assert, never zero for the entire labor force and rarely zero for any significant part of it. But it certainly may fall below the actual wage for some occupations in many industries and for many occupations in some industries. To the extent that it does, the excess of the actual over shadow wage bill in any industry or sector should be attributed as part of the true economic yield of capital, and should thus tend to produce a discount rate for cost-benefit analysis that is higher than the observed gross-of-tax rate of return to capital.

But—and this is an extremely important point—it is hardly something to be hoped for that the shadow wage should forever remain below the actual wage. Unemployment, underemployment, market imperfections, all the forces that make for a discrepancy between actual and shadow wages, are things that one would hope and expect to be substantially reduced if not eliminated as an economy develops successfully. This has

important implications for cost-benefit analysis, which I shall try
to bring out in a simple example. For this example, let me
assume that we can take, for each year, the ratio of estimated
shadow income from capital to total capital stock as the relevant shadow rate of return to capital applicable to benefit and
cost flows during that year.

Let us start with the prospective total national income stream
shown in column (1) of Table 1.2, and disaggregated into factor

TABLE 1.2

Year	(1) National Income	(2) Labor Share at Market Prices	(3) Capital Share at Market Prices	(4) Shadow Wage as Percent of Market Wage	(5) Labor Share at Shadow Wage	(6) Capital Share at Shadow Prices
1	1,000	600	400	70	420	580
2	1,060	640	420	75	480	580
3	1,120	680	440	80	546	574
4	1,180	720	460	84	605	575
5	1,250	760	490	88	669	581
6	1,320	800	520	91	728	592
7	1,400	850	550	93	790	610
8	1,480	900	580	95	855	625
9	1,560	950	610	97	922	638
10	1,650	1,000	650	99	990	660

shares at market prices in columns (2) and (3). Column (5) is
generated on the assumption that the shadow wage, as a percentage of the market wage, follows the path shown in column
(4), and column (6) is obtained by subtracting column (5)
from column (1).

Now assume the series in Table 1.3 for the prospective level
of capital stock in each year. This series was so selected as to
yield a market rate of return (gross of taxes, of course) to
capital of 10 percent in each year.

The re-estimation of the shadow rate of return to capital,
year by year, to take account of the expected gradual elimination of the discrepancy between shadow and actual wages
obviously has the effect of bringing the shadow rate of return
to capital gradually into correspondence with the market rate
of return. Moreover, it leads to a decision rule which is much

TABLE 1.3

Year	Capital Stock	Capital Share at Shadow Prices	Market Rate of Return to Capital (percent)	Shadow Rate of Return to Capital (percent)
1	4,000	580	10·0	14·5
2	4,200	580	10·0	13·8
3	4,400	574	10·0	13·0
4	4,600	575	10·0	12·5
5	4,900	581	10·0	11·8
6	5,200	592	10·0	11·4
7	5,500	610	10·0	11·1
8	5,800	625	10·0	10·8
9	6,100	638	10·0	10·5
10	6,500	660	10·0	10·2

less discriminatory against capital-intensive or long-lived projects than a rule based solely on the initially prevailing shadow wage and the initially prevailing shadow rate of return to capital.

The technique just outlined of obtaining the time path of the shadow rate of return to capital is appealing in other ways as well. First, it is consistent with the over-all approach that was recommended above for a situation in which market prices were taken as a guide; in effect the 10 percent market rate of return to capital could be the observed past average of that rate, or that average adjusted in the light of prospective market developments. Second, it develops the shadow rate of return to capital on the basis of macroeconomic magnitudes of the type likely to be estimated by development planners. And third, it recognizes that the setting of the shadow rate of return to capital as something distinct from the gross-of-tax market rate of return should be based on the discrepancy between the wages bill for the total economy valued at market prices and the wages bill for the total economy valued at shadow prices, rather than on these magnitudes by individual industries.

To elaborate a bit on the last point, assume that in Sector A the shadow wage is equal to half the market wage, while in Sector B the shadow wage and market wage are the same. Suppose the market rate of return to capital is 10 percent in both sectors, but that by imputing half the wages bill of Sector A to capital in that sector, we would thereby increase the computed rate of return to capital to 20 percent in that sector. It makes no sense at all to proceed with project evaluation in this case by using a 20 percent rate of return for projects in Sector A and a 10 percent rate of return for projects in Sector B. The same rate must be used in both sectors, and the above procedure would estimate the approximate rate by, in effect, obtaining a weighted average of the 20 percent return imputable to capital in Sector A and the 10 percent return of Sector B. Projects of Sector B would (and should) be burdened by being required to meet the test of a higher rate of return than the 10 percent market rate, while wages paid in B would be fully counted as costs. On the other hand, projects in Sector A would benefit from being allowed to exclude from costs half of their wages bill and include that amount as imputed income from capital, while being required to meet a 15 (not 20) percent test of capital yield at shadow prices.

The treatment of capital and labor in the above example is obviously different, and for a good reason. Discrepancies between shadow and market wages vary by skill of labor, by region, and by industry sector, among other things. Shadow prices should discriminate in favor of projects that actually draw into employment workers whose opportunity cost is less than the wages paid them, and should discriminate (at least in a relative sense) against projects that do not do so. This is done by assigning a share of the wages bill to capital in the former class of projects—a share that varies from project to project in accordance with the degree of discrepancy between their shadow and market wage bills. Once this is done, the accounts have been rectified, so to speak, and the projects should be free to compete for available capital funds by being required to meet the same rate-of-return or present-value test.

The main weakness of the procedure used in the tables above is that it requires one to specify—in advance, so to speak—the time path by which the gap between over-all shadow and actual wage bills will be reduced. Obviously, this time sequence cannot be drawn out of thin air or assumed at will; on the contrary, its estimation is a serious responsibility of the macroeconomic planners. Without attempting here to go into detail as to reasonable ways of guessing at this time path, let me just note that the most common alternative procedure also makes such a guess—by assuming that the shadow wage remains constant through time. The procedure advocated here simply makes explicit that a guess is required—and suggests that it be the best guess possible in the face of all available evidence and judgment.

TIME PATHS OF PRICES AND OF DEMAND

Let me begin this section by focusing on a particularly important price—the exchange rate—to indicate how its role differs from that assigned to the wage rate in the preceding section. The key point of the preceding section that is relevant here is that a shadow wage below the market wage had a direct implication with respect to the rate of return to capital. The situation is not nearly so clear when we consider a shadow exchange rate (defined as the price in local currency of foreign currency) different from (generally above) the market rate. A rise in the rate of exchange will enhance the profitability of export industries through its effect on their product prices. It may or may not enhance the profitability of import-competing industries, depending on whether imports were previously restricted (e.g. by licensing) to a volume determined by foreign exchange availabilities (in which case the effective internal price of imports might decline as a consequence of the rise in the exchange rate together with a relaxation of restrictions), or whether imports were freely admitted at the pre-existing exchange rate (in which case their price would surely rise). The rise in the exchange rate, on the other hand, would tend to reduce the profitability of investment in industries using imported materials and also in industries using imported capital equipment. The net effect of all these forces is uncertain in that there is no presumption that the introduction of a shadow exchange rate in place of a (lower) market rate will either typically raise or typically lower the shadow rate of return to capital.

The exchange rate differs from the wage rate in another important respect as well. Whereas the labor market imperfections that require the use of shadow as distinct from actual wage rates tend to be rather fundamental phenomena—not possible to eliminate quickly—there is no corresponding excuse for the use of shadow pricing with respect to the exchange rate. A simple act of devaluation can put into effect as the market rate whatever value one would choose to set as the shadow price of foreign currency. I feel that the policy of allowing the exchange rate to reflect the scarcity value of foreign currency is virtually essential for good project evaluation—as well as being good for other reasons. It obviates the need for readjusting a whole set of internal product prices and for revaluing amounts of capital actually invested. Moreover, even if the exchange rate is allowed to reflect the scarcity value of foreign currency, it still presents substantial problems for the project evaluator and the planner whenever it is expected that the rate will have to change through time. As in the case of investible funds, we may face circumstances of abnormal scarcity or glut of foreign currency that would require different expected exchange rates to be applied to different future years. I see no merit at all in compounding these problems by following exchange rate policies that require a complete reshuffling of the accounts for the present year as well.

Much of what has been said about the exchange rate applies to other prices as well. If the shadow price of a product is different from the actual price, this fact is not likely to have a profound effect upon the shadow rate of return to capital for the economy as a whole. But it does introduce serious problems in that purchasers of the product guide their own decisions by the actual price, while we would like them to guide their decisions by the shadow price. It may take ingenuity to make the actual price reasonably reflect the shadow price in some cases, but, as the experts of Electricité de France have shown, the job can be done well even in some very complicated cases.

Finally, just as with the exchange rate, even if we do permit market prices to reflect scarcity values on a current basis, we still have the substantial problem of estimating the future path of prices. With respect to this problem, there is one principle which is crucial to good project evaluation. One often hears projects justified, in practice, on the basis that even if they are not profitable today, they will become profitable in the future because of the growth of demand. There can indeed be such a justification for particular projects, but when this is the case it is more subtle than many people think. Almost any investment made today would become profitable with time if no competing investments were made in the future. But that does not say by any means that all such investments should be made today. In the first place, their postponement might result in their having even higher present value, and this should be taken into account in the process of analysis and decision-making. In the second place, and probably much more important, is the fact that the 'profitability' of today's investments should be estimated on the assumption that all 'profitable' future investments will also be made. This kind of consideration must of necessity enter into investment decision-making in a competitive industry, where one can more or less be sure that someone will undertake those investments that become profitable in the future even if they are inimical to the profitability of one's own investment of today. It is properly reflected, for example, by forecasts of declining prices where rapid technological advance is foreseen. In public-sector decision-making, one cannot rely on the expectation of 'someone's' future action to force upon the project analyst a pattern of a declining future price in the face, for example, of a rapidly rising total demand for the good or service in question. Here, of necessity, the project analyst himself has to estimate an expected time path of the price—not on the assumption that his project stands alone, nor on the assumption that future projects will be held up in order to 'protect' the profitability of his current project, but on the much more rigorous assumption that future investments will be made on their own merits and without consideration to their effect on the profitability of any past investments. All this can in most cases be summarized in the expected price path of the product through time, but it must be realized that the expected price path here means more than just a guess about future prices— it means rather a guess as to the prices that will be generated in the future by an essentially optimal investment policy or, perhaps better put, by the continuous application in the future of valid investment decision rules.

What has just been said about prices can be translated into corresponding statements about consumers' surplus. For simplicity, I shall represent this problem by a simple supply-and-demand diagram (Figure 1.2), but it should be borne in mind that the principle involved extends to much more complicated cases. Assume that the demand function for a product shifts, through time, from D_1 to D_2 to D_3, etc. Assume, furthermore,

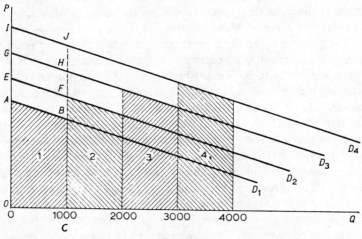

Figure 1.2

that in each period the installation of new capacity of 1,000 units is expected to be justified, following a valid decision rule.

The benefit stream attributable to the first year's investment will be (1) in the first year, (2) in the second, (3) in the third, (4) in the fourth, etc. It will not be *EFCO* in the second period, *GHCO* in the third, and *IJCO* in the fourth, because in these successive periods additional amounts of capacity of 1,000, 2,000, and 3,000 units must be assumed to be installed. Similarly, in evaluating the second year's investment, the benefit stream should be (2), (3), (4), etc.

One can, on occasion, count *ABCO*, *EFCO*, *GHCO*, and *IJCO* as the benefit stream from the first investment, but that only occurs if no further acceptable investments will be generated as demand grows through time—a condition that can be presumed to be highly unlikely.

The general principle involved here is that in assessing the contribution of any unit of capacity, it should be considered as the marginal unit in each year of its operation. Inframarginal benefits, which would have accrued in any event as a consequence of subsequent additions to capacity in the absence of, say, the first year's project, should not be attributed to part of the benefits of that project. Indeed, one can go further, for no benefits should be attributed to any given project which are greater in present value than the lowest alternative cost of achieving the same benefits. Following this principle, it is quite possible that the shaded areas in Figure 1.2 might overstate the benefits properly attributable to the first year's project. We can be sure, however, that they do not understate the relevant benefits.

Notes

[1] The example above assumes that the amount of labor required to produce a given output from the project in question remains constant through time, and is not reduced as a consequence of improvements in 'productivity'. This is the case for many types of projects, in which labor and materials requirements are established by the initial design of the project and its associated capital equipment. However, it is certainly possible that for some projects one might reasonably forecast a gradual improvement in labor productivity; in such cases the labor requirements should be projected independently, and the wage rate should, as in the example above, reflect the expected trend of real wages for the relevant categories of labor. Even where productivity on the project is expected to rise through time, there are no grounds for assuming that, project by project, the increase in productivity will just offset the anticipated rise in real wages.

[2] Robert H. Strotz, 'The Social Rate of Time Discount', mimeo., 1964, pp. 2–6.

[3] Strotz here cites the results reported in George J. Stigler, *Capital and Rates of Return in Manufacturing Industries*, Princeton, N.J., 1963.

[4] See A. K. Sen, 'On Optimizing the Rate of Saving', *Economic Journal*, September 1961; and Stephen A. Marglin, 'The Social Rate of Discount and the Optimal Rate of Saving', *Quarterly Journal of Economics*, February 1963.

[5] I have dealt with this subject at some length in 'Cost-Benefit Analysis and Economic Growth', *Economic Weekly*, Annual Number, February 1962, pp. 207–21.

CHAPTER TWO

SURVEY OF LITERATURE ON COST-BENEFIT ANALYSIS FOR INDUSTRIAL PROJECT EVALUATION

INTRODUCTION

The field of industrial project evaluation is a relatively new branch of economic analysis, and as such is still in its formative stages. Numerous gaps still exist in the available literature, and in many cases alternative approaches to problems have been suggested which entail differences of concept that are as yet unresolved. These facts have determined the design of this survey. An attempt has been made here to take a constructive and forward-looking approach, focusing on gaps, weaknesses and unresolved issues in the field and attempting to contribute to an improvement of existing procedures wherever possible.

Because the great bulk of the literature available in the United States concerns project evaluation in predominantly private enterprise or mixed economies, the present study has been confined to such cases, making no attempt to consider the case of completely centrally planned economies. But it is recognized in what follows that social benefits and costs do not always coincide with private pecuniary benefits and costs. Indeed, it may be said that one of the principal concerns of cost-benefit analysis is to appraise costs and benefits from a social point of view in cases where these diverge from the pecuniary costs and benefits perceived by the individuals in the marketplace.

Paper prepared for the Inter-Regional Symposium in Industrial Project Evaluation (Prague, October 1965). Published in United Nations Industrial Development Organization, *Evaluation of Industrial Projects* (1968), UN Sales No. E.67.11.B.23.

Section A focuses on the controversial problem of the relevant rate of discount for use in cost-benefit analysis. First the advantages and disadvantages of the internal rate of return are discussed, and it is concluded that, though useful as a summary indicator of a project's profitability, the internal rate of return should not be used as the basic criterion for project evaluation. Then market rates of interest on bonds, the 'social rate of time preference' and the marginal productivity of capital in the private sector are considered. It is concluded that the optimal rate for use in discounting costs and benefits, in a market economy, is the marginal productivity of capital in the private sector of the economy, defining this marginal productivity in such a way as to include all social benefits and costs in the calculations. Finally, the question of the variation of the discount rate through time is considered. It is concluded that the appropriate discounting of flows of benefits and costs should normally be done at rates which may vary from year to year, the principle being that flows occurring in year ten should be discounted back to year nine at the marginal productivity of capital expected to prevail in year nine; that these flows, in turn, should be discounted back to year eight at the marginal productivity of capital expected to prevail in that year, and so on.

This principle of a variable discount rate is necessary in order to reach proper decisions on project timing and scale, and is particularly important in reaching valid decisions in years in which investible funds are either particularly abundant or particularly scarce relative to existing investment opportunities.

Section B focuses on the measurement of benefits and costs, and particularly on how to project the path of expected benefits and costs through time. Initially, the basic principles underlying demand projections are reviewed, and subsequently the principles underlying the projection of prices, wages and other costs are considered. The main conclusion of section B is that it is necessary to project the prospective costs and benefits of a project year by year through the entire expected life of the project, incorporating expected changes in prices and costs directly into the analysis. Projects can then be evaluated and compared on the basis of the excess of discounted benefits over discounted costs, thus projected. Particular importance is attached to the fact that, in a developing economy, wages must be expected to rise relative to product prices in general, so that the excess of the price of a project's output (which is the first-approximation measure of its benefits per unit of output) over costs may frequently be expected to decline as real wages rise through time. Attention is also paid to the problem of projecting the path through time of the exchange rate and of cost components other than wages. Finally, the problem of measuring the indirect costs and benefits of a project is briefly surveyed.

Section C discusses the use of accounting prices in project evaluation. It finds that divergences between social costs and market prices can be significant in many cases, and thus endorses in principle the use of accounting prices. The main effort of this section is, however, to discuss the appropriate ways of estimating accounting prices.

In the case of labor, the need for having distinct accounting prices for labor of different skills and types, and in different regions, is emphasized. It is suggested that a minimum estimate of the accounting price for urban labor of a given type may often be obtained from the wage rate received by labor of that type employed within the urban complex in activities in which wages are not influenced either by minimum wage legislation or by union agreements. It is explicitly concluded that the marginal productivity of labor in agriculture is not a relevant measure of the accounting price of urban labor.

The method of setting the accounting price of foreign exchange is then outlined, the principle involved being the estimation of the market value of the goods that would probably be imported as a consequence of the availability of additional foreign exchange. The possibility of using accounting prices for materials inputs is then examined, the conclusion here being that, although accounting prices may in some cases be justified for such inputs, equivalent results are achieved by generally valuing all materials inputs at their market prices, and considering separately, as indirect benefits of the project, any surplus of benefits over costs generated in the material-producing industry as a direct consequence of the project in question.

Finally, the question of accounting prices for the output of a project is considered, the focus being particularly on cases in which this output is subject to indirect taxation. The conclusion is reached that, except in unusual instances in which the indirect tax was itself placed on the product in order to counteract an existing external diseconomy associated with the product's production or consumption, the social benefit associated with the output of a project is to be measured by its price including tax.

A brief addendum to section C considers the possibility of obtaining appropriate accounting prices through the use of linear programming models for the entire economy. Here it is concluded that in order to make a linear programming model for the whole economy feasible, the characteristics of the economy must be so drastically oversimplified as to make the resulting accounting prices highly unreliable.

In section D, problems of timing are considered. First, the influence of high discount rates on projects of different productive lives and gestation periods is reviewed, then the question of when to construct a given project is considered, and finally the question of how to deal with risk is faced. The key conclusions are, first, that the timing of the construction of a project is a problem of considerable importance. Construction should not be undertaken at the moment when the present value of benefits exceeds the present value of costs, but should be delayed to the point where the excess of the present value of benefits over the present value of costs is a maximum. For a particular class of cases, it is shown that this rule entails the delay of a project until such time as the benefits of its first year of operation exceed the interest charge on the capital investment in the project. Secondly, if benefits and costs are appropriately projected, so as to take account of possible reductions in the value of benefits of a project stemming from future improvements in productive technique, there is no need to add a risk factor to the discount rate used in cost-benefit analysis.

In section E, interrelations among projects are considered. The importance of analyzing separately the contribution of all separable components of a project is emphasized. Finally, the principles for deciding which of a set of interrelated projects should be undertaken are briefly set out.

A. PRESENT VALUE CRITERIA VERSUS THE INTERNAL RATE OF RETURN

1. *Advantages and defects of the internal rate of return*

The internal rate of return on a project (ρ) is obtained by the solution of the following quotation

$$\sum_{t=0}^{N} \frac{B_t - C_t}{(1+\rho)^t} = 0,$$

where B_t represents the benefits anticipated to accrue in year t of a project's life and C_t represents the costs anticipated to be incurred in year t. N is the length of life of the project. Costs are defined to include capital outlays, labor, materials, energy and transport costs, and maintenance and repair expenditures. Costs do not include depreciation charges or actual or imputed interest charges, as the internal rate of return itself reflects the implicit 'net interest yield' of the project, and in this sense allows for the depreciation of the project's cost. Thus, if a project has a capital cost of 100 in year 0, and yields a benefit of 120 in year 1, with an operating cost of 20, the net effect of the operation of the project would be -100 in year 0 and $+100$ in year 1. The capital invested would be just barely recovered one year later. Such a project would have an internal rate of return of zero, indicating that no more than capital recovery can be expected from it. On the other hand, if the project were to have a benefit of 130 in year 1, with an operating cost of 20 in that year, its internal rate of return would be 10 percent, indicating that the capital invested in the project will produce a yield of 10 percent after allowing for capital recovery. Finally, if the benefit in year 1 were merely 110, together with an operating cost of 20, the value of $B_1 - C_1$ would be 90, and the internal rate of return would be -10 percent, indicating that the project is incapable of yielding sufficient benefits to cover the cost of the invested capital.

The great advantage of the internal rate of return lies in the fact that it can be calculated on the basis of project data alone. In particular, its calculation does not require data on the opportunity cost of capital which, as will be seen below, is critical to the present value technique and can often be exceedingly

difficult to estimate. Thus, when a project evaluator has several
different projects to be surveyed, he may independently calculate the internal rate of return on each, and use the resulting
figures as one basis of comparison among the projects.

The disadvantages of the internal rate of return are severe,
however—so severe as to warrant the greatest caution in its use.
In the first place, there are some projects for which it is not
possible to determine the internal rate of return uniquely.
Figure 2.1a shows the time-profile of net benefits $(B_t - C_t)$ for

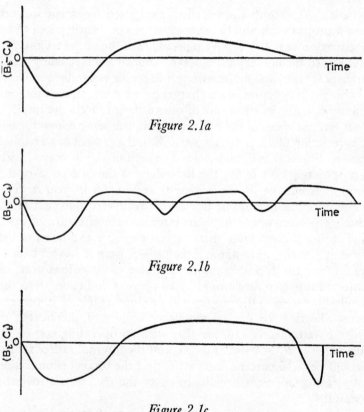

Figure 2.1a

Figure 2.1b

Figure 2.1c

a typical project. In it an initial period of investment, during
which the value of $B_t - C_t$ is negative, is followed by a period
in which the net benefit of the project is always positive. For

all cases of this type there is a unique solution for the internal rate of return. However, if the time-profile of net benefits crosses zero more than once, there will be multiple solutions for the internal rate of return. Examples of such projects are cases in which major items of equipment must be replaced relatively frequently, giving rise to negative net benefits, say, every five years when these replacements are accomplished (see Figure 2.1b); or cases in which the termination of a project entails substantial net costs (such as restoring rented facilities to their former state) (see Figure 2.1c).

All cases of the types illustrated in Figures 2.1b and 2.1c will yield multiple solutions for the internal rate of return; these multiple solutions are a mathematical necessity and present a problem of choice from which there is no escape. Consider the simple case of an investment of 900 in year 0, a net benefit of 1,900 in year 1, and a net cost of 1,000 in year 2. Obviously, one solution for the internal rate of return is zero, for at a zero discount rate the present value of benefits is just equal to the present value of costs. But another solution is a 11·11 percent rate, for setting

$$\left(\frac{1}{1+\rho}\right) = \cdot 9, \text{ and } \left(\frac{1}{1+\rho}\right)^2 = \cdot 81 \text{ we obtain}$$

$$-900 + \frac{1900}{1+\rho} - \frac{100}{(1+\rho)^2} = -900 + 1710 - 810 = 0.$$

Even where the internal rate of return can be unambiguously calculated for each project under consideration, its use as an investment criterion encounters other difficulties when some of the projects in question are alternatives to each other. Consider first a case in which all projects are strictly independent. In such a case, the internal rate of return criterion will work well. By arranging the projects in descending order of internal rates of return, one can select first that project with the highest internal rate, then that with the next highest, etc., proceeding in this way until the available investible funds are exhausted. Suppose that the last project qualifying under this procedure has an internal rate of return of 8 percent. Then 8 percent will represent the opportunity cost of investible capital, and it becomes appropriate to evaluate the costs and benefits of all projects using

this rate. Given that all the projects accepted under the internal
rate of return criterion have internal rates higher than 8 percent,
and assuming these internal rates to be unique (i.e. assuming
that the projects have net benefit profiles of the kind shown in
Figure 2.1a), the present value of all accepted projects, evaluated at 8 percent, will be positive, and the present value of all
rejected projects, again evaluated at the 8 percent rate, will be
negative. In this case the internal rate of return criterion leads
to no contradictions.

Now, however, consider a case in which two projects are
alternatives. Let project *A* have an internal rate of return of
20 percent and project *B* have one of 12 percent. The internal
rate of return criterion would lead one always to choose project
A, yet it can be shown that *B* might very well be preferable. If
the available investible funds are exhausted, as in the previous
example, at an 8 percent rate of return, we take 8 percent to
be the opportunity cost of investible capital, and calculate the
net present values of all projects using this rate. It can very
well occur that project *B*, in spite of its lower internal rate of
return, has a higher present value than project *A*. For example,
suppose that project *B* has a net benefit of $240,000 per year in
perpetuity on a capital investment of $2 million, while project
A has a net benefit of $64,000 per year in perpetuity on a
capital investment of $320,000. The present value of project
B's benefits, evaluated at 8 percent, is $3 million, while the
project cost is $2 million, yielding a net excess of benefits over
costs of $1 million. On the other hand, the present value of
project *A*'s benefits is $800,000 from which, deducting the pro-
ject cost of $320,000, we obtain a net excess of benefits over
costs of $480,000. In spite of project *A*'s higher ratio of benefits
to costs, project *B* is preferable, because if $320,000 is invested
in *A* rather than $2 million in *B*, the best alternative use for the
$1,680,000 thus saved is a 'marginal' investment with an in-
ternal rate of return of only 8 percent, on which the excess of
benefits over costs, evaluated at the opportunity cost rate of
8 percent, would be nil.

Discussions of the internal rate of return as a criterion can
be found in Friedrich and Vera Lutz, *The Theory of Investment
of the Firm*,[1] in Roland N. McKean, *Efficiency in Government
through Systems Analysis*[2] and in J. Hirshleifer, 'On the theory of

optimal investment decision'.[3] All these writers recognize the disadvantages indicated above.

2. *Choice of discount rates for use in connection with a present value criterion*

(a) *The marginal productivity of capital in the private sector.* It was shown above that the use of capital in a given project was justified if the benefits of the project exceeded its costs, evaluated at a discount rate reflecting the opportunity cost of capital. One highly recommended measure of the opportunity cost of capital is the expected marginal productivity of typical capital investments in the private sector of the economy. If a public sector project is to be financed by borrowing from the private sector, it is to be presumed that the funds so mobilized could, in the absence of this project, have been used to finance private-sector investments; hence in this case there is a direct sense in which private-sector investment can be considered as the relevant alternative to the project. When, on the other hand, the funds to be used are part of the savings of the public sector, the connection between a public-sector project and its private-sector alternatives need not be so clear-cut. If the funds available to the public sector investment authorities are sufficiently ample, it may work out that, in order to use all the available funds within a given set of projects being considered, the public sector authorities make investments having a yield of 5 percent, even though capital in the private sector has an expected rate of marginal productivity equal to 10 percent. Given that the yields in both cases are worked up on the basis of social benefits and social costs, the acceptance of public-sector projects with rates of return lower than those to be anticipated from additional private sector investments must be considered uneconomic. It would be preferable in this case to accept only those public-sector projects exhibiting a social yield of 10 percent or more, and to invest any remaining public-sector funds in financing additional private-sector investments with an expected yield of 10 percent or more. Thus in this case the optimal use of the funds available to the public sector leads to a result in which the private-sector investments are the relevant alternatives to marginal investments in the public sector.

One case in which the marginal productivity of investments in the private sector might not be the appropriate criterion for public-sector decision-making is where the investible funds of the public sector are so severely limited that they can be exhausted on public-sector projects, all of which have a higher expected yield than a typical private-sector investment. In such a case, if the limitation on public-sector funds is a binding constraint, the relevant opportunity cost for public-sector investments would be that rate of discount which, when used as the basis of a present value criterion, would result in the acceptance of a group of projects whose cost was just barely sufficient to exhaust the available funds. For example, in a case of severe budgetary stringency, it might turn out that, using a 16 percent rate of discount, the projects yielding a positive excess of benefits over costs would not fully exhaust the available funds, but that, using a 15 percent rate of discount, sufficient additional projects would pass the present value test so as just to exhaust the given budget. In this case, the opportunity cost of capital for a public-sector project would be 15 percent, in spite of the fact that private-sector investments have an expected marginal yield of only 10 percent. However, this result occurs only when the budgetary restriction on public-sector projects is binding. Otherwise, in a case such as that just described, the optimal result can be achieved by the public-sector authorities accepting all projects having benefits greater than their costs, evaluated at a discount rate of 10 percent, and borrowing the required additional funds from the private sector.

Thus, the opportunity cost of capital is best measured by the marginal productivity of capital in the private sector in virtually all cases, the only serious exception being the case of a binding budgetary constraint on the investible funds of the public sector, in which case the private-sector marginal productivity of capital still remains as a lower limit to the discount rate relevant for public-sector investment decisions.

We turn therefore to the problem of estimating the marginal productivity of private-sector capital. Consider any line of activity in the private sector, the line of activity being defined as including all operations producing a given product by similar production methods, for sale in the same market. An increase in the amount of capital invested in such a line of activity will augment the supply of the product in question, and may affect its price. If it does affect the price of the product, it will alter the marginal productivity of the capital previously invested in the line of activity in question, but it will similarly affect the rate of return perceived by the owners of this previously invested capital. Thus, where the newly invested capital is of the same type as that already existing, the private rate of return to capital in the line of activity in question may be taken as a rough first approximation to the marginal productivity of capital in that line.

Some problems must, however, be noted immediately. If a technological advance has occurred, it may be true that new investment, using the new technique, will have a marginal productivity, and a rate of return, equal to, say, 20 percent, but the introduction of this technique may reduce the price of the product to the point where the return on capital invested in the old technique is but 5 percent. The rate of return on all capital invested in the industry will be a weighted average of the 20 percent rate on the new technique and 5 percent on the old. And indeed it will be true, if no other complications enter into the calculation, that the marginal productivity of capital is 20 percent for that invested in the new technique and 5 percent for that invested in the old technique. The over-all marginal productivity of capital in the activity in question will also, in this case, be a weighted average of 20 and 5 percent, and will be measured (again barring additional complications) by the rate of return on the total capital invested in that activity.

The problem here is that any new investment that occurs will use the new technique, so that the marginal productivity of capital that is relevant for current and future decisions is that 20 percent rate obtainable from the new technique. The use of the observed rate of return in the entire activity (on both old and new techniques) therefore underestimates the rate relevant for the evaluation of current and future projects.

This error could be avoided by considering the two techniques as separate lines of activity and using, in the calculation of the marginal productivity of capital to be used in project evaluation, only the 20 percent rate arising from investment in the new technique. The difficulty with this approach stems from the way in which the available data typically appear, that is, from the financial accounts of enterprises. In these accounts, there is no way of distinguishing how much capital is invested in a new technique and how much in an old one, and likewise there is no way of allocating the income earned by an enterprise into a part attributable to a new and a part attributable to an old technique. Thus the data automatically yield rates of return which are, in our example, weighted averages of the 20 percent and the 5 percent rate, and it must be recognized that these estimates are biased downward when significant technological advances have recently occurred.

A second source of bias in estimating the marginal productivity of capital on the basis of observed rates of return is the presence, in some lines of activity, of monopoly elements. The effect of monopoly is to restrict production of the monopolized product and to raise its price. As a consequence, the value of the marginal product of all factors of production is raised above their respective prices. If prices are raised 10 percent above costs, the consequence would be an element of monopoly profits consisting of 10 percent of the wages paid, 10 percent of the cost of materials used, and 10 percent of the true cost of capital. The difficulty presented for measuring the marginal product of capital by the observed rate of return is that the profits appearing on the accounts of a company include the full amount of monopoly profits plus the true cost of capital; whereas for a proper measurement of the marginal productivity, they should include, in this example, only 110 percent of the true cost of capital. Thus the measured rate of return tends to overstate the true marginal productivity of capital when monopoly elements are present.

The construction of series on the rate of return to capital in the private sector is dealt with in some detail by George J. Stigler in *Capital and Rates of Return in Manufacturing Industries*[4] and by John W. Kendrick in *Productivity Trends in the United States*,[5] the latter dealing principally with the problem of measuring the stock of capital. The literature on the subject is as yet very weak on the problems of measuring the social as distinct from the private yield on private sector capital.

There are a number of possible sources of divergence between the social and private benefits of private investment; but of these, by far the most important consists of taxes. Corporation income taxes typically account for between 25 and 50 percent of the income generated by capital in the corporate sector; the social yield of capital (including the corporation income taxes) can thus easily be 12 percent, even though the private yield is only 6 percent. It would accordingly be erroneous to proceed on the assumption that the private yield on capital reflected its full opportunity cost. Of two investments with the same private yield, one of which generates corporation income tax payments equal to its private yield, and the other of which generates no tax payments at all, the former is clearly socially preferable, as it either enables the public sector to have more command over real goods and services or, alternatively, it permits the public sector to reduce some other tax and thus permits the private sector to buy more real goods and services. The indicated procedure is therefore to include corporation tax payments generated in any industry as part of the social return to capital in that industry. And if the social rate of return to capital is estimated for the private sector as a whole, the entire yield of the corporation income tax should be added to the income perceived by private enterprises in order to convert the latter to a social concept of 'income generated by capital'.

Where indirect taxes exist on a final product, they lead to a situation in which the value of the marginal product of each factor of production involved in that good's production exceeds the income earned by that factor by the percentage rate of indirect tax. In this case, the income from capital (gross of corporation income tax) should be augmented by a fraction of the receipts from the indirect tax, the fraction being capital's share in the value added in the industry in question.

Other sources of divergence between the private and the social rate of return on capital can arise out of divergences of the market prices of factors of production from their opportunity costs. These will be discussed in section C, below, in some detail.

For an attempt at estimating the social rate of return to capital in a developing country, in which explicit account is taken of the effects of taxes and of certain possible divergences between market prices and opportunity costs, see A. C. Harberger, 'Investment in man versus investment in machines: the case of India'.[6]

(b) *Market interest rates.* The conventional way of converting costs and benefits to present values is by the use of some market rate of interest. Market rates of interest generally substantially underestimate the opportunity cost of capital, because they fail to reflect the taxes that are paid on account of the profits of private sector projects, and because they neglect other external benefits generated by private sector investments, particularly where there are divergences between market prices and opportunity costs of factors of production or goods.

Two examples of the conventional view follow:

It is recommended that estimates of benefits and costs accruing at various times should be made comparable by adjustment to a uniform time basis through the use of projected long-range interest rates. Pending the development of such rates, the average rate of return i.e., yield, on long-term federal bonds over a sufficiently long period of time to average out the influence of cyclical fluctuations is considered appropriate for uniform application by all agencies on the condition that adequate allowance has been made for uncertainties and risks.[7]

Interest rates are a measure of the value attached to time differences and, hence, provide a means of converting estimates to a common time period. In calculating the costs of developing a project, interest should be charged on the project for its entire economic life and reduced to an annual basis in order to compose annual costs and benefits. The rate of interest to charge a project depends upon the rate you must pay for financing the project. Generally, government financed projects can be financed at a lower rate than private industry. The government rate of borrowing is relatively risk free because the security is the general taxing power and because the over-all degree of security for the loan is relatively certain. In view of these considerations, it is recommended that the expected average long-term government bond rate be used as the basis for calculating public investment costs and that higher rates be used for private investment costs.[8]

The approach reflected in both of the above quotations fails to appreciate the difference between the market interest rate on bonds and the opportunity cost of capital. Tinbergen, in advocating the use of accounting prices, has a much clearer appreciation of this distinction. He says that

[accounting prices of factors of production] represent the value of the marginal product to be obtained with their aid. . . . The interest rate to be applied should express the real scarcity of capital, to be derived from the marginal yield of projects as well as from the marginal rates to be paid for foreign loans.[9]

Tinbergen suggests the use of a 10 percent interest rate, which is far above the rates applying to government bonds in most countries, and which undoubtedly lies closer to the opportunity cost of capital than the government bond rate.

Likewise, the United Nations Industrial Development Division recognizes the unsuitability of bond rates:

More specifically, . . . accounting interest rates may be set at least double the rates on government securities or on international loans, and possibly at as high as 20 per cent.[10]

(c) *Other methods for setting discount rates.* Some of the theoretical literature rejects both the rate of interest on bonds and the private sector marginal productivity of capital in favor of what is called the 'social rate of time preference' or the 'social rate of discount'. This concept attempts to represent the relative valuation which society puts on a marginal amount of consumption in different time periods. For example, if 'society' considered $1·10 of extra consumption next year to be subjectively equivalent to $1·00 of extra consumption this year, the social rate of time preference between the two years would be 10 percent.

The main ground on which this part of the literature rejects market rates of return is the belief that the market, which reflects the resultant of individual, atomistic savings and investment decisions, does not give any weight to the preferences of future generations and hence tends to save 'too little', with the result that the market rate of return on investment is 'too high'. As Eckstein puts it:

> Social policy, as derived from the political process, may prefer rejection of present intertemporal preferences in favour of a redistribution of income towards future generations. Much of the conservation philosophy can be interpreted in these terms. Resource development is a field particularly suited to this kind of redistribution because there are genuine opportunities for making investments, part of the benefit of which will accrue in the far future. And perhaps equally important is the fact that it is in the resource area that the idea of making provision for the future of the country has caught the imagination of the public. It is not logically inconsistent for the same person to be willing to borrow at high interest rates to increase his present consumption while voting to spend tax money to build a project from which future generations will benefit, for in the case of a vote to tax, he can be sure that the other individuals in the society will be compelled to act similarly. . . . Our notion of efficiency is relative to the distribution of income; should we seek to redistribute income to future generations, the interest rate loses its meaning as an efficient price.[11]

More detailed discussion of this view may be found in O. Eckstein, 'Investment criteria for economic development and the theory of inter-temporal welfare economics'.[12] A somewhat similar position is expressed by Stephen A. Marglin in 'The social rate of discount and the optimal rate of investment'[13] and by A. K. Sen in 'On optimizing the rate of saving'.[14]

The difficulty that emerges from the Eckstein-Marglin-Sen position is that, when the social rate of time preference is low, its use in evaluating benefits and costs is likely to lead to the acceptance of a great many projects—in all likelihood more than can be financed.

Eckstein says:

> I propose the following compromise, which is designed to preserve the long-term perspective of the federal pro-

gramme, yet would ensure that only projects are undertaken in which capital yields as great a value as it would in its alternative employments: let the Government use a relatively low interest rate for the design and evaluation of projects, but let projects be considered justified only if the benefit-cost ratio is well in excess of 1·0.[15]

Marglin, in a more elaborately developed discussion than Eckstein's, develops formulas for measuring the opportunity cost of public investment when the social rate of discount lies below the marginal productivity of capital in the private sector. His formulas depend on the manner in which the public sector funds are raised; he considers the 'cost' of $1 of public funds raised at the expense of current consumption to be $1, while the cost of $1 of funds raised at the expense of investment is considered in his basic model to be ρ/r, when ρ is the marginal productivity of capital in the private sector and r is the social rate of discount. This assumes that $1 of private investment would have a perpetual yield of ρ per year which, discounted back to the present at the social rate of discount, would have a present value of ρ/r. If the fraction θ of public funds is raised at the expense of investment, and the fraction $(1 - \theta)$ at the expense of consumption, the present value of the forgone alternatives of a dollar of public funds will be $[(\theta\rho/r) + (1 - \theta)]$. Marglin then proceeds to recommend that the present value of the benefits stemming from a dollar of public investment should be at least equal to $[\theta\rho/r + (1 - \theta)]$.[16] A somewhat similar approach is followed by Peter O. Steiner in 'Choosing among alternative public investments in the water resource field'.[17]

The solutions reached by Eckstein, Marglin and Steiner are all subject to a single, decisive criticism: they may lead to results in which the rate of return to investments in the public sector lies below that which could be obtained by placing the same funds at the disposal of the private sector, or by investing directly in private sector type activities. Future generations lose, rather than gain, if funds are used for a 5 percent public-sector investment rather than for a 10 percent private-sector investment. The public sector can, and in many countries does, provide both equity and debt financing for the private sector, and can thus assure itself that its financing of private-sector activities does not entail the granting of a subsidy to the private sector but rather simply enables the public sector to obtain the same rate of return that prevails on private-sector investments. Once the public sector is prepared to accept this degree of flexibility in its use of investible funds, the criterion for project evaluation reduces once again to the marginal productivity of capital in the private sector of the economy, discussed in A.2. (a) above.

The fact that the social rate of discount may lie below the marginal productivity of capital proves only that the rate of investment should be expanded; it does not prove that, for a given rate of investment, capital should have different marginal rates of productivity in the public and private sectors. The end result of an optimal investment policy, with the social rate of discount taken as given, would therefore be a situation in which the marginal productivity of capital in both the private and public sectors was equal to the social rate of discount. During the transition from a position in which the marginal productivity of capital in the private sector lies above the ultimate social rate of discount to a position where these are equal, the optimum path would entail so allocating the investible resources of the economy as to maintain continuing equality of the marginal rates of productivity of capital in the public and private sectors, with these rates declining together from their initial (high) level to their ultimate (lower) level as a consequence of a stepped-up rate of investment.[18]

(d) *Changes in the relevant discount rate through time.* The case cited in the preceding paragraph gives only one of many possible ways in which the relevant discount rate may vary through time. Another possibility—more optimistic from the standpoint of economic development—is that through adoption of superior techniques, through better management and organization, and through an improved mix of social overhead investments, the marginal productivity of capital might rise rather than fall through time. This corresponds, in technical economic language, to upward shifts in the production function through time, which more than outweigh the downward pressure on the marginal productivity of capital stemming from the effects of increased capital-intensity of production.

Actually, for those countries for which it has been possible to estimate the marginal productivity of capital over substantial periods of time, there appears to have been no very significant upward or downward trend in this magnitude. Stigler, for example, finds the private rate of return to capital in United States manufacturing to have fallen in the 1930s to less than half the level of the late 1920s, then to have risen in the late 1940s to about $1\frac{1}{2}$ times the level of the late 1920s, and finally to have fallen by the late 1950s to approximately the same level as that of the late 1920s.[19]

This experience is suggestive of the possibilities that may emerge in other contexts. In the 1930s, the conditions of the United States economy were such that an abnormally low rate of return on capital prevailed; in the late 1940s, on the other hand, the need to restore the capacity for production of non-military goods created a situation where an extraordinarily high yield on investment could be obtained. In neither of these instances could it reasonably be expected that the then-prevailing rate of marginal productivity would be maintained indefinitely into the future.

Similarly, it may occur that a developing country may face a situation in which investible funds are abnormally scarce relative to investment opportunities (as when large debt service payments are due and available investment opportunities are particularly good) or in which investible funds are abnormally abundant relative to opportunities (as when the country receives a particularly large amount of foreign aid, or when its main export product experiences a temporary large increase in price, without investment opportunities expanding correspondingly).

In circumstances like these, the country should attach a 'price' to the use of investible funds which is higher than the expected future price if funds are relatively scarce, and lower if funds are relatively abundant. This can be done by attaching to each year a discount rate that corresponds to the expected marginal productivity of capital in that year. Thus, if we have a project with an expected life of three years, we would discount benefits and costs expected to accrue one year hence at the rate r_1 to bring them back to the present. Likewise, we would discount benefits and costs accruing two years hence by the rate r_2 to bring them back to one year from now, and then by the rate r_1 to bring them back to the present. Thus, the acceptance or rejection of a three-year project would turn on whether the sum:

$$(B_0 - C_0) + \frac{(B_1 - C_1)}{(1 + r_1)} + \frac{(B_2 - C_2)}{(1 + r_1)(1 + r_2)}$$
$$+ \frac{(B_3 - C_3)}{(1 + r_1)(1 + r_2)(1 + r_3)}$$

was greater or less than zero. The general form of this criterion, for a project of N years duration, is

$$(B_0 - C_0) + \sum_{i=1}^{N} \frac{(B_i - C_i)}{\prod_{t=1}^{i} (1 + r_t)}$$

It is unfortunate that the great bulk of the literature on cost-benefit analysis has been based on the simplifying assumption of a constant discount rate, because this assumption fails to give guidance as to how to overcome periods of unusual stringency in the supply of capital funds or how best to take advantage of a temporarily large availability of such funds. One notable exception is the work of Pierre Massé, in which changing discount rates are discussed explicitly, and in which the analyses are carried out in such terms.[20]

B. MEASUREMENT OF BENEFITS AND COSTS

1. *Projections of demand for the affected product*

Projections of demand for the affected product are an important element in estimating the economic feasibility of a project and determining its appropriate scale. The techniques of projection appropriate to any given case can be determined only by a careful study of the case itself, but certain general statements can be made.

(a) The potential market for the product must be ascertained (local, regional, national, international).

(b) Factors influencing the intensity of demand for the product in this market must be isolated and projected.

(c) On the basis of (b), the over-all level of demand for the product must be projected.

(d) The prospects of expansion of existing alternative sources of supply must be examined and corresponding projections made.

(e) The prospects of new sources of supply appearing in the future must be evaluated and, if they are likely to appear, supply from these sources must be projected.

For any market, a key factor influencing demand is the level of income, and the projection of this magnitude is therefore of key importance. Unfortunately, there is no touchstone to estimating the rate of growth of income. In particular, the rate of growth of income is not directly tied to the rate of capital accumulation in the community, but is the resultant of many factors, of which capital accumulation is only one.[21]

This fact introduces considerable uncertainty into all income projections, and suggests that basing such projections mainly or exclusively on capital-output ratios is unwise. The most appropriate procedure appears to be to assess the relative contribution of certain key factors (capital formation, labor force increase, improvement in labor force quality and technical advance) to past economic growth, to assess their probable future strength and to estimate the likely rate of income growth on this basis.

Having projected the rates of growth of income, population and so on, the problem of estimating demand for a particular product depends on the nature of the product. For most consumer goods, income and relative price appear to be the key determinants of demand; so that demand, expressed as a function of price, can be projected once the course of income is known. However, for products which are materials or intermediate goods, the best procedure is to estimate the demand for each type of end-use separately, and to project the demand for the material according to the projected growth of each of its corresponding end-uses.[22] Care must be taken, however, to allow for possible future changes in the quantity of the material used per unit of each end-use product. Capital goods demand should be projected on the basis of the amounts expected to be required for replacement, plus the additional amounts needed to produce projected increases in the final product of the activity in which the capital goods are used.[23] Once again, it is important that prospective development of improved and competing types of equipment be taken into account.

2. *Projections of product prices*

Since the market price of the output of a project is the principal
element in estimating the benefits to be obtained, it is important
that a project analysis should include projections of the probable path of this price through time. Project analyses need not
be concerned with possible movements in the general level of
all prices (i.e. general price inflation or deflation), as a parallel
movement of all prices and costs would not alter the real cost-
benefit relationship. However, movements of relative prices can
have a determining influence on the worth-whileness of a
project.

The best general procedure for projecting the prices and costs
relevant for a project's analysis is to project their movements
relative to the general price level. Concerning the price of the
output of a project, one must therefore attempt to judge
whether the price will move more or less than the general price
level and, if so, by how much. Having projected in index form
the relationship P_i/P_g, where P_i is the price of the project's
output, and P_g is the general price level, for each year of the
expected life of the project, this index is then applied to the
initial year's product price, P_{io}, in order to express future years'
prices in monetary units of the initial year's purchasing power.
Thus the projected price series would be of the form

$$P_{io}(P_{it}/P_{io})(P_{go}/P_{gt}).$$

The factor $(P_{it}/P_{io})(P_{go}/P_{gt})$, will average out to unity over
the whole economy when the appropriate weighted average is
taken for

$$\sum_i \frac{Q_{io}P_{io}}{(\sum_i Q_{io}P_{io})} \cdot \frac{P_{it}}{P_{io}} \cdot \frac{P_{go}}{P_{gt}}$$

$$= \frac{\sum_i Q_{io}P_{it}}{\sum_i Q_{io}P_{io}} \cdot \frac{P_{go}}{P_{gt}} = \frac{P_{gt}}{P_{go}} \cdot \frac{P_{go}}{P_{gt}} = 1.$$

Thus for a typical commodity, the projection of a constant
product price is likely to be justified. However, relative prices
exhibit substantial variations over time, and it is important to
attempt to identify situations in which a particular price is

likely to rise or fall relative to the general index of prices. In general, for industrial products, the course of prices will be the resultant of changes in input costs on the one hand and improvements in technology (including economies of scale) on the other. Since the wage component of input prices is likely to rise over time, the question largely centers on whether future technological advances will be sufficient to offset this force. In many industries, some indication of the likely force of future technological advances can be obtained from the processes that today are being studied for possible future application, and projections can be made on that basis. In some cases, the present market for the product may be found to be abnormal, in the sense of a current shortage of output causing an unusually high price or a current glut of supply causing an unusually low price. It is particularly important that such situations be identified, as in these cases it is highly unlikely that the assumption that the price will remain at its present level will be warranted.

Although most discussions of cost-benefit analysis pay lip-service to the principle of taking expected price changes into account, they generally do not go beyond this. Probably the most extensive treatment of the problem—itself not very extensive but at least attempting to face the major issue—is to be found in the ECLA *Manual*, pp. 26–28.[24]

3. *Projections of cost components*

(a) *Wages.* One of the gravest deficiencies in the existing literature on project evaluation is its failure to allow, explicitly and systematically, for the expectation that wage rates will rise regularly in the future, relative to product prices. In an economy experiencing successful economic development, it can be anticipated that real wages will rise at a rate of 2 percent per year or more. Thus, whereas the price of the average product will change in accordance with movements in the general price level, wages will increase at a significantly greater rate. The rise of wages at a greater rate than that of prices is possible because of the continued improvement of productive techniques. But in a given project, the technique of production is often determined by the design of the project itself. In this case, labor requirements will be determined by the layout of the plant, the types of machinery installed, etc. Future rises in wages will not in this case be accompanied by reductions in labor requirements, hence project costs will increase to reflect the rise of real wages.

A proper evaluation procedure should surely take into account expected rises in real wages. In cases where future labor-saving innovations are anticipated, which will be applicable to the project in question, these may be taken into account, including in the project analysis the expected cost of introducing the innovations as well as the reduction in labor requirements that is expected to follow.

(b) *The exchange rate.* The exchange rate is an exceedingly important factor in project evaluation and an adequate projection of its expected future course through time is therefore necessary. As with other types of prices, what is of interest is movements of the exchange rate relative to the general price level. Three key questions should be borne in mind in developing exchange rate projections.

First, does the present exchange rate reflect the normal forces of demand and supply, or are certain abnormal forces present which produce an exchange rate that is unlikely to be maintained in the future? Abnormal forces might reflect unusually high or low prices for key export (or import) commodities, unusually large capital movements and/or receipts of foreign aid, etc.

Second, what are the likely trends in the basic demand for imports and the supply of exports? Here one must take into account not only the effects of secular income growth, but also the effects of the changing composition of production. Thus projected expansions of export production, or of import substitutes, would influence the probable future course of the exchange rate.

Third, what are the likely changes in government policy with regard to import restriction? Here one can expect that the liberalization of trade controls will produce a higher price of foreign currency, and their tightening a lower price, than would be the case with unchanged policies.

(c) *Other costs.* The prices of inputs that are manufactured products can generally be projected by the same method as was suggested above for projecting the price of the output of a given project, that is, as a resultant of expected changes in input costs and expected improvements in the technique of production. This procedure is based on the generally valid assumption that the prices of manufactured goods are largely cost-determined.

Minerals and agricultural products, however, are not typically as elastic in supply as manufactured goods. Hence their projection requires an analysis of the likely movements in both supply and demand. Moreover, because of the characteristically low price-elasticity of demand for these products, it can readily occur that the price observed currently is far different from the price to be expected in the longer term future, after the level of production can be adjusted to accommodate the demand situation.

(d) *'Annualized' benefits and costs.* The many possibilities listed above of prices and costs changing over time, as well as the likelihood (discussed in section A) that the relevant discount rate will itself change over the life of a project, indicate the necessity of carrying out project evaluation by projecting expected benefits and costs on a year-by-year basis, and then discounting them back to the present by the appropriate discount factors. The often recommended procedure of attempting to put all benefits and costs on an annualized basis[25] entails the possibility of dangerous oversimplification. As it leads one to presume that all the relevant components of benefits and costs will be (comparatively) constant over time, the 'annualization' approach tends to distract attention from the whole set of problems considered in this section.

4. *Indirect benefits and costs*

In addition to its direct benefits and costs, a project may induce a series of indirect effects, which in principle should be taken into account in its evaluation. These indirect effects are the result of changes that take place in the rest of the economy as a consequence of the project in question having been undertaken. Obviously, any project is likely to have some perceptible effect on the demand and supply of goods produced by other industries, the main effects of this type being in the industries which supply the materials used by the project, and the industries which supply goods which are either complementary to or competitive with the project's output. If, as a consequence of a project, changes occur in the output of an industry for which, at the margin, social benefits equal social costs, no adjustment need be made. But if changes occur in the output of industries for which benefits exceed or fall short of costs, at the margin, an adjustment is in order. The appropriate adjustment is the difference between marginal social benefit and marginal social cost, per unit of output in the industry in question, times the change in the output of that industry which is induced by the project under consideration.

The task of measuring indirect benefits can thus be reduced, first, to ascertaining those industries or activities in the economy for which marginal social benefit (MSB) is likely to differ from marginal social cost (MSC); second, estimating the magnitude of the difference, for each such industry, per unit change in its output and, third, estimating the likely change (ΔQ) in the output of such industries as a consequence of the project being evaluated. Having done this, the estimation of indirect benefits can be calculated by the formula $\sum_i (MSB_i - MSC_i)\Delta Q_i$, where the subscript i varies over all industries for which $MSB_i \neq MSC_i$.[26]

C. USE OF SOCIAL OR ACCOUNTING PRICES IN INDUSTRIAL PROJECT EVALUATION

The early work on cost-benefit analysis did not recommend the use of social or accounting prices. An example is the following:

Ideally, measurement standards in project evaluation should reflect the interest of society as a whole; as such, these standards should be concerned with 'real' costs and benefits. However, it is not practicable to establish and apply 'real' costs and values. Estimates would be in theoretical terms rather than in terms of a monetary unit. All things considered, the most satisfactory approach would result from using prices estimated as they are expected to be at the time when costs are incurred and benefits received. . . . This procedure is recommended as the best available method. It permits a useful working relationship with repayment determination. It takes account of future prices and price relationships based on the best judgment at hand.[27]

This view is in marked contrast with the tone of the more recent literature, as represented by the following:

The market price would represent the true value of goods and services if the law of supply and demand operated freely, under perfect competitive conditions, with full employment of all resources and complete mobility of all factors. If, because of any interference, obstacles, or regulations, these conditions do not exist, then the price system will be distorted; it will not correspond to that ideal system of equilibrium nor represent the value of the factors from the point of view of the community as a whole. It is therefore considered necessary to correct market prices in order to obtain what has been termed the 'social cost' of the factors.[28]

As in the choice among sectors, the basic criterion that is recommended for comparing projects is the social return on the capital invested in each alternative use. . . . Labor, imported materials and export and import substitutes are valued at accounting prices. The remaining inputs are valued at market prices except for a few important elements, such as electric power and transport, for which the market price may seriously understate the amount of resources used in their production. In these cases, accounting prices should be calculated also.[29]

Under the circumstances, a selection of projects based on market prices will result in a misallocation of resources, in the sense that there will be a heavy strain on the resources that are under-priced while part of the resources that are over-priced will be left idle, so that the aggregate yield of the selected projects will fall short of the maximum yield that could have been obtained from the available resources. It is thus necessary to introduce into the evaluation procedure a device intended to restrain the use of under-priced factors and stimulate the use of the overpriced ones. This can be accomplished . . . [by basing] the evaluation on 'shadow' or 'accounting' prices instead of the market prices. The accounting prices are intended to reflect as accurately as possible the intrinsic values of the factors involved.[30]

There can be no doubt that the recent trend towards consideration of accounting prices represents in principle a substantial advance over the alternative position, since it attempts to take into account the effects of divergences between market prices and social costs, while the alternative approach does not. However, the problem still remains of obtaining adequate estimates of the appropriate accounting prices to use, and it must be admitted that this aspect of the problem has not been thoroughly explored in the literature. We turn, therefore, to the examination of this question for the main types of prices.

1. *Accounting prices for labor*

The 'shadow wage,' or accounting price of labor, is an elusive magnitude to estimate, particularly because of the great variety of skills and types of labor, and because of regional immobility of that factor. It can therefore readily occur that the opportunity cost of agricultural labor may be quite low, while the opportunity cost of employing the same labor in industrial projects in the cities is considerably higher. It is necessary, when considering the accounting price of labor, to be specific both as to region and as to skill, and to recognize that it is generally not possible to obtain even the most unskilled labor in urban areas at wage rates similar to those paid such labor in rural places. Thus the accounting price of urban labor should not be considered to be the actual wage received by similar labor in rural employments, but should rather be based, first, on the wage that is required in order to attract this type of labor from rural to urban employment, and second, on an adjustment factor reflecting the higher costs of providing social overhead facilities for urban as against rural workers and their families. It is not correct, as suggested on page 205 of the ECLA *Manual*,[31] to consider the agricultural wage as the opportunity cost or accounting price of labor diverted to urban employment.

Similarly, the existence of unemployment should not be taken to mean that the accounting price of labor is zero, unless the unemployment is so widespread as to include substantial fractions of the labor force of every type and skill. In general, it is likely that the more highly skilled grades of labor will have accounting prices at or very near to their market prices, as these grades of labor are typically in relatively scarce supply, even in periods when the unemployment rate for the total labor force is relatively high. Even for the lower skill grades, the phenomenon of unemployment cannot be taken as direct evidence that the accounting price of labor is substantially below its market price. The unemployment rate must be viewed as the outcome of a number of forces: plant shutdowns, normal labor force turnover, migration to the city and so on. Suppose that, as a consequence of these forces, 6 percent of the urban labor force is at any moment unemployed, and that a new project is established which will occupy 1,000 workers. This new project will also have plant shutdowns, seasonal variation in its demand for labor, normal turnover, etc., and it can very well be that over the year this new plant will engender for these reasons an average unemployment equal to 6 or more percent of its own labor force. In this case it might be concluded that the opportunity cost of labor for the new plant was given by the market wage rate, in the sense that at that wage rate it would be drawing 1,000 workers from the market, who would have been employed 94 percent of the time and unemployed 6 percent of the time, and it will itself employ them 94 percent of the time and leave them unemployed for the remainder.

It is not contended that the above type of calculation should be used as a guide in attempting to arrive at accounting prices for labor; it is merely presented as an example of a case in which the existence of reasonably significant unemployment might plausibly be interpreted as being consistent with an accounting wage equal to the market wage.

Actually, the estimation of accounting wage rates for labor classified by different skills, types and regions is an extremely complex and important area of research which deserves much deeper study than it has had. Such research should take into account not only the forces of seasonality, normal turnover and shutdowns mentioned above, but also should investigate the forces which are operating to keep the market price of labor above its opportunity cost. These latter forces include wage rates set either legally or by union agreement, but often there are large segments of the labor force which are unprotected by either of these means. It is generally to be presumed that in these segments of the labor force the wage rate reflects opportunity cost; and such wage rates can often be taken as minimum estimates of the accounting prices of labor of similar skills and types in the industries and activities in the same region in which labour is protected by minimum wage rates and/or union agreements.

Attempts to specify the nature of the discrepancies between market and accounting prices for labor are necessary for another reason as well—the projection of how these discrepancies are expected to change in the future. It is to be anticipated that, in a developing economy, gross differences between market and accounting wages will tend to be eliminated over time, but the process and speed by which this occurs depend upon the source of the initial discrepancy. In any event, it is reasonable that a cost-benefit analysis should allow for at least the gradual reduction over time of such discrepancies—thus confronting us once more with the importance of carrying out a project analysis through a year-by-year projection of benefits and costs rather than attempting to summarize these solely through annualized estimates largely based on the current situation.

2. *The accounting price of foreign exchange*

Whereas labor is characterized by great heterogeneity and substantial immobility, foreign exchange, at least in a world of convertible currencies, is a basically homogeneous commodity that can readily be shifted from one use to another. Thus, where in principle numerous accounting prices will be required for labor, only one will typically be required for convertible foreign exchange. Nonetheless, serious difficulties arise in estimating this accounting price, owing to the many distinct uses to which foreign exchange can be put. This can easily be seen by considering a tariff structure in which some items are not taxed at all, while others are taxed at, say, 20 percent, and still others at, say, 50 percent. If the exchange rate is 5 rupees to the dollar, a dollar spent on imports of category 1 will bring in goods having an internal value of 5 rupees, while a dollar spent on category 2 will bring in goods having an internal value of

6 rupees, and the same dollar spent on category 3 will bring in goods having the internal value of $7\frac{1}{2}$ rupees. The value produced by the dollar thus varies with its use.

The key to estimating the accounting price of foreign exchange is to estimate the likely pattern in which incremental dollars would be distributed over the various categories of goods. If it was anticipated that extra dollars would be spent 50 percent on category 1, 30 percent on category 2, and 20 percent on category 3, then the internal value of a marginal dollar would be $(\cdot5)(5) + (\cdot3)(6) + (\cdot2)(7\cdot5)$, or 5·8 rupees.

This procedure for estimating the accounting price of foreign exchange can also be applied to goods which are subject to licensing or other restrictions rather then tariffs, but here one must estimate independently on the basis of available market evidence what is the internal value of a dollar's worth of each type of goods so restricted.

The basic difficulty with the suggested procedure is estimating the pattern in which incremental foreign exchange will be distributed among imports, but this can be at least roughly estimated on the basis of past marginal distributions of foreign exchange, for instance, by ascertaining from import statistics how the increase in foreign exchange availabilities from, say, 1960 to 1965 was in fact used. More accurate estimates could be obtained by serious econometric study of the demand for different categories of imports. In some cases, the exchange licensing authorities might themselves have a policy indicating how they would allocate any additional sums becoming available.

The procedure outlined above assumes that the incremental foreign exchange will be used to augment the total supply, that is, that it will not force down the price exporters receive for foreign currency. If it does this, then the above procedure would be applied to estimate the value of the net increment to the supply of foreign currency, and the rate of exchange applicable to exports would reflect the value attaching to the use of incremental foreign currency for displaced exports.

This procedure is closely attuned to the economic reality; as such it is far preferable to the procedure recommended in the ECLA *Manual* (p. 204) of arriving at the accounting price of foreign currency on the basis of a purchasing power parity formula. The great difficulty with the purchasing power parity approach is that it is valid only when the casual factors at work between the two situations being compared were completely monetary, as in the case of differential rates of inflation in the two countries whose currencies are being compared. But the function of the exchange rate in cost-benefit analysis is basically as a guide to resource allocation. Rather than looking backward to a base year and being concerned with monetary changes having taken place in the past, cost-benefit analysis looks at the present and the future, and attempts to evaluate alternative projects in 'real' terms. There can be no doubt that a direct effort at estimating the value to the economy today of the goods an extra dollar is likely to buy forms a better basis of judgment of the value of foreign exchange than a mechanical extrapolation from some past year. By the same token, the analysis of the current value of foreign exchange, in the manner indicated above, provides the most reasonable starting point for the projection of the time path of this variable in the future.

3. *Accounting prices for inputs of materials*

The problem of arriving at accounting prices for materials is in some respects similar to that for foreign exchange. Suppose that the market price of a material is $5 and its social cost of production is $4. A project under consideration will use some of this material, and the question arises of setting the appropriate accounting price. The problem that faces us can be summarized by considering two extreme possibilities. On the one hand, the output of the material may remain constant, and the supply for the project under consideration may be diverted from other uses. In this case the appropriate accounting price is the market price which can be taken to represent the marginal value of the material in its other uses. On the other hand, the project's demand for the material might be met by increasing its supply: in this case it appears that the appropriate accounting price is $4, the true economic cost of producing each added unit.

This apparently plausible conclusion, however, is not always correct. For, suppose that the materials-producing industry were to augment its output by the same amount, in the absence of the project being considered. This increased output could, presumably, be sold at prices in the neighbourhood of $5—say, between \$4·90 and \$5·00—on the open market. Some reduction in price would presumably have to occur to induce additional sales, but unless the demand of the project in question were very great indeed relative to the initial level of production of the material, or unless the overall demand for the material were very inelastic, the required reduction in price would not be very great. Thus even if the production of the material expands in response to the project's additional demand, the opportunity cost of the project's use of the material can be approximated by the market price of the material rather than by its social cost of production.

The use of the market price of materials as their social or accounting price has another advantage in avoiding the double-counting of benefits among projects. Suppose that project *A* is a construction project, in which substantial amounts of cement will be used. Suppose, further, that project *B* is a project to expand capacity in the cement industry. If cement is valued at its market price in evaluating project *B*, and is also valued at its market price in evaluating project *A*, we can be sure that there will be no double counting of benefits. But if cement is valued at \$5 in evaluating project *B* and at \$4 in evaluating project *A*, the difference of \$1 per unit will be counted as benefits for both projects—clearly a dubious procedure. In order for \$4 to be a valid accounting price for the cement used in project *A*, project *B* must meet two stringent conditions: first, present value of benefits equals present value of costs, when the cement is priced at \$4 and, secondly, the cement produced by project *B* must have a value no greater than \$4 in alternative uses (other than project *A*).

Having thus indicated the grounds for preferring the use of market prices for materials inputs, it is imperative to qualify this preference by noting that, when the output of a material in fact expands as a consequence of a given material-using project, and where that material does not have an alternative use in which its value lies above the cost of producing the material, and where the market price is nonetheless above the cost of producing the material, an accounting price equal to the cost of production of the material is appropriate for use in evaluating the material-using project.

Examples of cases meeting these conditions can indeed be

found. Perhaps the clearest case is one in which, first, the material has an infinite elasticity of supply at a price equal to its unit cost of production and, second, a tax exists which makes the market price higher than unit production cost. In this case, any expansion in the industry has social benefits greater than social costs by the amount of the additional tax collections. Moreover, even though with a cost of $4 and a market price of $5 (= $4 plus $1 tax), added production of the material could be sold if offered at a price of $4.95, it will not be so sold because this would entail a loss to the producers. In fact, the expansion of output of the material is strictly contingent on the emergence of additional demand at a price of $5 and, so long as the tax remains at $1 and the net-of-tax supply price remains at $4, each increment of demand at the price of $5 will in fact generate the additional supply necessary to meet it. And, assuming the supply price truly reflects the social costs involved, the net-of-tax price can in such cases be used as the accounting price of the material.

Even in such a case, however, it might be preferable to use the market price of the material in the basic calculations of the direct costs and benefits of the material-using project, and to count the extra tax payment generated by the project on account of the expansion of material supply as an indirect benefit of the project. The two procedures amount to the same thing, and counting as indirect benefits the excess of benefits over costs generated in other activities as a consequence of a given project permits the adoption of the standard rule that accounting prices of materials should always be their market prices.

4. *Accounting prices for the output of a project*

Where products are freely sold at the market price, the social benefit attaching to such products should be measured by their market prices. Where, however, goods are subject to rationing or licensing, accounting prices different from market prices are indicated. In this case the accounting prices should attempt to reflect the intrinsic value of an increment of output to those who purchase it.

Where products are subject to indirect taxation, the market price inclusive of tax should be used as the measure of benefits.

This is clearly seen by the United States Inter-Agency Committee on Water Resources:

> To the extent that taxes are reflected in the market prices of goods and services, such taxes . . . will have been considered in estimating the value of the goods and services produced by . . . development projects. No deductions for taxes in market prices should be made, since this would reduce the value of benefits below the actual appraisal of the market as indicated by consumers' preferences of willingness to pay.[32]

The ECLA *Manual*, on the other hand, recommends elimination of taxes and subsidies on the ground that 'greater or lesser customs duties or sales taxes cause variations in selling prices, unrelated to the effort involved. . . . Thus variations in the amount of sales tax, or the list of goods to which it is applicable, can vary the apparent productivity of projects employing such goods or services, distorting their relative position in the priority scale, although there have been in fact no changes in productivity. Similar observations can be made for subsidies, inasmuch as they are "negative taxes".'[33]

The position taken in the ECLA *Manual* is difficult to interpret as it does not distinguish clearly between taxes upon materials inputs and taxes upon the output of a project. In the example given, the reference appears to be to materials inputs. If correction for taxes and subsidies on materials inputs is all that is meant, then no exception can be taken to the statement. Taxes on materials, as indicated above, mean that benefits exceed costs in the materials-producing industry, and a project can in this case legitimately consider the additional taxes generated on account of its increased use of materials to be an indirect benefit of the project.

On the other hand, if the statement is taken to refer to taxes on the output of a project as well as on materials, one must take exception to it, the value to purchasers of the product being the price that they pay for it, which clearly includes the tax.

The only exception to the general rule that taxes paid on the product of an activity are to be included in the benefits of that activity is the case in which the taxes are designed to correct a previously existing disequilibrium between social benefits and market price. Thus, if an activity produces a product with a price of $1, but the consumption or production of that product engenders external diseconomies of $.10, the market equilibrium will be one in which, at the margin, consumers of the product receive a benefit of $1, but others suffer an added cost of $.10 for each unit consumed. In this case a tax of $.10 would be indicated as a corrective measure. The price, including tax, would be $1.10, the consumers of the product would have a benefit, at the margin, of $1.10, but other consumers would lose $.10 per unit, so that the total social benefit would be $1 per unit, in this case being the market price less the tax. Since in fact virtually no taxes are levied for the purpose of overcoming the extrenal diseconomies associated with the consumption or production of a product, the general rule should be to measure benefits by market prices including taxes, and to deduct from such benefits any identifiable external diseconomies.

In short, since no presumption can be established that the existing taxes are an appropriate measure of external diseconomies, or that existing subsidies are an appropriate measure of external economies, market prices gross of taxes should be taken as the proximate measure of benefits, and in the project analysis itself the attempt should be made to correct for external economies or diseconomies associated with a project, either in the production of the project's output or in its consumption. It is to be anticipated that cases of significant external effects of this type will be rare, and not closely related to the amounts of tax or subsidy on the product in question.

5. *Accounting prices obtained from linear programming models*

It has sometimes been suggested that accounting prices be obtained on the basis of a linear programming model.[34] This approach has proved highly valuable in the programming of activities within a firm, and its successful extension to problems of greater scope is a distinct possibility. However, it is unlikely that this technique will be able to yield relevant accounting prices for a national economy as a whole. In principle, this would require an accurate description of all actual and potential productive processes within the economy, and an accurate inventory of its resources. Moreover, it should also entail a study of the transferability of resources from one category to another (i.e., how many factory operatives could work effectively as carpenters? how many could be trained to do so at a given cost? etc.). These requirements of basic data go far beyond the foreseeable possibilities.

As a consequence, the application of linear programming techniques in practice requires that the problem be drastically oversimplified—by assuming that one or two or three processes can describe the activities available to an industry by aggregating industries into a few broad groups, by considering all labour to be homogeneous, and so on. The resulting 'shadow prices' that emerge from the analysis can, unfortunately, be very sensitive to the way in which the simplification is done, and as a consequence little faith can be placed in the results of any particular simplification. Since drastic simplification is an unavoidable necessity in using linear programming models for an entire economy, there is no way of avoiding serious uncertainty as to the validity of the resulting 'shadow prices.'

D. PROBLEMS OF TIMING

1. *Choices among projects of different productive lives and different gestation periods*

As the analysis of section *A* showed, the problem of placing projects with different time profiles on a comparable footing is reduced to the problem of obtaining an appropriate set of discount rates, reflecting for each point in time the opportunity cost of capital at that time. Once this set of discount rates $(r_1, r_2, \ldots, r_N,$ for years $1, 2, \ldots, N$ in the future) is obtained, the relevant criterion for project choice is to maximize the net present value of the entire investment operation, considering investments to be made this year as well as investments to be made in future years.

The particular relevance of the pattern of discount rates to choices among projects lies in the fact that high discount rates weigh heavily against projects with long gestation periods and long productive lives. Thus a project with a one-year gestation period and a total cost of $1,000 would have to yield $200 per year in perpetuity in order to be justified at a 20 percent discount rate, starting a year from now. But a project whose construction costs were spread out over five years, in equal quotas of $200 per year, would have to yield $318 per year in perpetuity, starting five years from now, in order to pass the 20 percent test. The required absolute benefit increases rapidly with the length of the gestation period; if the same $1,000 of investment were spread evenly over a ten-year gestation period, the required yield would be $559 per year in perpetuity in order to make the investment worth-while at a 20 percent rate of discount.

By the same token, the length of duration of the benefit stream takes on less importance at high discount rates than at low ones. The present value of $100 per year, in perpetuity, at a 20 percent rate, is $500; but the present value of $100 per year for just the next ten years is $419, or nearly as much as that of the perpetual stream.

These considerations come to be of crucial importance when the relevant discount rates are high, which is likely to be the case for most developing countries. Not only is it true that the private rate of return tends to be high (probably 10 percent or more) in these countries, but this rate of return has also to be adjusted upward to reflect both taxes attributable to capital and differences between the market prices and opportunity costs of associated factors of production, in order to arrive at an estimate of the social rate of return. In particular, any substantial excess of the market price of labor over its opportunity cost is likely to raise the social rate of return to capital significantly above the market rate. This point is clearly seen by Tinbergen, when he says, 'Very probably the equilibrium level of wage rates will be considerably less than market wages. On the other hand, equilibrium interest rates probably are much higher than market rates.'[35]

Considerations of gestation periods and productive life are important in the choice of the scale of a project as well as in choosing among different projects. Obviously, the scale of a project will affect the pattern of both costs and benefits through time. The optimal scale for a project at any given point in time is that for which the present value of benefits minus costs is a maximum. If scale is a continuous variable, then optimum scale is reached when the increment to the present value of benefits stemming from a small expansion of scale is just equal to the increment in present value of costs associated with that same expansion.[36]

2. *Criteria for deciding when to postpone a given project*

The existing literature on cost-benefit analysis typically is not at all explicit on the question of when to initiate a project. Failure to consider this choice can lead to serious mistakes, however. Suppose, for example, that a project could be constructed this year for a capital cost of $1,000, and would then produce a stream of expected net benefits having a present value of $1,050, evaluated at the relevant set of discount rates. It appears that this project is worth doing. Yet suppose that the same project, constructed next year, would have an expected capital cost of $1,050, and an expected present value of net benefits of $1,150. The net present value of the project would be $100, evaluated as of next year, or $100/(1 + r_1), evaluated as of this year. Obviously, it pays to postpone construction of the project, so long as r_1, the rate of discount applicable for comparisons between this year and next, is less than 100 per cent.

The solution to the pure timing problem, as to when to do a particular project, is simply an application of the general present value rule. Let N_i be the net present value, evaluated as of today, of the project in question if it is to be constructed in the year i. The optimum construction time is then that year i^* for which N_i is at its maximum. N_i can vary with i because the capital costs of the project will depend on the date of its construction, and/or because the net benefit accruing in any future year will vary, depending on the date of construction (that is, depending on the age of the project), and/or because by postponing a project for a year we lose the first year's net benefits and gain an extra year's net benefits at the end of the project's life. All these elements are incorporated in the calculation of N_i for various starting times, and in the procedure of choice which chooses i^* to maximize N_i.

A particularly simple special case of the timing choice occurs when net benefits accruing in any year depend only on the year (in the sense of calendar time) and not on the age of the project, and in which the anticipated capital cost of constructing the project does not change through time, and in which the project has an infinite life. In this case, provided that the net benefit stream is an increasing function of time in the neighbourhood of the optimal construction date, the optimal construction date is that point in time i^* in which the first year net benefits of the project are just equal to its cost of construction times the interest rate r_{i^*+1}.

The reasoning behind this is simple. Regardless whether the project is constructed in the year 0 or in year 1, it will be in operation from year 2 onwards. Therefore all net benefits from year 2 onwards will be present in either case, and the decision whether or not to postpone the construction of the project from 0 to 1 cannot depend on them. The postponement decision turns simply on the question whether the net benefits to be obtained in the year 1, which will be enjoyed if the project is already constructed by then, are sufficient to compensate for the cost of constructing the project one year earlier (in year 0 rather than year 1). The cost entailed in constructing earlier is simply the interest rate reflecting the opportunity cost of capital between 0 and 1, which we have denominated r_i. Thus the fact that net benefits will increase in the future does not justify the construction of a project now. The time to construct the project is when the immediately forthcoming benefits are sufficient to justify the immediate use of the capital funds in question.

In a slightly less simple case, if construction costs are expected to increase between this year and next, the requirement for construction this year is that the net costs of postponement (which now consist of the net benefit of year 1 plus the increase in construction costs between year 0 and year 1) be less than r_1 times the capital cost of constructing the project in year 0. Thus a project whose capital costs are expected to increase with postponement will qualify for earlier construction, while one whose capital costs are expected to decrease with postponement will require further delay of construction than was indicated in the previous example, which assumed capital costs not to vary with the date of construction. These modifications can be of some importance, for in some industries expected improvements in technology can lead to reduction over time in the capital cost of a project, while in other lines expected rises in labor and materials costs can work in the opposite direction.

An excellent discussion of the timing problem, including a

consideration of the case of projects of finite life, which reveals only minor differences from that just outlined for the case of infinite life projects, is to be found in Stephen A. Marglin, *Approaches to Dynamic Investment Planning*.[37]

3. *The relation of investment decisions and timing to uncertainty and risk*

The conventional approach to making allowance for risk is well reflected in the following quotation:

> It is recommended that net returns exclude all predictable risks, either by deducting them from benefits or adding them to project costs, usually on a present worth or annual equivalent basis. Allowance for uncertainties or unpredictable risks in benefit accrual should be made indirectly by use of conservative estimates of net benefits, requirement of safety margins in planning, or including a risk component in the discount rate.[38]

The difficulty with this statement, and indeed with most discussions of the subject, is that it is not explicit on how to cope with uncertainties or 'unpredictable risks'. Virtually all writers agree that predictable risks of fire, hazard, etc., should be dealt with on an insurance basis. But when it comes to other types of risk or uncertainty, a wide divergence of opinion emerges. Eckstein argues that a premium in the interest rate is 'the most useful adjustment for risk in project evaluation'[39] and Hirschleifer comes to a similar conclusion.[40] Arrow, however, argues[41] that the Government should not display risk aversion, that is, should not incorporate a risk premium in the discount rate it uses, and Marglin maintains[42] that where the net-benefit stream is rising over time, the criteria arrived at in section D, 2, above, give appropriate guides to investment decisions and their timing, without adjustment for uncertainty.

The issue in question appears to be in large part (although not entirely) semantic. Eckstein asserts that future changes in technology will, if they occur at all, be improvements, reducing the net benefit to be obtained from an investment made today (which would in this case become obsolescent). Clearly, if the probability of such changes has not already been taken into account in the estimation of future net benefits, it must be considered at some point, and one way to do this is to give relatively less weight to future benefits by raising the discount rate applicable to them. Likewise, if future technological changes have not been adequately foreseen, taking them into account may alter the shape of Marglin's rising net benefit stream, and turn it into one which first rises and then falls, or one which falls uniformly with time. In this case the fact that next year's net benefits covered the interest cost on this year's investment in a project would not be a sufficient basis for justifying the project's construction; there would have to be further checking to see whether the present value of the (adjusted) net benefit stream was in fact greater than or equal to the capital cost.

In principle, Arrow and Marglin appear to be closer to the truth than those who would place an explicit risk premium on future net benefits, but this assumes that all estimates of future benefits and costs have been adjusted to incorporate our best guesses as to expected changes in these magnitudes. It may be concluded that an adjustment of the discount rate for a risk premium on future benefits is, by its nature, likely to be applied quite generally, implicitly assuming that 'unadjusted' calculations of future benefits should be adjusted in the same way regardless of the type of investment, line of activity, etc. Since expected changes in product prices and factor costs, and expected improvements in technology as such are likely to be very different for different types and lines of investment, the adjustment for these changes should be carried out by as detailed as possible an extrapolation of individual cost and benefit items on each project separately, rather than being dealt with by a global risk premium attached to future discount rates.

The procedure suggested here implicitly assumes that the government does not have risk aversion as such, which appears to be a fair assumption since the wide variety of governmental investments ensures a substantial amount of risk-reduction through diversification. Moreover, the private-sector investments which yield the marginal productivity of capital that should be used as the discount rate in public investment decisions are themselves extremely widely diversified, and when taken in the aggregate as distinct from individually, appear to entail very little risk. Thus with both the public-sector package of investments and its private-sector alternative being widely diversified and therefore of relatively low risk, the assumption that the public authorities are neutral to risk appears quite reasonable.

E. INTERRELATIONS AMONG PROJECTS

1. *Separability of components of a project*

Like the choice of scale of a project, the problem of dealing with separable components is readily handled using the present value rule. As the United States Federal Inter-Agency Committee on Water Resources puts it:

> Net benefits are maximized if the scale of development is extended to the point where the benefits added by the last increment of scale or scope are equal to the cost of adding that increment. The increments to be considered in this way are the smallest increments on which there is a practical choice as to inclusion or omission from the project. The same principle applies when selecting a number of projects to form a programme or system of projects to meet a given objective. To be justified for inclusion in a plan, each project in a group, each purpose of a project, and each separable segment of a project should add as much or more benefits as it adds costs.[43]

This principle is indeed the correct one to apply so long as all projects having a positive excess of benefits over costs can be financed, a proviso that we have assumed to be met, given the possibility of government borrowing. However, it is important to recognize that the principle applies to large as well as small components of a project. A case in point occurred in the evaluation of the benefits of the publicly owned beet-sugar refining industry in Chile. Here large benefits were attributed to the indirect effect of the extension services given to farmers upon their general efficiency of operation. On the presumption that similar extension services could be given even if no sugar-beets were cultivated, the benefits in question should be attributed to the extension operation and not to the over-all sugar-beet project. Thus the extension operation could be viewed as a separable component, and evaluated separately from the rest of the project. When this was done, the main project turned out to be of dubious validity, even though the extension component was quite clearly worth-while.[44]

The careful examination of possibilities of separating components from a project is as important an aspect of appropriate design and evaluation procedures as the study of possibilities of adding components. It is, moreover, an aspect of cost-benefit analysis which has not received sufficient attention to date.

2. *Criteria for the evaluation of groups of projects*

The evaluation of groups of projects is quite similar in nature to the problem of dealing with separable components. There is no need to consider groupings of projects when their benefits and costs are independent, but when the benefits or cost associated with one project is to be different, depending upon whether or not another project is undertaken, the analysis of the projects so related should be done jointly. The appropriate method is shown below.

Let $PVB\ (A)$ stand for the present value of the benefits of project A if it is undertaken alone, and $PVC\ (A)$ stand for the present value of its costs (including both capital and operating costs) if undertaken alone. Correspondingly, $PVB\ (B)$ represents the present value of the benefits of project B, undertaken alone, and $PVB\ (AB)$ represents the present value of benefits of A and B taken together. A similar notation will be used for costs. Two projects are independent on the benefit side when $PVB\ (AB) = PVB\ (A) + PVB\ (B)$; they are independent on the cost side when $PVC\ (AB) = PVC\ (A) + PVC\ (B)$. The projects are:

(a) Complementary on the benefit side when

$$PVB\ (AB) > PVB\ (A) + PVB\ (B);$$

(b) Substitutes on the benefit side when

$$PVB\ (AB) < PVB\ (A) + PVB\ (B);$$

(c) Complementary on the cost side when

$$PVC\ (AB) < PVC\ (A) + PVC\ (B);$$

(d) Substitutes on the cost side when

$$PVC\ (AB) > PVC\ (A) + PVC\ (B).$$

Let $N = PVB - PVC$ be the net present value of any project or group of projects. The principle of choice is to maximize the total net present value. Thus if there are three projects which are interrelated on either the demand or cost side or on both, there will be seven possible options. A, B, or C can be undertaken alone, or A and B together, A and C together, or B and C together, or, finally, all three projects together. The criterion for choice in this case is reduced to finding which of the following seven magnitudes is the largest: $N(A)$, $N(B)$, $N(C)$, $N(AB)$, $N(AC)$, $N(BC)$, $N(ABC)$, and investing in that project or combination of projects.

This criterion for choice among groups of projects can be extended to any number of interrelated projects. It automatically takes account of the effects of any given project on the benefits and/or costs of other projects in the group. Moreover, it can also handle the problem of timing, simply by including as separate projects in the list of possibilities of constructing a given project at different times. Thus if we had two projects, A and B, and were considering the benefits of constructing either or both of them, with options of timing in years 1, 2, and 3, there would be fifteen possible options whose net present values would have to be compared: A_1, A_2, A_3, B_1, B_2, B_3, A_1B_1, A_1B_2, A_1B_3, A_2B_1, A_2B_2, A_2B_3, A_3B_1, A_3B_2, A_3B_3, and the problem would be reduced to finding which of these options had the greatest net present value, when the benefits and costs of all of them were discounted back to the same point in time.

Notes

[1] Princeton: Princeton University Press, 1951, pp. 16–48.

[2] New York: John Wiley, 1958, pp. 89–92.

[3] *Journal of Political Economy*, University of Chicago Press, August 1958.

[4] Princeton: Princeton University Press, 1963, appendix A.

[5] Princeton: Princeton University Press, 1961.

[6] In C. A. Anderson and M. J. Bowman, eds., *Education and Economic Development*, Chicago: Aldine, 1965.

[7] United States Inter-Agency Committee on Water Resources, *Proposed Practices for Economic Analysis of River Basin Projects*, Washington, D.C.: U.S. Government Printing Office, 1958, p. 24.

[8] H. W. Singer, 'Development projects as part of national development programmes', in *Formulation and Economic Appraisal of Development Projects*, United Nations publication, Sales No.: 51.II.B.3, pp. 123–24.

[9] J. Tinbergen, *The Design of Development*, Baltimore: Johns Hopkins University Press, 1958, pp. 40, 42.

[10] 'Evaluation of projects in predominantly private enterprise economies', *Bulletin on Industrialization and Productivity*, No. 5, United Nations publication, Sales No.: 62.II.B.1, p. 30.

[11] Otto Eckstein, *Water Resource Development: the Economics of Project Evaluation,* Cambridge, Mass.: Harvard University Press, 1958, pp. 99–100.

[12] *Quarterly Journal of Economics,* Cambridge, Mass.: Harvard University Press, February 1957.

[13] *Ibid.,* February 1963.

[14] *Economic Journal,* Cambridge, England: September 1961.

[15] *Op. cit.* (see footnote 11, above). See also J. V. Krutilla and O. Eckstein, *Multiple Purpose River Development,* Baltimore: Johns Hopkins University Press, 1958.

[16] See Stephen A. Marglin, 'The opportunity costs of public investment', *Quarterly Journal of Economics,* Cambridge, Mass.: Harvard University Press, May 1963.

[17] *American Economic Review,* Evanston, Ill.: Northwestern University Press, December 1959.

[18] This view is supported in a recent paper by Arrow, who says that, so long as public investment can be financed by bonds or taxation, 'the rates of return in the two sectors (public and private) should be equated at every instant of time, but the government through its bond and tax policies should aim at driving the common rate towards the natural rate of interest. The optimal policy may well involve negative bond financing, i.e. government lending or retirement of the national debt' (Kenneth J. Arrow, 'Discounting and public investment criteria', paper presented at the 1965 Western Resources Conference, Seminar on Water Resources Research, 6 July 1965).

[19] Stigler, *op. cit.* (see footnote 4, above).

[20] See Pierre Massé, *Optimal Investment Decisions,* Englewood Cliffs, N.J.: Prentice-Hall, 1962, pp. 10–20. For an earlier discussion of the same problem, see Irving Fisher, *The Theory of Interest,* New York: Macmillan, 1930.

[21] See, for example, R. M. Solow, 'Technical change and the aggregate production function', *Review of Economics and Statistics,* August 1957, and E. F. Denison, *The Sources of Economic Growth in the United States and the Alternatives Before Us,* New York: Committee for Economic Development, 1962.

[22] See United States President's Materials Policy Commission, *Resources for Freedom,* Washington, D.C.: Government Printing Office, 1952, vol. II, chap. 22, 'Projection of 1975 materials demand': United Nations Economic Commission for Latin America (ECLA), *Analyses and Projections of Economic Development,* vol. I, United Nations publication, Sales No.: 55.I.G.2, pp. 32–33, and the ECLA *Manual on Economic Development Projects,* United Nations publication, Sales No.: 58.II.G.5, p. 24.

[23] For an example, see 'Projection of demand for industrial equipment' in *Industrialization and Productivity Bulletin* No. 7, United Nations publication, Sales No.: 64.II.B.1.

[24] See footnote 22, above.

[25] See ECLA *Manual* (see footnote 22, above), pp. 198 ff.

[26] See United States Inter-Agency Committee on Water Resources, *op. cit.* (see footnote 7, above), p. 3.

[27] H. W. Singer, 'Development projects as part of national development programmes', in *Formulation and Economic Appraisal of Development Projects,* United Nations publication, Sales No.: 51.II.B.4/vol. I, pp. 121–22.

[28] ECLA *Manual* (see footnote 22, above), p. 203.

[29] Economic Commission for Asia and the Far East (ECAFE). *Formulating Industrial Development Programmes,* United Nations publication, Sales No.: 61.II.F.7, p. 39.

[30] 'Evaluation of projects in predominantly private enterprise economies', *Bulletin on Industrialization and Productivity,* No. 5, United Nations publication, Sales No.: 62.II.B.1, p. 29.

[31] See footnote 22, above.

[32] *Op. cit.* (see footnote 26, above), p. 30.

[33] *Op. cit.* (see footnote 22, above), p. 203.

[34] See H. B. Chenery and Paul G. Clark, *Interindustry Economics*, New York: Wiley, 1959, chap. 11.

[35] *Op. cit.* (see footnote 9, above), p. 39.

[36] On these points, see Friedrich and Vera Lutz, *op. cit.* (see footnote 1, above), pp. 22–32, and Pierre Massé, *op. cit.* (see footnote 20, above), pp. 42–81.

[37] Amsterdam: North-Holland Publishing Co., 1963; see especially pp. 9 to 34.

[38] United States Inter-Agency Committee on Water Resources, *op. cit.* (see footnote 7, above), p. 23.

[39] *Op. cit.* (see footnote 11, above), p. 90.

[40] 'Risk, the discount rate and investment decisions', *American Economic Review*, Evanston, Ill.: Northwestern University Press, May 1961.

[41] *Op. cit.* (see footnote 18, above).

[42] *Op. cit.* (see footnote 16, above), pp. 31, 71–72.

[43] *Op. cit.* (see footnote 7, above), p. 14.

[44] See Ernesto R. Fontaine, 'Un analisis de los costos y beneficios sociales de la industria azucarera nacional, S.A.', in *Estudios de Economia*, Santiago: Catholic University of Chile, 1961, pp. 31–32.

CHAPTER THREE

ON DISCOUNT RATES FOR COST-BENEFIT ANALYSIS

I. INTRODUCTION

This paper is concerned with the choice of the appropriate rate of discount for use in cost-benefit analysis and project appraisal. In particular, attention is focused on the manner in which the appropriate discount rate depends upon the conditions prevailing in the labor market of the economy in question. Where labor is genuinely in excess supply, to the point where all workers to be employed in the operation of a project can be assumed to be drawn from a large pool of unemployed, the wages to be paid to labor should not be counted as an economic cost, and should therefore not be deducted from the gross benefit stemming from the investment in the project. The consequence of this procedure is to produce high estimated returns to investment, and consequently a high discount rate for cost-benefit work. For India in particular, the assumption of a superabundant labor supply, in the sense just mentioned, would appear to require that a discount rate of over 30 percent be used in cost-benefit analysis.

When, on the other hand, the labor market of an economy is functioning well, and is expected to produce relatively full employment in future years, the wage payments involved in the operation of a project should normally be counted as true economic costs of that project, and should therefore be deducted, along with costs of materials, etc., from the gross benefits of the

This paper was published as 'Sobre las Tasas de Descuento en el Analisis de Beneficio-Costo', Economic Development Institute (World Bank), *Trabajos Sobre Desarrollo Economico*, 1966–67 (Washington, 1967); reprinted in *Revista del Banco Hypotecario de el Salvador*, January–March 1969 and (in Portuguese) in *Revista de Teoria e Pesquisa Economica* (October 1969).

project before arriving at its expected net benefit stream. This more traditional approach leads to an estimated discount rate far lower than that obtained on the assumption of truly super-abundant labor, but even so the resulting rate for India appears to be well in excess of 10 percent per annum—a figure substantially above the rates used in official Indian project evaluation procedures.

Between the extremes of superabundant labor on the one hand and a 'tight' labor market on the other lie a whole continuum of possible 'hybrid' situations, in which part but not all of the wage bill should be treated as a project cost. Associated with these intermediate situations are discount rates for cost-benefit analysis that are higher, the lower the fraction of the wage bill that is considered to be a true economic cost of the project's operation. These rates for India would range from something above 10 to something above 30 percent as one reduced from 100 to zero percent the fraction of the wages bill assigned as project cost.

II. THE RELEVANCE OF THE MARGINAL PRODUCTIVITY OF CAPITAL IN THE PRIVATE SECTOR

In the calculation of the appropriate rate of discount to be applied in India under any given set of assumptions, I have tried to estimate what would be the marginal productivity of capital in the private sector of the Indian economy under these assumptions.

I justify this approach by noting that if a government wishes to use a certain amount of its financial resources to provide benefits (via investment) for future generations, among the avenues open to it are investments in industrial establishments similar in nature to those already existing in the private sector. Such investments could be made directly in government-owned establishments, or indirectly by providing equity and debt financing for the establishment or expansion of basically private enterprises. It should be noted here that many precedents exist for both of these ways of using public-sector funds. Many countries (and particularly India) have established government-owned firms in areas traditionally served by the private sector, and the mixed corporation (owned partly by government and partly by individuals) is a familiar element on the economic landscape of a number of countries.

Two important caveats must be borne in mind in using the private-sector rate of return as the criterion for public-sector projects. The first is that, in measuring the private-sector rate of return, social benefits which do not accrue to the private investors themselves but are attributable to their investments must be counted as part of the return to capital. This simply reflects the fact that government decisions on the uses of public funds within the public sector can (and should) be governed by weighing against their costs the total benefits produced by such projects; thus in order to place private-sector investments on a comparable basis the same procedure should be used. This entails attributing as benefits (a) such taxes as are paid out of the income generated by investments, (b) any net increment to consumer surplus that would result from a typical marginal investment in the private sector, (c) any excess of wages paid over the alternative earnings of the workers employed, and (d) any external benefits associated with private-sector investments.

The second caveat concerns the use of the observed average 'social' rate of return on private investments rather than the expected future 'social' rate of return on such investments. Obviously, when we consider the various possible uses of today's investible funds, what we should compare are the future rates of return that are expected to accrue from investments in alternative projects. The rate of return that is observed today on past investments in the private sector can therefore be no more than a guide to the probable outcome of new investments in this area. It is likely to be a better guide if it has maintained its level over a relatively long period than if it has shown a significant upward or downward trend, but even so it is still only a guide. Particular care must be taken to avoid using the private-sector rate of return in a particular narrow class of investments as the criterion rate for social projects, if it is felt that any significant expansion of the capital stock in that private-sector activity would have the effect of significantly reducing the rate of return.

If, on the other hand, a fairly broad class of private-sector activities is considered as the alternative outlet for public-sector investible funds, and if these are activities for which demand is likely to grow significantly in the future, then the likelihood is strong that these activities will be able to absorb substantial amounts of public-sector funds, without a significant reduction in their rate of return, and the use of their currently-measured rate of return as the criterion-rate for public-sector projects is more readily justified.

Thus if one can demonstrate the existence of ample investment opportunities in the private sector having 'social' marginal productivities of, say, 15 percent per annum or more, we cannot in the face of this evidence justify public-sector investments promising a 'social' yield of only 10 percent. The ideal investment policy would strive to equalize the 'social' marginal productivity of capital in all lines of activity. But even a less than ideal policy—one recognizing the existence of numerous market and other imperfections—would nonetheless require that public-sector projects produce an expected yield equal to the average 'social' rate of marginal productivity in the private sector of the economy or in a relevant subsegment thereof. Particularly in India, where the public sector has invested in a wide range of activities that in many other countries remain in private hands, one of the reasonable alternatives to doing any given public-sector project would be to invest in one or more lines of activity now dominated by the private sector. The rates of return obtainable on such investments thus become directly meaningful for decisions on the allocation of the investible resources of the public sector, and investment of substantial funds at expected rates of social return significantly below those obtainable within the private sector would appear to reflect poor decision-making and/or implementation. If policies can be pursued, and funds mobilized to drive the social rate of return down to 10 percent everywhere, well and good; but in the meantime the social rate of return in the private sector represents a challenge that public-sector projects should be called upon to meet. If not enough public-sector projects can be found that meet this challenge, the surplus investible funds of the public sector should be channeled, directly or indirectly, into the (presently private-sector) activities of highest yield.

III. MEASURING THE SOCIAL YIELD OF PRIVATE IN-
VESTMENTS ASSUMING A 'SHADOW WAGE' OF ZERO

In this section I shall outline the procedures followed and summarize the results obtained in calculations designed to estimate the social rate of marginal productivity of capital in the 'modern' private sector of the Indian economy, on the assumption that the 'shadow wage' is zero. This last assumption reflects a belief that is widespread in the literature on under-developed countries in general and especially on India. I shall not for the moment attempt to argue the merits of this assumption, but simply follow through its logical consequences in the field of project evaluation. Operating on this assumption, we must attribute the full value added of an operation to the capital invested therein: the rate of return to capital becomes, in effect, the value-added/capital ratio. Since we are concerned with social rather than private benefits, value added should be calculated gross of taxes—both direct and indirect—paid by the enterprise in question. The resulting sum of private net-of-tax return to capital plus wage bill plus tax payments is our estimate of social net income attributable to the capital invested in an enterprise, when a zero shadow wage is assumed.

Our estimates were designed to measure the rate of productivity of capital invested in physical assets. Hence the capital stock figures for an enterprise or activity should represent net fixed assets plus inventory holdings. However, most firms hold significant amounts of financial assets (cash, securities, receivables), at least some of which generate interest or dividend income for the firm. It would obviously be improper to attribute income generated by financial assets to the physical assets owned by the firm. Hence we deducted from social net income as defined above an amount equal to 10 percent of the excess of financial assets over short-term financial liabilities (principally accounts payable). This procedure undoubtedly overstates the actual earnings on financial assets and, hence, leads to an understatement of the social net income attributable to physical assets.

Both the figures on social net income attributable to physical assets and the figures on the value of the stock of physical assets were then expressed in 1955 prices, so as to value both income and capital in units of constant purchasing power. The deflation procedures were crude, owing to the fact that only price indexes of rather broad coverage are available for India. To offset to some extent the crudeness of the deflating indexes, procedures were consciously adopted that would tend to overstate the value of physical assets in 1955 prices while understating the amount of income—also in 1955 prices—attributable to these assets.[1] Thus at a second point in the estimation procedure, the estimates were biased in the direction of understating the desired rate of return.

Additional biases in the same direction were introduced to take account of the tendency of business firms to overstate depreciation whenever possible in order to enjoy the maximum possible tax advantage. A number of alternative methods for doing this were outlined in the paper just cited, but two of them proved to be uniformly the most conservative; that is, to produce the lowest estimates of the rate of return to physical capital. The first of these (Method A) operates on the identities

true net income ≡ gross income − true depreciation
                                             allowance
true net assets ≡ gross assets − true accumulated
                                             depreciation

From these it follows that

$$TNI \geqq GI \quad \text{as} \quad TDA \leqq GI$$
$$TNA < GA \quad \quad TAD > GA$$

Now even though tax considerations make actual depreciation allowances exceed the 'true' (that is, economically appropriate) allowance, and to make the actual accumulated depreciation exceed its 'true' counterpart, there is no presumption that the ratio of actual depreciation allowances to actual accumulated depreciation will be similarly strongly biased as an estimate of the true ratio. Hence, when the ratio of ADA/AAD is less than the ratio of gross income to gross assets, Method A uses (GI/GA) as an *under*estimate of the (TNI/TNA). This, for the data examined, is typically the case. In the infrequent cases where (ADA/AAD) exceeded (GI/GA), the ratio of net income to net assets derived from the books of the enterprises (with, of course, all the adjustments previously discussed) was used as the estimate of (TNI/TNA) in Method A.

Method B is based on the modern approach to capital budgeting in that it calculates internal rates of return on a cash-flow basis. The annual cash flow associated with the physical assets of an enterprise is estimated by taking the difference between gross income attributable to physical assets and the outlay on new physical assets. Neither of these figures is influenced by arbitrary depreciation procedures. Having calculated the normal cash flows for a series of years on this basis, the initial cash flow (the amount 'invested') is taken to be the gross assets of the firm prior to the first year of normal cash flows, and the final cash flow (the 'final repayment' on the investment) is taken to be the gross assets of the firm at the end of the last year for which normal cash flows were measured. A typical pattern of cash flows would, for example, be − 13600. + 2994, + 3383, + 4709, + 5649, + 19933. The first figure in this sequence represents gross assets at the end of 1955, the subsequent four figures represent net cash flows during the years 1956 through 1959, and the final figure represents gross assets at the end of 1959—all, of course, expressed in 1955 prices. The internal rate of return implied by the above series—dating the initial and terminal flows at 31 December, and the intermediate flows at 30 June of the corresponding years—is 38·5 percent per annum.

The data underlying Table 3.1 are produced by a survey of 1,001 companies, regularly conducted by the Reserve Bank of India.[2] The sample is large and well representative of the 'modern' private sector in India. In fact, the 1,001 companies, taken together, regularly account for more than two-thirds of all corporate investment in India. The Reserve Bank of India consolidates the accounts of reporting companies on an industry and sector basis, as well as for the sample as a whole. It is these consolidated figures that were used in making the computations lying behind Table 3.1. In the case of Method A, rates of return for each industry were calculated separately for each of the years 1955 through 1959, and the resulting estimates were then averaged to yield the figure reported in the table.

It is important to realize that, despite the high estimates emerging from the table, there is a strong presumption that they understate the correct figures. First, the estimating procedures

TABLE 3.1

Estimates of the Social Rate of Return to Capital in Indian Industry, Assuming a Shadow Wage of Zero
(Based on Data from Reserve Bank of India Survey of 1,001 Companies, 1955–59)

Percent per Year

Industry	Method A	Method B	Method A (excluding indirect taxes)
Total	*33·6*	*38·5*	*27·4*
Tobacco manufactures	110·3	101·0	41·1
Rubber and rubber manufactures	50·1	62·0	32·6
Mining and quarrying	47·0	58·5	46·8
Cotton textiles	41·2	47·5	33·8
Sugar	40·7	61·5	19·5
Processing of grains and pulses	40·5	47·5	34·5
Mineral oils	39·9	49·5	23·8
Coffee plantations	38·9	47·5	38·8
Tea plantations	38·7	45·5	38·4
Trading	38·3	39·5	38·2
Edible oils	36·2	39·0	24·8
Machinery (except transportation and electrical)	35·9	42·5	35·6
Pottery, china, earthenware	34·8	42·0	34·8
Electrical machinery	34·7	39·5	33·6
Medicines and pharmaceuticals	34·2	39·0	32·4
Rubber plantations	32·9	37·5	32·2
Processing and manufacturing, n.e.c.	32·3	38·0	23·7
Construction	31·7	35·0	31·7
Chemical products, n.e.c.	31·5	35·5	29·8
Paper and paper products	30·6	36·0	23·1
Cement	27·8	32·0	20·0
Jute textiles	27·1	28·0	27·1
Hotels, restaurants, eating houses	25·0	27·0	24·5
Iron and steel	23·9	25·5	22·2
Transportation equipment	22·2	23·5	22·0
Silk and woolen textiles	21·3	24·5	19·5
Aluminum	20·5	23·5	20·5
Basic industrial chemicals	17·0	19·0	16·8
Shipping	13·1	16·0	13·1
Electricity generation and supply	11·1	11·5	11·1

were consciously biased to produce underestimates. Second, no account was taken of consumers' surplus in developing the estimates. Third, the procedures used develop estimates of the marginal productivity of capital on the basis of the observed average rate of return (adjusted as indicated above) in each line of activity. Where the relevant production function is characterized by constant returns to scale, the marginal productivity of capital will tend to equal the average rate of return, but where increasing returns to scale are present, as may be the case in several of the covered industries, the marginal productivity of capital will tend to exceed the average rate of return on which our estimates were based.

By and large, the highest estimated rates of return in Table 3.1 are those affected by indirect taxes. The third column of the table presents estimates in which indirect taxes are not incorporated in the social return to capital; it can be compared with column (1) to indicate the importance of indirect taxes in any sector. Nonetheless, not much relevance should be attributed to column (3), since, in general, the taxes generated by a new investment should be considered as part of the benefit it produces.

IV. IMPLICATIONS AND RELEVANCE OF A ZERO SHADOW WAGE

Table 3.1 shows clearly that there are many lines of activity in the private sector of the Indian economy in which the social marginal productivity of capital would exceed 30 percent per annum if the shadow wage were indeed equal to zero. In fact two-thirds of the listed industries fall into this category when Method A is used, and nearly three-fourths when Method B is used. For the total sample, Method A yields an estimated overall marginal productivity of capital of 33·6 percent, and Method B produces an estimate of 38·5 percent per year. Other lines of approach tend to confirm this conclusion. If labor is so abundant that its scarcity value is zero, then the whole output of the economy must be attributed to capital (broadly defined so as to include land and the like). The social rate of return on capital for the economy as a whole then becomes the ratio of net national product to the capital stock. Even though we have no good estimates of the capital stock of India, there are no grounds to presume that it exceeds three times the net national product. Thus it must be assumed that an exercise similar to the present one, carried out for the whole Indian economy, would produce an estimated social marginal productivity of capital of 33⅓ or more percent per annum.

It thus appears that if the hypothesis of a zero shadow wage is correct, Indian planners should be using a discount rate of at least 30 percent in evaluating the alternative projects confronting them. This high rate is counterbalanced, so to speak, by the fact that the assumption of a zero shadow wage permits one to include the entire wages bill to be generated once a project gets into operation as a part of the yield of the capital invested in that project. In the net, the use of a zero shadow wage will substantially benefit labor-intensive activities, and will weigh heavily against capital-intensive activities, as a glance at Table 3.1, in which the industries are arranged in descending order of social rate of return (under Method A), will verify.

Not only does a high discount rate weigh against capital-intensive projects, it also discriminates strongly against projects with long gestation periods and/or with long economic lives. At a 30 percent rate of return, an invested sum should more than double in three years, and should multiply by nearly five in six years. An investment of 100 today in a project with a six-year gestation period must produce, starting with the seventh year, an *annual* yield of 145 in order to pay off at 30 percent. By the same token the present value of 100 six years hence is only around 20, evaluated at a discount rate of 3 percent per year, and the present value of 100 twelve years hence is only a little over 4.

These simple relationships have tremendous implications as to the sorts of projects that would be acceptable when high discount rates are used. Large irrigation projects would have to be tremendously productive in order to justify their long gestation periods. Investments with long lives, such as houses and roads, would benefit little from their longevity—the 'economic' annual rental of a house, for example, would be a third or more of its value, if a 30 percent discount rate were used.

In the long run, if the policy implications of a zero shadow wage were followed through consistently, there would have to be a massive readjustment of relative prices in the economy. By concentrating investment in those lines with the highest ratios of value added (gross of indirect taxes) to capital and short gestation periods, the prices of their products would tend to be

driven down while increasing scarcity would drive up the prices
of products produced in lines with low ratios of value added to
capital and/or long gestation periods. By such a process of price
adjustment, projects of types initially neglected because their
ratios of value added to capital were too low would ultimately
become acceptable. Indeed, if a 30 percent discount rate were
applied consistently throughout the economy for a sufficiently
long period, the ratios of value added to capital-at-charge
would tend toward equality at approximately 30 percent in all
lines of activity. (Capital-at-charge is obtained by accumulating past capital outlays at the critical discount rate—
here 30 percent—and of course adjusting the capital-at-charge
for depreciation during each year of its use.)

The implications of a zero shadow wage, sketched briefly
above, suggest very different directions for Indian economic
planning than have in fact been followed. Should we therefore
conclude that Indian planning has been grossly wrong? I think
not, at least not on the basis of the evidence and arguments
presented, for up to now we have been operating on the assumption that the shadow wage is in fact zero. In point of fact, there
is substantial evidence suggesting that this assumption is quite
inappropriate for India, and it is to this evidence that we now
turn.

The idea that labor is so superabundant in India that its
shadow price should be zero is deeply rooted in the situation
of Indian agriculture—a sector employing some 70 percent of
the Indian labor force. Here, it is said, one confronts an
enormous pool of labor, whose marginal productivity is (virtually) zero. Large quantities of this labor could be withdrawn
from Indian agriculture, the argument goes, without occasion-
ing any significant reduction in agricultural output.

There is considerable and good evidence that weighs against
this argument. More than a quarter of the Indian agricultural
labor force works for wages, which are voluntarily paid to
the workers by their employers. It is to be presumed that
these employers are getting, in return, a marginal product
per worker that is at least equal to the wage being paid. If
the marginal productivity of labor were below the wage paid,
the first to suffer would be the wage laborers who would
then be put out of work. Yet the average adult male wage-

laborer in Indian agriculture worked, in 1956 to 1957, over 250 full-time equivalent days per year at wages averaging 1 rupee or more per day. The average agricultural labor household in India had an income of nearly 400 rupees per year, while even the landless, casual-labor households had an average income of over 335 rupees per year.[3] When agricultural households are classified according to their per capita consumer expenditures in 1956 to 1957, the lowest 28 percent of the households had per capita expenditures averaging 71 rupees and per household expenditures of some 380 rupees per year.[4]

The high number of days worked by adult male laborers in Indian agriculture is in part explained by the fact that there are typically two plantings and two harvests per year, and partly by the fact that the seasonal peaks of employment in agriculture are filled by women and children entering the work force at such times, and by a seasonal reflux of some male workers from the cities.

The important conclusions that follow from this evidence are (a) that even the most disadvantaged groups of agricultural workers in India work more days per year than is common for farmers in most advanced countries and (b) that they earn incomes per worker in excess of the national per capita income, which was 292 rupees at the time to which the data cited above apply. An Indian income of 335 rupees per year, in 1956 to 1957, would correspond to a U.S. income of nearly $3,000 per year in 1964, when both are expressed relative to the respective per capita national incomes. Yet the average member of the U.S. agricultural labor force did not obtain in 1964 significantly more than $3,000 of personal income from all sources. We obviously do not conclude that labor has a zero marginal productivity in U.S. agriculture, and by the same token I fail to see how we can reach this conclusion for the Indian labor forces in the face of the relationships just indicated.

Further evidence strongly suggesting that the marginal productivity of labor in agriculture is not zero in the Indian economy has recently been assembled by Professor T. W. Schultz.[5] Schultz analyzes the effects of the influenza epidemic of 1918–19 on agricultural production in India. This epidemic

82 *Project Evaluation*

cost the lives of millions of people throughout India, and struck at different rates in different areas. Comparing periods of similar climatic conditions prior to and subsequent to the year of the epidemic itself, Schultz obtained a high correlation between the percentage drop in population in an area, on the one hand, and the percentage fall in agricultural output on the other, between the 'before' and 'after' years. Moreover, the elasticity of output with respect to changes in labor force, implied by Schultz's data, suggest that the marginal productivity of labor in Indian agriculture is approximately equal to the average wage. Schultz's test of the hypothesis of zero marginal productivity is a direct one, and its results are powerful. Its only weakness is that it refers to the India of some 45 years ago—but it is well to recall that India was commonly regarded as overpopulated then, and that its per capita income was undoubtedly somewhat lower than it is now. It should be added that in spite of the substantial difference in time, the results of Schultz's test lead to the same general conclusions as the National Sample Survey evidence presented above.

A final piece of evidence negating the idea of a zero marginal productivity of labor in Indian agriculture comes from Professor K. N. Raj's study of the great Bhakra Nangal Dam project. In discussing the recruitment of labor for this project, Professor Raj states:

It is a common assumption to make, on theoretical analyses, that the supply of unskilled labor in underdeveloped countries is almost infinitely elastic. This, obviously, is not always true. For instance, the additional demand for unskilled labor created by the Bhakra Nangal project, even at the peak level of activity during the construction of the canals, cannot be regarded as very large, when considered with reference to the investment undertaken or the area (and population) over which the construction work was spread. Yet the supply of unskilled labor from the areas adjoining the work proved hardly adequate. In March 1954, when the total number employed on the Bhakra Canals was around 100,000, it would appear that as much as 60 per cent of the labor required had to be imported from other States.[6]

This result was observed in spite of the fact that the wages paid were good (typically 2 rupees per day plus free housing). It is obviously hardly consistent with the notion of a large pool of labor having zero marginal productivity, which can readily be drawn upon to meet additional labor requirements.

I believe that the evidence cited above warrants our rejecting the hypothesis of zero marginal productivity of labor in Indian agriculture, and with it the hypothesis of a zero shadow wage for the labor used in Indian industry. We can, however, attempt to estimate at this point what would be the minimum shadow wage for the labor used in the modern industrial sector of India. We have seen that the average casual laborer in Indian agriculture earns over 300 rupees per year. Yet such workers will not willingly present themselves for work in a typical industrial establishment for 300 rupees a year. By and large, modern industrial establishments are located in the urban sector, where the real costs of housing, food, transportation to and from work, and the like, are significantly greater than they are in the villages of rural India. Moreover, other 'costs' are associated with the migration of rural labor to urban areas, notably the transportation costs that many workers feel impelled to bear in order to maintain periodic contacts with their native villages. Many urban workers in fact leave their families in the village, returning there as often as they can, providing maintenance for their families, and, of course for their own separate maintenance in the city. Factors like these, on the labor supply side, explain why even the lowest paid of urban workers obtain incomes substantially in excess of those earned by their rural counterparts. These factors need not always be operative, that is, if the pattern of economic development required a migration flow, in the net, from city to country, some of the forces listed above might even work to produce a differentially higher wage in agriculture. But in the Indian context the forces of economic development are in fact drawing population to the urban areas, and to do this urban wages must be sufficient to attract the required flow.

In point of fact, the lowest paid urban workers—household sweepers, ricksha drivers, casual construction labourers, for example—appear to earn approximately 2 rupees per day (including some income in kind in the case of sweepers). These occupations are unorganized, have completely free entry, and are subject to no legal minimum wages; thus no 'artificial' forces are at work to press their wage levels above. Moreover, these occupations do not require any special skills, and in fact are often entered by rural-urban migrants. It is reasonable, under these circumstances, to interpret the differential between wages in these occupations and the wages of casual rural laborers as reflecting the premium needed to elicit the required amount of migration. This being the case, we can consider the wage of 2 rupees per day, as roughly 600 rupees per year, to be the effective shadow price of completely unskilled labor in the cities. This judgment is confirmed by data from the National Sample Survey. In 1957–58, for example, the 26 percent of the urban population with lowest per capita incomes lived in households in which per household consumption expenditures were over 720 rupees per year.[7] This amount is roughly consistent with the figure of 600 rupees of income per worker, as some of the households in this category had more than one income earner.

V. MEASURING THE SOCIAL YIELD OF PRIVATE INVESTMENTS ON THE ASSUMPTION THAT SHADOW WAGES EQUAL ACTUAL WAGES

This section presents estimates of the social yield of capital in Indian industry, based on the assumption that the shadow wage is equal to the actual wage paid in each line of activity. This means, of course, that the shadow wage is not the same as among industries and activities, but it is quite appropriate that the shadow wage should vary with the skill of labor and with region. The assumption that the shadow wage everywhere equals the actual wage in effect attributes all variations in wages to factors like skill and region, and leaves no room for 'artificial' factors—such as legal minimum wages in given lines of activity —to explain wage differentials. As was the case with the assumption of a zero shadow wage, we shall examine the implications of the assumption that shadow wages equal actual wages without for the moment inquiring into its validity. This is done in Table 3.2. The concept of social return to capital used in Table 3.2 is similar to that underlying Table 3.1, ex-

TABLE 3.2

Estimates of the Social Rate of Return to Capital in Indian Industry, Assuming Shadow Wages equal Actual Wages (Based on Data from Reserve Bank of India Survey of 1,001 Companies, 1955–59)

(Percent per year)

	Method A	Method B	Method A (excluding indirect taxes)
Total	*13·2*	*13·0*	*10·9*
Tobacco	44·6	47·5	15·5
Mineral oils	32·4	39·5	18·8
Processing of grains and pulses	26·1	28·5	22·3
Sugar	21·7	23·0	11·1
Rubber and rubber manufactures	21·2	23·0	14·1
Processing and manufacturing, n.e.c.	19·2	21·0	14·0
Coffee plantations	18·1	19·0	18·1
Electrical machinery	17·6	17·0	17·1
Paper and paper products	16·9	18·5	12·9
Cement	15·8	16·5	11·0
Rubber plantations	15·7	16·0	15·4
Machinery (except transportation and electrical)	15·1	15·0	15·1
Pottery, china, and earthenware	14·8	15·5	14·8
Construction	13·2	12·5	13·2
Chemical products, n.e.c.	12·7	13·5	11·9
Tea plantations	12·6	12·5	12·5
Iron and steel	12·2	12·0	11·2
Medicines and pharmaceuticals	12·1	12·0	11·5
Silk and woolen textiles	12·0	16·0	11·0
Trading	11·6	9·5	11·6
Edible oils	11·5	10·0	8·1
Aluminum	10·2	12·0	10·2
Transportation equipment	10·2	11·0	10·1
Cotton textiles	9·7	8·0	8·2
Mining and quarrying	9·5	9·0	9·5
Electricity generation and supply	7·7	8·0	7·7
Basic industrial chemicals	7·5	9·5	7·4
Hotels, restaurants, and eating houses	6·4	5·5	6·2
Shipping	5·3	9·5	5·3
Jute textiles	5·1	5·0	5·1

cept for two adjustments. In the first place, the wage bill is not imputed as part of the return to capital here, since we are treating wages as a true economic cost. In the second place, only a part of indirect taxes is imputed to capital: namely, that fraction which the net income from capital bears to value added in the activity in question.[8] Thus 'capital's share' of indirect taxes is assigned as part of the social return to capital, a procedure consistent with that underlying Table 3.1 because the assumptions behind that table assigned 100 per cent of value added as return to capital.

The full costing of labor has a dramatic effect upon the rate of return to capital. Whereas in Table 3.1, two-thirds of the industries covered had social rates of return to capital above 30 percent, and the overall rate for the total sample was above 33 percent, in Table 3.2 slightly over one-third of the industries covered have rates of return below 12 percent, and the average for the total sample is only about 13 percent.

Column 3 of Table 3.2 excludes capital's share of indirect taxes and thus shows the gross-of-income-tax rate of return to physical capital in the covered industries. It is notable that this series shows a marked central tendency—half the industries covered had rates of return between 10 and 15 percent, and three-quarters between 7 and 17 percent.

Despite the fact that the rates of return estimated in Table 3.2 are low when compared with Table 3.1, they are quite high when compared to the rates of return (3 to 5 percent) commonly used for cost-benefit analysis in India. And it should be emphasized that Table 3.2 is based on extremely conservative assumptions. Not only does the estimation procedure contain a downward bias, but also a very narrow concept of social benefit is used. In fact, the only element of nonprivate benefit entering into the return to capital measured in Table 3.2 consists of taxes. The results therefore strongly suggest a drastic upward revision of the discount rate used for project evaluation in India.

VI. MEASURING THE SOCIAL YIELD OF CAPITAL ON 'INTERMEDIATE' ASSUMPTIONS

We now inquire into the validity of the assumption that the actual wage and the shadow wage are equal. We take as the point of departure the conclusion—reached in section IV— that the minimum plausible value of the shadow wage for unskilled workers in urban employments in India was around

600 rupees per year. Now although we do not have direct data on the wages per man-year paid by the 1,001 companies in the Reserve Bank of India Survey, we do know that in modern factory establishments in India the average annual earnings per worker averaged between 1,000 and 1,200 rupees per year in 1956–58.[9] These earnings obviously apply to the average of the skill-mix of workers used in factory establishments, and not just to unskilled labor. Clearly the shadow wage for this skill-mix will substantially exceed the minimum 600 rupees figure that was estimated for the least skilled class of workers. But granting that the shadow wage relevant for the companies in the Reserve Bank survey is higher than 600 rupees, the key question is by how much. Most employers undoubtedly do try to obtain labor of a given quality at the minimum possible cost, a policy which tends to produce a situation in which actual wages and shadow wages are the same. On the other hand, not all employers succeed in this aim—union pressure and government policy being the principal forces leading to wage rates above the supply price of labor—and some employers appear to pursue a conscious policy of paying wage rates that are somewhat above the going market. In any event, regardless of why wages are higher than required, we can be quite sure that they sometimes are so in fact. This is demonstrated by the fact that some industrial enterprises—particularly the larger and more modern ones—have long waiting lists of qualified applicants for work, who are ready and willing to work at the wages these enterprises pay, but who must typically settle for jobs in other lines of activity which pay less.

Thus, particularly when we look at the combined group of 1,001 companies in the Reserve Bank survey, we should properly allow for some excess of actual wages over shadow wages. It is the size of this excess rather than its existence which is open to doubt. Some observers of the Indian scene feel that the excess is so small that it can be neglected for practical purposes; these people would consider the results of Table 3.2 to be sufficiently accurate to serve as a reasonable guide for setting the rate of discount to be used in cost-benefit work. Other observers, however, feel that the excess of actual over shadow wages in the modern industrial sector may be quite large—perhaps as high as 15 or 20 percent. Table 3.3 is presented as illustrative of the sort of measure of the social rate of return to capital that these people would regard as relevant.

Table 3.3 is similar to the previous tables, except that here

TABLE 3.3

Estimates of the Social Rate of Return to Capital in Indian Industry, Assuming Shadow Wages equal eighty percent of Actual Wages

(Based on Data from Reserve Bank of India Survey of 1,001 Companies, 1955–59)

(Percent per year)

	Method A	Method B	Method A (excluding indirect taxes)
Total	*17·3*	*17·5*	*14·3*
Tobacco	57·7	66·0	20·9
Sugar	36·2	39·0	24·8
Mineral oils	33·9	41·5	19·8
Processing of grains and pulses	29·0	32·0	24·7
Rubber and rubber manufactures	27·0	30·5	17·8
Coffee plantations	22·3	24·5	22·3
Processing and manufacturing, n.e.c.	21·8	24·0	16·2
Electrical machinery	21·0	21·5	20·4
Paper and paper products	19·6	22·0	15·1
Machinery (except transportation and electrical)	19·3	20·0	19·2
Rubber plantations	19·2	20·0	18·8
Pottery, china, earthenware	18·8	20·5	18·8
Cement	18·2	19·5	13·0
Tea plantations	17·9	18·5	17·7
Trading	17·2	15·0	17·1
Construction	17·1	16·5	17·1
Mining and quarrying	17·0	18·0	16·9
Chemical products, n.e.c.	16·9	18·0	16·0
Medicines and pharmaceuticals	16·5	17·0	15·7
Edible oils	16·5	15·0	11·8
Cotton textiles	16·2	15·0	13·6
Iron and steel	14·6	14·5	13·5
Silk and woolen textiles	13·9	17·5	12·7
Transportation equipment	12·8	13·5	12·7
Aluminium	12·6	14·0	12·6
Hotels, restaurants, and eating houses	10·1	9·5	9·9
Jute textiles	9·9	9·0	9·9
Basic industrial chemicals	9·4	11·5	9·3
Electricity generation and supply	8·5	9·0	8·5
Shipping	6·8	10·5	6·8

80 percent of the wage bill has been treated as a cost and the remaining 20 percent has been assigned as part of the social return to capital. In allocating indirect taxes, capital was assigned that fraction of indirect taxes which the adjusted return to capital (that is, including 20 percent of the wage bill) bears to value added in each industry.

Obviously, a careful effort to measure the social rate of return to capital in any industry would properly entail an investigation into the various types of labor used by that industry, and into their likely employment alternatives and/or supply prices. One would presumably arrive at a different ratio of shadow to actual wages for each category of labor. The relevant ratio for the industry as a whole would be the weighted average of these separate ratios for each class of labor. Similarly, the relevant industry ratios would surely differ from industry to industry; this is why Table 3.3 should be regarded as merely illustrative. Nonetheless, if the weighted average of the respective industry ratios of shadow to actual wages were ·8, the figures given in Table 3.3 for all 1,001 companies taken together would be appropriate measures of the social rate of return to capital for the overall group, subject of course to the downward biases mentioned earlier.

Comparing the results of Tables 3.2 and 3.3 for the overall sample, we conclude that the social rate of return to capital in Indian industry is either somewhat in excess of 13 percent (Table 3.2) or somewhat in excess of 17 percent (Table 3.3). The importance of this difference should, however, not be exaggerated, for if we were to use the 13 percent rate to evaluate a project, we should not assign any of the wage bill as part of the return to capital, while if we were to use the 17 percent rate, we would presumably have to assign a portion of the wage bill. A proportion that would equal 20 percent of the difference between actual and shadow wages in the project being evaluated was representative of the corresponding difference assumed for the 1,001 companies in the construction of Table 3.3. Although a 17 percent rate is itself harder to achieve than a 13 percent rate, the assignment of a portion of wages to the return to capital eases the task, particularly for relatively labor-intensive activities.

The differences in the assumptions underlying Tables 3.2

and 3.3 roughly reflect, I believe, our present degree of uncertainty. We cannot be sure that the shadow wage equals 100 percent of the actual wage, nor can we be sure that it equals 80 percent of the actual wage. We can be reasonably certain that it lies somewhere in between. Given this range of uncertainty, it is comforting to know that it does not create any very serious problems for cost-benefit analysis. Many projects that pass a 13 percent rate-of-return test when wages are counted as social costs will also pass a 17 percent rate-of-return test when 20 percent of wages are counted as social benefits. Likewise, many projects that pass a 17 percent test when 20 percent of wages are counted as benefits will·also pass a 13 percent test when no wages are counted. This, of course, does not say that the two sets of criteria will always lead to the same decision in respect of a project—the 17 percent test is biased, relatively, in favor of labor-intensive projects, and the 13 percent in favour of capital intensive projects. These differences can be perceived in the relative rankings of the different industries in Tables 3.2 and 3.3. Mining and quarrying—a labor-intensive industry in India—ranks much higher in Table 3.3 than in Table 3.2, and jute textiles and trading, also labor-intensive industries, rank somewhat higher.

Despite the differences in concept underlying the two tables, however, there is a striking degree of correspondence in their rankings of the industries by rate of return. For example, the top nine industries in Table 3.2 are also the top nine in Table 3.3, and the bottom five industries are also the same in both tables. Moreover, very few of the industries changed their ranking by more than two or three places between Tables 3.2 and 3.3. This correspondence reflects the fact that the two sets of criteria are not really very different, and suggests that project evaluation under either set would not lead us into gross errors of judgment.

VII. SUMMARY AND CONCLUSIONS

One way of viewing the intent of this paper is to juxtapose, initially, conventional project evaluation procedures with those implied by the hypothesis of zero marginal productivity of labor. The conventional procedures use rates of discount of 3 to 5 percent and consider all labor costs as true social costs. The zero marginal productivity of labor hypothesis, on the other hand, appears to require, for India, the use of a rate of discount well above 30 percent per annum, and would consider no labor costs as true social costs. These two sets of criteria have vastly different implications as to which projects should be accepted and which rejected.

The evidence presented in this paper, however, leads to the rejection of both these extreme positions. Even if one follows convention in counting all wages as social costs, the data on India suggest that the social rate of return to capital is near 13 percent rather than 3 to 5 percent. On the other hand, the data lead to the rejection of the hypothesis underlying a zero shadow wage, and suggest that the maximum plausible allowance for an excess of private over social cost of labor would, for Indian industry, be something like 20 percent of the wage bill. When this allowance is made in calculating the social rate of return to capital in Indian industry, the resulting estimate is somewhat over 17 percent per annum, but far below the over-30 percent figure that was implied by the hypothesis of a zero shadow wage. With the narrowing of the range of uncertainty with respect to the discount rate from 3 to 30 percent to 13 to 17 percent, one obtains a great reduction in the degree of divergence of the implications of alternative criteria within the uncertain range. Thus, even though for lack of adequately precise data we may have to live with some uncertainty with respect to the relationships between actual and shadow wages for some time to come, this uncertainty does not appear to be so great as to stand in the way of a very substantial improvement of present project evaluation criteria.

APPENDIX

A NOTE ON THE SOCIAL COST OF LABOR USED IN INVESTMENT PROJECTS

Where, in this paper, we have taken the shadow wage to be different from the actual wage, we have permitted this assumption to be reflected in a reallocation of the value added produced by a project, once in operation. We have not permitted it to be reflected in the capital cost of the investment itself. Thus, a zero shadow wage for textile operatives led to an upward adjustment of the social return to capital in the textile industry, but it did not lead to a downward adjustment of the value of the capital employed in the textile industry, to reflect the fact that some labor was used in the making of that capital equipment. How can this apparent asymmetry of treatment be justified?

The answer lies in the fact that the investible surplus of the Indian economy (represented by both private and public savings) is for various reasons—social and political as well as economic—rather stringently limited. Assume, for simplicity, that in a given period it is strictly given. Then the question of promoting maximal growth amounts to getting the most out of a given sum of available savings. The investible funds are just as much 'spent' when they are paid out for labor services as when they are paid out for machinery or for capital services. Maximizing the rate of growth from a given investible surplus therefore entails getting the most per rupee of investible funds paid out, regardless of whether the payment is made for the services of labor or for those of capital. Thus if one accepts the commonly-held (and I believe correct) view that the investible surplus in India is very hard to expand, and if one is interested in maximizing the net increment to output that can be generated by this surplus, one cannot escape valuing capital expenditures at, so to speak, their full cash cost, as we have done in this paper.

Notes

[1] These procedures are discussed in detail in Arnold C. Harberger, 'Investment in Man vs. Investment in Machines: The Case of India', in C. A. Anderson and M. J. Bowman, eds., *Education and Economic Development* (Chicago: Aldine Press, 1965). The procedures were applied there to estimate the global rate of return to investment in physical capital in Indian industry; in the present paper they are applied to obtain estimates of rates of return by industry class.

[2] See *Reserve Bank of India Bulletin*, September 1961, pp. 1403–57; October 1961, pp. 1752–76.

[3] See Government of India, The Cabinet Secretariat, *The National Sample Survey*, No. 33: *Wages, Employment, Income and Indebtedness of Agricultural Labor Households in Rural Areas*, Delhi, 1960, pp. 18, 23, 61.

[4] See Government of India, The Cabinet Secretariat, *The National Sample Survey*, No. 46: *Consumer Expenditure of Agricultural Labor Households in Rural Areas*, Delhi, 1961, pp. 31, 37.

[5] See T. W. Schultz, *Transforming Traditional Agriculture*, New Haven, Conn.: Yale University Press, 1964, pp. 53–70.

[6] K. N. Raj, *Economic Aspects of the Bhakra Nangal Project*, Bombay: Asia Publishing House, 1960, pp. 77–78.

[7] Indian Statistical Institute, *The National Sample Survey*, No. 80: *Tables with Notes on Consumer Expenditure*, Calcutta: Indian Statistical Institute, 1961, Tables 2.3.0 and 2.5.0.

[8] For a justification of this procedure see my paper, 'The Measurement of Waste', *American Economic Review* 54 (May 1964): 65.

[9] Government of India, Ministry of Information and Broadcasting, *India, 1961*, Delhi: 1961, p. 377.

CHAPTER FOUR

ON MEASURING THE SOCIAL OPPORTUNITY COST OF PUBLIC FUNDS

I. THE BASIC MODEL

The literature on project evaluation abounds with competing recommendations as to what rate of interest should be used to discount to a single point in time the estimated costs and benefits of public-sector projects. Official policy in the United States, as established in the *Green Book*[1] and in Senate Resolutions, is to base public-sector investment decisions on interest rates prevailing or expected to prevail in the market for government bonds. An alternative, proposed by such authors as Hirshleifer, DeHaven and Milliman, Strotz, and Stockfisch, is to discount benefits and costs at the estimated marginal productivity of capital in the private sector of the economy. A third group, to which Marglin and Sen belong, asserts that market interest rates give an exaggerated picture of the rate of 'social time preference', and suggests that that rate be chosen which represents the consensus of the policy-makers (or of the society as a whole) concerning what the social time preference rate really is or should be. I shall defer discussion of social time preference rates, thus arbitrarily defined, to a later point, and shall instead assume that the 'social rate of time preference' refers to an appropriately weighted average of the different marginal rates of time preference applicable to the individuals who compose the society.

I propose here to present a simple analytical framework

Reprinted in *The Discount Rate in Public Investment Evaluation* (Conference Proceedings of the Committee on the Economics of Water Resources Development, Western Agricultural Economics Research Council, Report No. 17, Denver, Colorado, 17–18 December 1969), pp. 1–24.

which is sufficiently general to yield the market rate of interest, the private-sector marginal productivity of capital, and the social rate of time preference (as defined above) as the appropriate rate of discount under special circumstances. The solution that emerges in the general case is, however, equal to none of these but to a weighted average of the last two or, equivalently, to the market interest rate adjusted for distortions in the capital market. For simplicity, I shall initially assume that the capital market of the economy in question functions perfectly and that there are no risk premia of any kind. Thus, the equilibrium rate of return on private investment, net of business taxes, is assumed in this section to be equal to the rate of interest on government bonds.

In assuming that the capital market functions perfectly, however, I do not mean to imply that it is undistorted. Distortions exist in all capital markets, and the most important and pervasive form they take is taxes. I shall, therefore, assume that a tax of 50 percent (similar to the corporation income tax) applies to all income from private-sector investment, and that a flat-rate personal income tax of 25 percent applies to all personal income. If the equilibrium interest rate is 6 percent, these assumptions imply an equilibrium gross-of-tax rate of return on private-sector investment (that is, a marginal productivity of private-sector capital) equal to 12 percent, and an equilibrium net-of-tax rate of return to private-sector saving (that is, a marginal rate of time preference of private savers) equal to 4·5 percent.

The situation postulated is depicted in Figure 4.1. The investment demand schedule $I(\rho)$ expresses investment demand as a function of the gross-of-tax cost of capital, ρ, assuming full employment of the economy's resources. Presumably, investment will be carried to the point where its expected marginal productivity is equal to the cost of capital; hence, the $I(\rho)$ function can be identified as a schedule of the marginal productivity of investment. The $I(i)$ function represents investment as a function of its yield after the business income tax; for any volume of investment, its ordinate is just half that of the $I(\rho)$ schedule, reflecting the 50 percent tax that has been assumed.

The $S(i)$ schedule depicts private-sector saving as a function of the market rate of interest (again assuming full employment),

Project Evaluation

while the $S(r)$ schedule shows savings as a function of their net-of-personal-tax yield (r) to the individual saver. Market equilibrium is determined by the condition that $S = I + B$, where B is the amount of net government borrowing occurring in the period in question. Thus, if government borrowing is initially equal to the amount $CH (= DN)$ the market interest rate will be i_0, the amount of private investment OC, and the amount of private savings OH.

If the government now, to finance additional investment projects, decides to borrow $AJ (= EM)$ rather than CH, the result will be a slight rise in the market interest rate (from i_0 to i'), which has as its consequences a reduction in private investment equal to AC and an increase in private savings equal to HJ. The additional capital $(AC + HJ)$ raised by the government is obtained at an opportunity cost equal to the areas $ACGF$ plus $HJKL$, as will be shown below.

There are two alternative interpretations of the $I(\rho)$ relationship in Figure 4.1, but fortunately the social yield of private

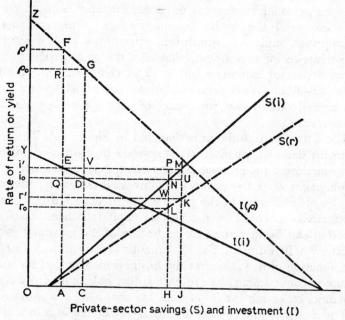

Figure 4.1

investment is the same under either of them. Under the first interpretation, the investment demand schedule consists of separate projects, arrayed in descending order of their expected yield. If the cost of capital is lowered, under this interpretation, the yield of inframarginal projects remains unaffected; the only impact of the lower capital cost is to permit the undertaking of additional projects of lower yield than was previously profitable. In this case, the expected gross-of-tax earnings from investments currently being undertaken are measured by the area $ZGCO$, the net-of-tax earnings are measured by $YDCO$, and the business-income-tax yield to be produced by the level of current investment associated with an interest rate of i_0 is $ZGDY$. When, as a consequence of additional government borrowing, the interest rate rises to i', expected gross-of-tax earnings from current investments fall to $ZFAO$, expected net-of-tax earnings drop to $YEAO$, and expected business-tax receipts decline to $ZFEY$. The loss to the economy as a consequence of the reduction of investment by the amount AC is a forgone return equal to $ACGF$, consisting of $EDGF$ of business-income taxes forgone by the government, and $ACDE$ of net-of-business-tax yield forgone by those private citizens who otherwise would have financed AC of private investment. As these private citizens presumably have instead bought government obligations yielding i' percent per year, they achieve from the switch a net gain of EDV, and the social cost of the forgone private-sector investment is simply the interest paid by the government on the funds obtained at the expense of private investment ($ACVE$) plus the business-tax loss to the government ($EDGF$), minus the gain (EDV) accruing to those who shifted their funds from marginal private-sector investments to the purchase of government bonds.[2]

The second interpretation of the $I(\rho)$ schedule is that a lowering of the cost of capital reduces, through competition, the yield on inframarginal investments, at the same time as it attracts more capital investment generally. Thus, if the cost of capital were to fall from ρ' to ρ_0, competition would beat down the yield on all inframarginal investments to ρ_0, producing a gain in consumer surplus equal to $\rho_0 GF\rho'$. Conversely, when government operations in the capital market raise the interest rate from i_0 to i' and the cost of private-sector capital from ρ_0

to ρ', there is a consequent loss of $\rho_0 GF\rho'$ in consumer surplus.

As the interest rate moves from i_0 to i', expected government business-tax revenues from current private investment fall from $i_0 DG\rho_0$ to $i'EF\rho'$, the net reduction being equal to $QDGR$ plus $i_0 QEi'$ minus $\rho_0 RF\rho'$. $\rho_0 RF\rho'$ is outweighed by the loss in consumer surplus of $\rho_0 GF\rho'$, leaving a net loss on these two accounts equal to RGF. Similarly, the revenue loss reflected in $i_0 QEi'$ is counterbalanced by a gain to those private investors who are responsible for financing OA of investment.

Thus, the social cost of diverting AC of investment from the private sector is $ACGF$, which can be broken down in two ways: (a) RGF of forgone consumer surplus not offset by increased taxes, plus $QDGR$ of forgone tax revenues not offset by private gains, plus $ACDQ$ of net-of-business-tax income forgone by private investors; alternatively, (b) RGF, as above, plus $QDGR$, as above, plus $ACVE$ of interest cost to the government on the funds diverted from private investment, minus $QDVE$ of extra earnings to those investors whose funds were diverted from AC of private investment, earning i_0, to the purchase of public-sector securities earning i'.

Regardless of which interpretation of the $I(\rho)$ schedule is relevant, the area $ACGF$ represents the social opportunity cost of the amount AC of capital which was diverted from private-sector investment to the public sector. Under either interpretation it can be readily identified with the marginal productivity of the diverted funds in their alternative private-sector use, and hereafter it will be so labeled. In the real world, of course, the investment demand function can reflect cases of both of the types treated above: that is, there may be some investments whose marginal productivity is for one reason or another insulated from the competition of new investments when the cost of capital falls, and there may be others for which a highly competitive market will keep marginal productivity closely tied to the cost of capital. Such hybrid situations do not alter the conclusion reached above; displacement of private investment of either type will have a social opportunity cost equal to the social marginal productivity of the investment in question.

On the savings side, the consequence of additional borrowing by the government is a rise of the interest rate from i_0 to i', and a resulting increase in private savings from OH to OJ. What is the social opportunity cost of these incremental savings? From the standpoint of the private savers the area $HJKL$ reflects the accumulated 'supply price' of each incremental unit of savings, and hence its opportunity cost.

Looking at the same problem in another way, the government pays $HJMP$ in interest on the bonds bought by the suppliers of additional savings. Of this amount $PMKW$ comes back to the government in the form of taxes on the newly-induced savings, so the net cost to the government of these added funds is $HJKW$. However, a part of this net cost, LKW, represents a surplus accruing to the incremental savers, so that, from a social point of view, $HJKL$ measures the true opportunity cost of the extra savings.[3]

If the amount of incremental government borrowing is small in relation to the size of the capital market, the change in interest rates is likely to be very small, so that triangles RFG and LKW become negligible in size relative to $ACGR$ and $HJKW$. The social opportunity cost of capital, ω, can then be defined as $\left(r\,\dfrac{\partial S}{\partial i} - \rho\,\dfrac{\partial I}{\partial i} \right) \Big/ \left(\dfrac{\partial S}{\partial i} - \dfrac{\partial I}{\partial i} \right)$, where the presumptive signs of $\dfrac{\partial S}{\partial i}$ and $\dfrac{\partial I}{\partial i}$ are positive and negative, respectively.

Expressed in terms of elasticities, this can be written $\omega = (rS\epsilon_S - \rho I\eta_I) \,/\, (S\epsilon_S - I\eta_I)$ where η_I (<0) is the elasticity of private-sector investment and ϵ_S (>0) that of private-sector savings with respect to changes in the rate of interest.

The above expressions define the social opportunity cost of government borrowing at a point on the excess-supply schedule of funds available for government use. This supply schedule is simply the lateral excess of the private savings schedule over the private investment schedule; that is, $S(i) - I(i) \equiv E(i)$. $E(i)$ will be a rising function of i, with slope $\dfrac{\partial E}{\partial i} = \dfrac{\partial S}{\partial i} - \dfrac{\partial I}{\partial i}$ and elasticity $\epsilon_E = \dfrac{S}{E}\,\epsilon_S + \dfrac{I}{E}\,|\eta_I|$. Any given i determines a given set: S, I, E, ρ, r, ϵ_S, and η_I; and this set contains all the data necessary to calculate the value of ω, the social opportunity cost of capital, corresponding to that i. Calculating the values of ω and E corresponding to different values of i enables one to ultimately express the social opportunity cost of capital as a function of the amount of government borrowing, B, in the capital market under the equilibrium condition $B = E$ (which is equivalent to $I + B = S$). The normal slopes of the savings and investment function determine that ω will be a rising function of B. With the aid of an estimate of such a function, the relevant opportunity costs of large as well as small changes in government borrowing can be assessed.

The simple model set out above can be readily generalized to deal with cases in which the marginal productivity of investment differs as among the various sectors of the private economy, and in which the marginal rate of time preference differs as among various groups of savers. The excess supply schedule of funds available for government use now becomes

$$E = \sum_k S_k - \sum_j I_j, \tag{1}$$

where S_k represents the flow of savings generated by the kth class of savers, and I_j the flow of investment occurring in the jth sector. The social opportunity cost of capital can then be expressed as:

$$\omega = \left(\sum_k r_k \frac{\partial S_k}{\partial i} - \sum_j \rho_j \frac{\partial I_j}{\partial i} \right) \Big/ \left(\sum_k \frac{\partial S_k}{\partial i} - \sum_j \frac{\partial I_j}{\partial i} \right). \tag{2}$$

This in turn can be transformed into

$$\omega = (\bar{r} S \epsilon_S - \bar{\rho} I \eta_I)/(S \epsilon_S - I \eta_I) \text{ using the following definitions:} \tag{3}$$

$$\bar{r} = \left(\sum_k r_k \frac{\partial S_k}{\partial i} \right) \Big/ \left(\sum_k \frac{\partial S_k}{\partial i} \right) = \left(\sum_k r_k S_k \epsilon_k \right) \Big/ \left(\sum_k S_k \epsilon_k \right); \tag{4}$$

$$\epsilon_S = \frac{i}{S} \frac{\partial S}{\partial i} = \frac{i}{S} \sum_k \frac{\partial S_k}{\partial i} = \sum_k \frac{S_k}{S} \epsilon_k; \tag{5}$$

$$\bar{\rho} = \left(\sum_j \rho_j \frac{\partial I_j}{\partial i} \right) \Big/ \left(\sum_j \frac{\partial I_j}{\partial i} \right) = \left(\sum_j \rho_j I_j \eta_j \right) \Big/ \left(\sum_j I_j \eta_j \right) \tag{6}$$

$$\eta_I = \frac{i}{I} \frac{\partial I}{\partial i} = \frac{i}{I} \sum_j \frac{\partial I_j}{\partial i} = \sum_j \frac{I_j}{I} \eta_j. \tag{7}$$

Expression (3) is identical to that obtained from the simpler model analyzed earlier in this section. The only adjustments required in moving from the simpler to the more general model entail the interpretation of the symbols. In the more general model we have

$\bar{\rho}$ = the marginal productivity of capital in the private economy = a weighted average of the separate marginal productivities of capital in the separate sectors.

η_I = the overall elasticity of private-sector investment with respect to the rate of interest = a weighted average of the elasticities of sectoral investment with respect to the rate of interest.

$\bar{r}$ = the net-of-tax yield on private savings = a weighted average of the net-of-tax yields applying to the various tax brackets or other relevant groups.

ϵ_S = the overall elasticity of private savings with respect to the rate of interest = a weighted average of the elasticities of saving in the various tax brackets with respect to the rate of interest.

Whereas in the simpler case ρ, η_I, r, and ϵ_S were derived from single investment or savings functions, in the more general case they are weighted averages of the corresponding values derived from investment functions of the several sectors or the savings functions of the various relevant groups of savers. The social opportunity cost of capital, therefore, is a weighted average of the private-sector marginal productivity of capital and the net-of-tax yield on private savings, which we have previously identified as a measure of the marginal rate of time-preference in the private sector. It is this rate which in principle should be used to discount the costs and benefits of public projects, at least where a reasonably well-functioning capital market exists.

To illustrate the calculation of the social opportunity cost of capital in the more general case, and also to bring some additional elements of realism into the picture, I here present a simple numerical example entailing two sectors of investment and three relevant classes of savers. Once again a perfect capital market is assumed, with a going rate of interest (after business taxes but before personal taxes) of 6 percent. Taxes applying to business consist of (a) a general property tax at the rate of

2 percent per annum on the true market value of all physical (but not financial) assets, (b) a corporation income tax at the rate of 50 percent on the income accruing to corporate equity capital, and (c) a general value-added tax at the rate of 20 percent on all productive processes in the private sector. A personal income tax also applies to individual incomes (including each shareholder's portion of corporate savings), with marginal rates in successive brackets of 0, 25, and 50 percent.

Let us now examine the nature of equilibrium in this perfectly functioning though distorted capital market. The equilibrium rate of interest on bonds (government and private), the rate of return to noncorporate equity (after property and value-added taxes), and the rate of return to corporate equity (after corporation, property, and value-added taxes) will all be 6 percent. The cost of equity capital to firms in the corporate sector will therefore be $17\frac{1}{2}$ percent, and the cost, ρ_N, of private debt capital and of noncorporate equity capital will be 10 percent.[4]

Now it is clear that unless corporations faced some constraints on their access to debt capital, they would finance themselves wholly in this way, and the equilibrium level for the marginal productivity of corporate capital would be 10 percent. In the real world it is largely considerations of risk (both lender's and borrower's) that limit the degree to which a company can avoid the corporation tax by 'fleeing' into debt and thereby determine a firm's optimum financial structure. Since risk premia have been assumed away in order to simplify this exercise; I shall simply assume that banking practices and other institutional constraints have determined that corporations finance themselves two-thirds by equity and one-third by debt. This assumption determines that the over-all cost of capital to corporations will be 15 percent $[=(\frac{2}{3})(\cdot 175)+(\frac{1}{3})(\cdot 10)]$. This figure, therefore, represents the equilibrium level of the marginal productivity of corporate sector investment, while the marginal productivity of non corporate investment will be 10 percent in equilibrium.[5]

We now turn to the marginal rates of time preference that are relevant to our example. These are obtained by reducing the 6 percent market rate of return to capital by the rates of personal tax corresponding to the different tax brackets. All groups of savers receive the same market rate of interest, i, here 6 percent, but their behavior is governed by their net-of-tax rates of return, which will vary, in our example, all the way from 6 percent for the zero-marginal-tax-rate group down to 3 percent for the group with a 50 percent marginal tax rate.[6] Thus in accommodating his plans to whatever market interest rate appears, each individual will adjust his portfolio behavior and consumption program to the point where his marginal rate of time preference reflects the net-of-tax marginal yield on his savings.

Table 4.1 summarizes the values for the ρ_j and the r_k that emerge from the above specifications. It also introduces assumed initial values for the I_j and the S_k, and for the sectoral or class elasticities, η_j and ϵ_k. From the data of Table 4.1, equations (4)–(7) can be solved to obtain $\bar{r} = \cdot04$; $\epsilon_S = \cdot225$; $\bar{\rho} = \cdot14$, and $\eta_I = -1\cdot67$. These values, in turn, can be substituted into (3) to yield the estimated value of the social opportunity cost of capital, $\omega = \cdot1244$.

TABLE 4.1

Investment Sectors	ρ_j	I_j	η_j
Corporate	·15	40	−2·0
Noncorporate	·10	20	−1·0
Total (I)		60	

Classes of savers	r_k	S_k	ϵ_k
Zero tax bracket	·06	20	0·1
25% tax bracket	·045	40	0·2
50% tax bracket	·03	20	0·4
Total (S)		80	

II. AN ALTERNATIVE FORMULATION: EXTERNAL EFFECTS OF GOVERNMENT BORROWING

The social opportunity cost of capital can be represented by an alternative expression which is useful in a number of contexts. Adding and subtracting the interest rate i on the right-hand side of (2), we obtain

$$\omega = i + \frac{\left[\sum_k (r_k - i) \frac{\partial S_k}{\partial i} - \sum_j (\rho_j - i) \frac{\partial I_j}{\partial i} \right]}{\left(\sum_k \frac{\partial S_k}{\partial i} - \sum_j \frac{\partial I_j}{\partial i} \right)}. \tag{8}$$

In the example treated thus far, where the rate of return on capital, net-of-business-taxes and gross of personal taxes, was equal to i in all applications, and the only distortions present were taxes $(r_k - i)$, a negative number, can be identified with $-t_k i$, where t_k is the marginal rate of personal income tax applicable to the kth income class, and $(\rho_j - i)$, a positive number, can be identified with $t_j \rho_j$, where t_j is the effective rate of business taxation of the income from capital in activity j.[7] Both $(r_k - i)$ and $(\rho_j - i)$, therefore, measure the distortions δ_k and δ_j affecting, respectively, savings by the kth income class and investment in the jth activity. δ_k (<0), which has the same dimensionality as the interest rate, reflects the fact that personal taxes will be paid on the income produced by any savings that are stimulated by additional government borrowing, while δ_j (>0) reflects the fact that taxes will be forgone on the income from investible funds that are diverted from private investment as a result of an increment of government borrowing. We therefore have:

$$\omega = i + \left[\left(\sum_k \delta_k \frac{\partial S_k}{\partial i} - \sum_j \delta_j \frac{\partial I_j}{\partial i} \right) \Big/ \left(\sum_k \frac{\partial S_k}{\partial i} - \sum_j \frac{\partial I_j}{\partial i} \right) \right]. \tag{9}$$

Measuring the social opportunity cost of capital as the interest rate paid by the government plus an adjustment factor representing the relevant weighted average degree of distortion in the private capital market permits us to abandon the assumption, maintained up to this point, that the net-of-business-tax yields on all forms of investment were equal. Let i_j represent the supply price of funds for investment in the jth activity, that is, the expected yield after business taxes which is just barely necessary to attract additional funds to that activity. Similarly let i_k be the supply price of additional savings coming from the kth income class.

The i_j obviously incorporates premia for risk and for whatever other factors influence portfolio decisions. They can be represented as $i_j = i_g + \lambda_j$, where λ_j is the (quite possibly variable) 'risk premium' required for investment in the jth activity and i_g is the (risk-free) rate of interest on government bonds. In this expanded framework the counterpart of (9) becomes

$$\omega = i_g + \left[\left(\sum_k \delta_k \frac{\partial S_k}{\partial B} - \sum_j \delta_j \frac{\partial I_j}{\partial B} \right) \middle/ \left(\sum_k \frac{\partial S_k}{\partial B} - \sum_i \frac{\partial I_j}{\partial B} \right) \right], \quad (10)$$

where δ_k is now defined as $(r_k - i_k)$, δ_j as $(\rho_j - i_j)$ and B is the amount of government borrowing. Note that the weights attaching to the δ_k and δ_j in (10) are derivatives of saving and investment with respect to B, whereas in (9) they were derivatives with respect to i. This change is required because whereas in the simplified model underlying (9), an increase in government borrowing (at a given level of national income) works out its effects on the capital market solely through a change in *the* interest rate i, in the more complicated model underlying (10) there can be changes of differing amounts in all of the separate interest rates i_j and i_k. $\partial S_k/\partial B$ and $\partial I_j/\partial B$ measure the net effect of an increment of government borrowing upon S_k and I_j and incorporate the influences of such borrowing upon saving and investment through all components of the structure of interest rates and yields.[8]

The distortion measures, δ_j and δ_k, consist almost exclusively of taxes, the principal exception to this rule being monopoly profits (and even monopoly profits can plausibly be viewed as the proceeds of privately-imposed and privately-collected taxes). One has no difficulty in identifying property taxes and corporation income taxes as distortions which create a differential between the marginal productivity of investment and the supply price of investible funds. Likewise, a value-added tax of x percent will lead to a situation in which (in equilibrium) both the marginal productivity of capital and that of labor will be x percent higher, in relation to the supply prices of these factors, than they would otherwise be. Thus, capital's share (defined as $1 - \dfrac{\text{wages and salaries}}{\text{value added}}$) of value added taxes should be incorporated as part of T_j when estimating the distortion affecting ivestment in sector j.

Some problems emerge, however, in connection with excise or sales taxes. Standard price theory tells us that such taxes introduce gaps of equal proportion between the marginal revenue productivity and the marginal factor cost of all variable factors of production. This suggests that a 10 percent excise tax in and of itself causes the marginal revenue productivity of capital, labor, and materials inputs to exceed their supply prices by 10 percent. However, if materials enter production in fixed proportions (a close approximation to reality in most cases) a tax of t percent on the output of an activity is equivalent in all its effects to a tax of $t/(1 - \alpha_M)$ on the value added by labor and capital in that activity, where α_M represents the fraction that materials costs bear to total costs.[9] Hence, whereever the fixed-coefficient assumption is deemed to be appropriate for materials inputs, T_j should include capital's share of all excise and sales taxes generated by activity j, where capital's share is once again $1 - \dfrac{\text{wages and salaries}}{\text{value added}}$.

Monopoly profits (defined as any excess of profits in a given activity over the supply price of capital to that activity which is attributable to the exploitation of monopoly power) should be treated in a fashion analogous to excise taxes. In the formula $t_j = T_j/\pi_j$, both T_j and π_j should include capital's share and exclude labor's share of monopoly profits.

The approach outlined above is a special case of a more general treatment of the external effects of any given disturbance. If D_l represents the excess of marginal social benefit over marginal social cost per unit change in the level of activity Z_l, then the sum total of the external effects of an amount ΔB of government borrowing can be expressed as $\sum\limits_l D_l \dfrac{\partial Z_l}{\partial B} \Delta B$.

The last terms of equations (9) and (10) represent the external effects per unit of government borrowing when the only relevant non-zero distortions D_i are those affecting the savings and investment sides of the capital market.[10]

Obviously, if there are other relevant distortions, it is appropriate to take them into account in measuring the social opportunity cost of capital, and the way to do so is to subtract from (9) or (10) $\sum\limits_l D_l \dfrac{\partial Z_l}{\partial B}$, where l is allowed to vary over all activities other than the savings and investment activities directly taken to account in the equations in question. The ways in which these other distortions could affect the social opportunity cost of capital are too numerous to even attempt a listing of all possibilities, but a few examples can be given here. If more labor is used in an activity subject to excise taxation as a consequence of the government's increased borrowing, a net external benefit is created equal to $t/(1 - \alpha_M)$ times the value of the additional labor employed in that activity. If, in a given area, the wage for whatever reason exceeds the supply price of labor at the margin, and if the added government borrowing leads to more labor being employed in that area, there is an external benefit equal to the excess of the wage rate over the supply price of labor times the increment to employment in the area in question. If imports contract owing to the increased tightness in the private capital market, the duties forgone as a consequence represent an external cost attributable to the added government borrowing.

It is obviously difficult to identify all the relevant sources of externalities above and beyond those in the capital market itself, and even more difficult to estimate the effect of added government borrowing on the levels of the corresponding activities. Yet, even if one cannot surmount these difficulties it may in many cases be possible to reach the judgment that the net effect of externalities other than those explicitly taken into account in (9) and (10) will be small. The capital market is directly affected by government borrowing, being required to yield up the funds required by the government. In a context of full-employment, then, either private investment or private savings or both must change to reflect added government borrowing. By the same token we have divergences (δ_k and δ_j) between marginal social benefits and costs of added savings and investment which can be clearly identified and quite accurately measured. Thus, within the capital market area there is a presumption that both D_i and $\partial Z_i/\partial B$ will be significantly different from zero. Outside the capital market area, however, there may be many activities for which the relevant distortion is zero or nearly so, and for these the size of $\partial Z_i/\partial B$ is of essentially no moment. Similarly, there are probably many activities which can be judged with a fair degree of certainty to be very insensitive to changes in B, and for these there is no need to inquire into the size of the distortions D_i.

Thus, the number of activities for which the product $D_i(\partial Z_i/\partial B)$ is of significant enough magnitude to warrant its being taken explicitly into account is likely to be sufficiently small to be manageable.

III. IMPLICATIONS OF THE ABOVE ANALYSIS

Two special cases

The first and most obvious implication emerging from formula (3) is that the social opportunity cost of capital will be equal to the marginal productivity of capital in the private sector, $\bar{\rho}$, *only* when the elasticity of savings with respect to the interest rate is zero (assuming $\bar{r}$ and S to be positive), and will be equal to the marginal rate of time preference, $\bar{r}$, *only* when the elasticity of investment with respect to the cost of capital is zero. The traditional extreme positions thus correspond to quite specific behavior assumptions whose plausibility can be examined. In my judgment, the accumulated econometric evidence on investment functions clearly shows that many categories of investment are quite sensitive to changes in interest rates, while evidence that saving is responsive to interest-rate changes is, to date, only scanty. There is thus a reasonable presumption that the relevant weighted average will be reasonably close, if not precisely equal, to the marginal productivity of capital in the private sector.

On the use of a sectoral opportunity cost of capital

The second implication is somewhat more subtle. It has sometimes been suggested that the government use as its discount rate the gross-of-tax rate of return on capital in some such aggregate as manufacturing industry or the corporate sector. If the productivity of capital is 15 percent per year in the corporate sector, could not the government, rather than build a particular dam or bridge, invest the same money in financing new corporate investment (say by buying a share of all new equity and debt issues) and thus obtain for itself, including the taxes on the investment it is financing, the full 15 percent yield referred to above? And since the government can expend this yield on future generations so as to produce a distribution of benefits among groups and through time similar to that which would have been produced by any given project, *should* the government not insist that each of its projects produce as a minimum the 15 percent per annum that it can obtain in the corporate sector under the suggested investment policy?

Despite the plausibility of positive replies to these apparently rhetorical questions, the answer in each case is negative. And the reason is simply that in a well-functioning capital market one can neither inject funds into nor extract funds from any given segment of that market. If the government is extracting funds, interest rates will rise in all segments of the market, and investment will be curtailed in all sectors in accordance with their elasticities of response to interest-rate changes. If the government is introducing new funds into the market, interest rates will fall throughout the market, and all sectors will expand investment in accordance with their rates of response to interest-rate changes. It matters not whether the government injects $1 billion into the mortgage market or into the market for new corporate securities; if the overall capital market is functioning well, the end result should be the same.[11] The ancient principle of arbitrage will see to it that all sectors of the market share in any influx of funds and contribute to any outflow. This means, among other things, that when government demand for funds increases, mortgage rates as well as the cost of corporate capital tighten, a phenomenon that does not lack empirical support.

There is indeed a way in which the marginal productivity of capital in the corporate sector could be *made* to be the social opportunity cost of capital, but it would require rather special efforts. In particular it would entail insulating the rest of the market from the effects of the government's action of, say, purchasing $1 billion of new corporate securities. In the simple model of our exercise, this entails keeping the interest rate constant at 6 percent per year, while offering capital to the corporate sector which was previously in equilibrium at a 15 percent per annum rate of productivity. If 15 percent represents where the corporate sector would be *in the absence* of any government funds, the government would have to reduce the cost of capital slightly below 15 percent in order for the corporate sector to absorb the $1 billion in question. To accomplish this without affecting the interest rates facing other sectors, either the corporation income tax would have to be slightly reduced, or some equivalent measure would have to be taken that reduced the cost of capital in the corporate sector but not elsewhere.

In a similar vein, the government could, if it chose to, create a situation in which the marginal rate of time preference for the highest income-tax bracket would measure the effective social opportunity cost of capital, so long as the savings of this group were sufficiently responsive to changes in yield. But once again this could not be done merely by selling bonds to this group, which would cause interest rates, savings yields and capital costs to change in all segments of the market. Actions would have to be taken to cause the highest income-tax bracket to demand more bonds at the prevailing market interest rate (6 percent in our example); and to accomplish this the yield on savings to this group must be raised, either by reducing somewhat their marginal income-tax rate or by some essentially equivalent measure.

In my view, it is totally unrealistic to think that a government would make the kinds of continuous adjustments in its tax structure that would be necessary to 'validate' any particular sector's marginal productivity of capital or any particular group's marginal rate of time preference as the social opportunity cost of capital. In general, social project evaluation is carried out within a given institutional framework which includes, among other things, the tax structure. A project evaluation office has neither the legislative power to change the tax structure nor, typically, even the administrative prerogative of a Finance Ministry or a Treasury to propose such changes to the legislature. It must, in such cases, operate within the confines of the given tax policy, which means that the private investments that are curtailed and the private savings that are stimulated by the government's drawing funds from the capital market will be market-determined according to the principles embodied in equation (3). It is simply not within the power of a project evaluation or government investment authority to determine the ultimate 'sources' of the funds it draws from the private capital market or the ultimate 'uses' of any funds it might put into the private sector.[12]

The 'uniqueness' of ω

The third implication, already touched upon above, but deserving of further elaboration, is the 'uniqueness' of formula (3) as a measure of the social opportunity cost of capital. Let me state at the outset that what I call uniqueness is in a sense more a matter of convention than of pure logic, yet I shall contend that this is an area in which some convention is necessary, and that the assumptions underlying formula (3) provide the best basis for such a convention.

The problem is a familiar one in public finance, where one can develop a separate analysis of any tax for each possible way the proceeds can be spent, and a separate analysis of each possible expenditure for each possible way the money can be raised. In the present context, the questions can be put of what would be the social opportunity cost of funds raised through a reduction in personal exemption levels on the income tax; through an increase in high-bracket rates; through an across-the-board increase in income tax rates, through a rise in the cigarette tax, or the corporation income tax, through the imposition of selective excises on particular commodities, and the like. Quite obviously, each of these different ways of raising public funds is likely to have a different impact on consumption and investment, and within these broad aggregates the various groups of savers and the various categories of investment are likely to be differently affected by each. It is equally clear that if after tracing out the respective effects of each tax measure, we were to construct an estimate of the opportunity cost of public funds raised in that way, we would likely end up with as many values of opportunity cost as the number of tax measures we analyzed.

This multiplicity of tax-based measures of opportunity cost would not necessarily be embarrassing if only we knew the true source of the funds to be obtained, or the relative contributions that various sources would have in financing movements of government expenditure. But in point of fact we do not have this information, nor are we likely to get it.

The 'convention' that I would adopt to resolve the problem of multiplicity is to treat the capital market as a 'sponge' which absorbs any increment of government funds that may come

from an increase in tax yields, and which yields up the funds
to finance any increment of government expenditures. That the
capital market in a very real sense serves this function is clear.
If, as a consequence of an unexpected spurt in economic activity, tax revenues rise above the anticipated levels, the government will as a consequence either reduce its borrowings or pay
off existing debt. By the same token, at least if rational project-
evaluation procedures are in force, the failure of a particular
project to pass muster will simply mean that much less government borrowing or that much more reduction of outstanding
debt. In this sense one can say that incremental tax funds have
a social yield of ω, as measured by (3), and incremental government expenditures have a social opportunity cost of ω.

Note that we have attributed to incremental tax funds a
social yield, not a social cost, of ω. The resource-allocation costs
of raising additional funds will vary with the manner in which
they are raised, and may be very large in certain cases and
strongly negative in others.[13] Moreover, their analysis is highly
complex and is not an appropriate function of a project-
evaluation office. Those who do recommend tax changes
should, if they operate on appropriate economic criteria,
evaluate particular changes in terms of whether they are justified in the light of a yield of ω, and those who evaluate projects
should ask whether the projects are justified in the light of
an opportunity cost of ω. ω therefore plays the true role of
a shadow price in creating the possibility for decentralized
decision-making both on the side of sources and on that of uses
of funds.

Though project evaluation is, under the suggested convention,
in a sense insulated from tax policy decisions, it is not totally
unaffected by them for tax changes can shift the savings and
investment schedules of various groups and sectors, thus changing the underlying functions on which formula (3) is based.
The course of ω through time will be a function, among other
things, of tax policy. An extreme example is the case of a society
attempting to employ a 'social rate of time preference' derived
without direct reference to capital market phenomena to reach
its decisions on the allocation of resources between present and
future generations. This is the approach suggested by Marglin
and Sen, both of whom believe that the appropriate 'social rate

of time preference' lies far below the current opportunity cost of capital.

Let us suppose that the opportunity cost of capital (our ω) is currently equal to 10 percent, while the 'social rate of time preference' is only 4 percent. This does not mean that public-sector projects should be evaluated at a 4 percent rate, since marginal increments of public funds could be put into the private capital market where they would have a social yield of 10 percent. The appropriate policy is for public projects to be continuously evaluated at ω, and for the fiscal authorities to design their policies so as to gradually bring ω down to 4 percent. This would undoubtedly take a long time (perhaps forever) to accomplish, and would likely entail the dismantling of such taxes as the corporate income and property taxes in a fashion similar to that referred to in note 12.[14] But the important point is that in the process ω would continue to guide investment decisions. If the 'social rate of time preference' is a guide for anyone, it is for fiscal authorities and overall planners, not for project evaluators.

ω as a measure of the social opportunity cost of private investment and of the social yield of private savings

In the model presented in Section I, where a single interest rate prevails in the market and no risk premia, etc., are present, ω, as measured by equation (3), represents not only the social opportunity cost of public borrowing, but also the social opportunity cost of private investment and the social yield on private savings. In Section I, the disturbance that was analyzed was an increment in the rate of public-sector borrowing, with given private-sector investment and savings functions. But exactly the same results are obtained when the disturbance being analyzed is an autonomous shift of the private-sector investment function or of the private-sector savings function. If additional (new) private-sector investment demand appears on the scene, interest rates are bid up in precisely the same way as in the case of incremental public-sector borrowing, and the real resources needed to make the new investment are in part bid away from other private-sector investments and, in part, provided by the increment to savings that the rise in the interest rate itself generates. By the same token, an autonomous rightward shift in the private savings schedule has the effect of lowering the level of interest rates; the "new' saving thus in part displaces (through its effect on interest rates) 'old' saving that would otherwise have occurred and, in part, stimulates an increment to private investment.

This can easily be seen if we let $S(i)$ and $I(i)$ be the 'old' savings and investment functions, and S_a' and I_a' be hypothetical autonomous shifts in these functions. Then we have

$$B = S(i) + S_a' - I(i) - I_a'. \tag{11}$$

It is clear from the above that $\partial S/\partial B = \partial S/\partial I_a' = -\partial S/\partial S_a'$, that $\partial I/\partial B = \partial I/\partial I_a' = -\partial I/\partial S_a'$, and that $\partial i/\partial B = \partial i/\partial I_a' = -\partial i/\partial S_a'$. This is because government borrowing B, and the private-sector savings and investment shifts S_a' and I_a' are all autonomous within the context of this model. A dollar change in the quantity $(B + I_a' - S_a')$ will have the same effects on S (non-autonomous saving), I (nonautonomous investment) and i (the market interest rate), regardless of which of the three autonomous elements was responsible for the change. Thus, in the absence of risk premia ω represents the social opportunity cost of private as well as public investment, and at the same time reflects the social yield of private savings as well as public tax revenues.

APPENDIX

1. *Changes in the discount rate through time*

Up to this point we have glossed over the problems associated with the term structure of interest rates. Here we treat these problems within the framework of the Fisher-Hicks expectations model. Let ω_1 represent the social opportunity cost of an additional dollar borrowed by the government in year 0 and paid back in year 1. To a first-order approximation the increase in savings generated in year 0 will be counterbalanced by a decrease in year 1, and the decline in investment in year 0 will be offset by an increase in year 1. Thus, the private sector's holdings of real assets and government obligations at the end of period 1 will, to a first-order approximation, be essentially the same as they would have been in the absence of the added borrowing of a dollar for one year. The opportunity costs of the operation in question are therefore represented by (a) the forgone product during year 1 of the investment displaced by the added borrowing in year 0, plus (b) the supply price (that is, the net-of-personal-tax yield) of the added savings generated as a consequence of the increased borrowing in year 0. The sum of (a) and (b), plus the initial dollar borrowed, is what the government would require in order to pay back to the private sector in year 1 the supply price of the funds in question and to compensate the net tax losses that the added government borrowing has generated through its effects on private investment and saving.[15]

If now a project is contemplated which has costs of C_0 in year 0 and benefits of B_2 in year 2, its benefits would have to exceed $C_0(1 + \omega_1)(1 + \omega_2)$ in order for it to be socially advantageous, where ω_2 is the social opportunity cost of borrowing in year 1 for repayment in year 2. If the government borrowed C_0 in year 0, it would have to generate $C_0(1 + \omega_1)$ in year 1 in order to fully compensate the private sector and itself for their respective forgone opportunities. Real benefits of the project are not yet present in period 1, so the government to accomplish the required compensation, in effect, reborrows $C_0(1 + \omega_1)$ for which it must repay in period 2 the amount $C_0(1 + \omega_1)(1 + \omega_2)$ in order to compensate the private sector and itself for the opportunities forgone.

In a similar fashion it can be shown that the criterion for choosing any project with costs of C_j concentrated in period j and benefits of B_k concentrated in period k is $C_j \prod\limits_{t=j+1}^{k} (1 + \omega_{t-j})$ $\leq B_k$, where ω_t is the social opportunity cost of the government's borrowing in year $t - 1$ for repayment in year t. If we call project profiles with costs in just one year (j) and benefits in just one other year (k) 'canonical' profiles, then what we have shown is that for such profiles the criterion for project choice is that the present value of benefits should exceed costs when benefits are discounted to the initial year of the project

(j) by multiplying by the factor $1 / \prod\limits_{t=j+1}^{k} (1 + \omega_{t-j})$. Since the time profile of net benefit flows $F_t(= B_t - C_t)$ of any project can be decomposed into a sequence of 'canonical' profiles, it follows that the criterion for accepting any project initiated in year j and terminating in year k is:

$$F_j + \sum_{t=j+1}^{k} \left[F_t / \prod_{j+1}^{t} (1 + \omega_{t-j}) \right] \geq 0. \tag{12}$$

The ω's in (12) are clearly estimates of the expected future social opportunity costs of borrowing in year $t - 1$ for repayment in year t. Implicit in any such estimates are anticipations of (a) how the behavioral relationships $I(\rho)$ and $S(r)$ will shift in the future, (b) how tax rates (or other distortions which cause differences to emerge between ρ and r and the market rate of interest (i) will be altered through time, and (c) how much net borrowing the government will actually do in each future year. The answer to (a) determines the expected location of the $I(\rho)$ and $S(r)$ schedules, that to (b) determines that of the $S(i)$ and $I(i)$ schedules, and that to (c), together with the elasticities of the relevant schedules, determines how far above or below the intersection of $S(i)$ and $I(i)$ the actual market interest rate will lie.

It is worth emphasizing in this connection that the approach here outlined for measuring the social opportunity cost of capital is relevant regardless of the extent to which the government relies on tax financing (short of operating without any government debt at all), and regardless of the types of taxes imposed. But both the amount and type of tax financing do influence, in the ways indicated, what actual figures will be obtained for the ω_t's.

To see how the process of projecting the ω_i's might work, suppose that the interest rate currently is at 6 percent, but that an upward movement of interest rates is judged to be required to stem an actual or prospective gold drain (I assume fixed exchange rates here). The current market rate of interest, i, might be 6 percent, and ω_0, the social opportunity cost of capital in the current year might be 8 percent—a weighted average of a marginal productivity of private-sector capital of 12 percent and a net-of-personal-tax yield on savings of 4 percent. If the government is to have higher interest rates and still maintain full employment, it will have to pursue an easier fiscal policy. This might be accomplished by cutting the corporation income tax rate, say, from 50 percent to 30 percent, and the end result might be ρ = 10 percent, i = 7 percent, and r = $4\frac{2}{3}$ percent. The same effect on over-all tax revenues might also be obtained by reducing the personal income tax rate from $33\frac{1}{3}$ to 25 per cent, and this might result in ρ = 12·8 percent, i = 6·4 percent, and r = 4·8 percent. Using weights of ·5 for averaging ρ and r, the relevant value for ω_2 in the corporate-tax-reduction case would be $7\frac{1}{3}$ percent while in the personal-tax-reduction case it would be 7·8 percent.

Obviously the projection of the ω_t's into far future years will have to be based on general judgments concerning the probable productivity of capital in the economy and the types and rates of taxes likely to be in effect. In all likelihood, there will be no plausible ground for choosing a different level of ω for a year 5 years hence than for one 10 years in the future. Differences of ω_t are more likely to emerge, however, in respect to near-future years. A few of the possible cases can be distinguished: (a) when the current state of the capital market is judged to be abnormally weak (or strong), the current level of ω_t should be lower (higher) that what is judged to be its normal long-term level, and the successive annual ω_t's should be projected to approach the long-run normal level over the period during which it is expected that capital-market conditions will be moving back to 'normal'; (b) when changes are immediately foreseeable in tax rates that enter into the formula for ω (such as might occur after the termination of a military crisis or with the accession of a new administration), they should influence the pattern of ω_t's via a once-and-for-all shift in their level at the probable date of adoption of the tax changes; (c) when, as in the example presented above, a balance-of-payments crisis dictates a significant shift in the mix of monetary and fiscal policy, this should have the effect of raising ω_t above its long-run normal level for the period for which the crisis is expected to last.

While the idea of discount factors that change through time may seem at first glance to be an excessive embellishment, it is, in fact, the fundamental way in which the procedures of cost-benefit analysis can be adapted to reflect situations of abnormal glut or scarcity in a country's capital market, or to capture the effects of prospective institutional or policy changes on the true social opportunity cost of capital.

2. *Adjusting for anticipated inflation*

It is essential for the proper evaluation of projects to carry out the calculations of costs and benefits in real terms, and the customary way to accomplish this is to express estimated costs and benefits in terms of the price level prevailing at the time the project is being studied.[16] One cannot quarrel with this well-established procedure, but one must follow through what it implies with regard to the discount rate to be used in public project evaluation. Clearly, the relevant interest rate must reflect real forces and correction must be made in estimating ω for any 'contamination' of the basic data due to anticipated inflation. Such contamination enters the calculation through market interest rates and through a possible failure of depreciation changes to reflect true economic depreciation. With inflation anticipated to be at a rate of α percent per year, a market interest rate of i percent reflects a real rate of $(i - \alpha)$ percent. Since the prices of real assets are presumably rising in value at α percent per year, firms are making, on account of inflation, a capital gain of this amount, which offsets the extra α percentage points they have to pay on interest account. Their adjusted total interest costs are therefore $(i - \alpha)/i$ times the actual interest charges that they pay. In calculating the total income from capital, therefore, interest costs β_j must be separated from the after-tax earnings of equity E_j, with β_j being then adjusted downward by multiplying it by the factor $(i - \alpha)/i$ [or $(i_j - \alpha)/i_j$) in the case where the relevant i varies from sector to sector].

Attention should also be called to the fact that, where firms are not permitted to write up asset values to reflect the inflation before depreciation is charged, the depreciation expense appearing on their books will understate the true amount chargeable to depreciation at current prices, and earnings will be correspondingly overstated. The earnings of capital must accordingly be adjusted downward in such cases to reflect the implicit depreciation error.

Note that this approach does not assume that the tax system

is, in any sense, 'neutral' to inflation. If depreciation charges are understated taxable profits will be higher than true profits, and the taxes paid on the fictitious profits will be a part of the tax bill assessable against income from capital along with those based on true profits. Similarly, if property-tax assessments lag behind the inflation, the relevant tax bill will on that account be lower than it would be with continuous adjustment of assessed values.

In a similar vein, when it comes to estimating the rates of return to saving—net-of-personal income tax—interactions between inflation and the tax system can be accommodated. Whereas, without inflation the yield on bonds to the kth income class would be $r_k = i(1 - t_k)$, in the presence of inflation at α percent per year the real yield would be estimated as $r_k = i(1 - t_k) - \alpha$, reflecting the fact that income taxes have to be paid on the inflationary component of interest yields.

Other adjustments for anticipated inflation may also be required in order to implement fully the concept of social opportunity cost here put forward. This is not the place to attempt an exhaustive catalogue of all possibilities. My purpose is rather to alert readers to the necessity of incorporating such adjustments for anticipated inflation as appear to be relevant, in any empirical effort, to measure the social opportunity cost of capital.

Notes

[1] 'Proposed Practices for Economic Analysis of River Basin Projects', U.S. Interagency Committee on Water Resources, 1950.

[2] The net transfer from the government to the private sector is slightly smaller than EDV because private investors would, in the absence of the additional government borrowing, have been paying personal income taxes on $ACDE$, and in the presence of such borrowing will pay personal taxes on $ACVE$. This consideration, however, is of no moment for measuring the social opportunity cost of capital since, as was the case with EDV itself, what is involved is simply a transfer between the public and the private sectors.

[3] As with the case of the investment-effects of government borrowing, we ignore the implicit transfer of $r'WPi'$ minus $r_0LN i_0$ from the public sector to inframarginal private savers, the gain of the savers offsetting the extra cost to the government. To count this transfer as an added cost to the government is tantamount to the government's behaving as a monopsonist in the market for funds—treating private savers as antagonists to be exploited rather than as members of the over-all society with the welfare of which the government is concerned.

[4] If we call ρ_e the cost of corporate equity, its value under the assumed tax

setup is found by solving $\cdot5(\cdot8\rho_e - \cdot02) = \cdot06$. The factor $\cdot8$ multiplying ρ_e takes into account the 20 percent value-added tax (assumed to be of the income type); the deduction of $\cdot02$ reflects the property tax; and the factor $\cdot5$ takes into account the corporation income tax. In the case of private debt and noncorporate equity capital, no corporation income tax applies, so the relevant equation is $\cdot8\rho_N - \cdot02 = \cdot06$. As is appropriate for our purposes, the marginal productivity of capital is measured net of depreciation, as well as of materials and labor costs, and of that part of the value-added tax bill which is attributable to wage and salary payments.

[5] Obviously, if an activity could be carried on at equal cost in either sector, tax considerations would lead to its being noncorporate. In general, activities of low minimum economic scale are found in the noncorporate sector, while those for which the minimum economic scale is relatively high are carried on under the corporate form. In the United States the distinction between the two types of activities is extremely clear. More than three-fourths of all the income accruing to noncorporate equity capital comes from agriculture and from the ownership of residential housing; this fraction grows to 92 percent if wholesale and retail trade are included. By contrast, less than 2 percent of corporate income comes from agriculture and housing, and less than 15 percent from these sectors plus wholesale and retail trade. The picture, then, is of a quite strictly noncorporate sector consisting of agriculture and residential housing, and of a 'mixed' sector consisting of trade, with the great bulk of the rest of the private economy being overwhelmingly corporate. The after-tax income from capital comes in about equal proportions from the corporate and noncorporate sectors. See Leonard G. Rosenberg, 'Taxation of Income from Capital by Non-Financial Industry Group, Average 1953–59', in Arnold C. Harberger and Martin J. Bailey (eds.), *The Taxation of Income from Capital*, Washington, D.C.: The Brookings Institution, 1969, especially Table 1.

[6] Again for simplicity, I have abstracted from any complications stemming from the differential tax treatment (whether direct or via special treatment of capital gains) of distributed and undistributed profits. The exercise assumes that shareholders pay personal income tax on their share of corporate retained earnings as well as on the dividends that they receive, and that share prices rise to reflect the reinvestment of corporate retentions.

[7] If T_j represents the sum of corporation income taxes, property taxes, and other taxes allocable to capital in activity j, and π_j represents the gross-of-tax earnings of capital in that activity, then $t_j = T_j/\pi_j$.

[8] That is, $\dfrac{\partial S_1}{\partial B} = \sum_k \dfrac{\partial S_1}{\partial i_k} \dfrac{\partial i_k}{\partial B} + \sum_j \dfrac{\partial S_1}{\partial i_j} \dfrac{\partial i_j}{\partial B}$, where $\dfrac{\partial i_j}{\partial B}$ and $\dfrac{\partial i_k}{\partial B}$ are 'reduced form' coefficients measuring the responsiveness of the endogenous variables i_j and i_k to changes in the exogenous variable B.

[9] Another way of viewing the matter is to note that an increment of capital having a marginal productivity of \$1 will entail the use of $\$\alpha_M/(1 - \alpha_M)$ of materials. The increment to tax revenue will be $\$t + [t\alpha_M/(1 - \alpha_M)]$, which simplifies to $\$t/(1 - \alpha_M)$.

[10] If the only relevant distortions are in the private capital market on the savings and investment sides, the δ_j (defined as $\rho_j - i_j$) can be identified directly with the D_i's in the above formula, and the δ_k (defined as $r_k - i_k$) can be identified as the negative of the corresponding D_i's. Equation (10) can then be seen to be a special case of the general expression $\sum_i D_i \dfrac{\partial Z_i}{\partial B} \Delta B$. The externality connected with increased savings is positive, thus tending to reduce the social cost of government borrowing below the interest rate paid, and the externality connected with reduced investment is negative, thus tending to raise the social cost of government

borrowing above the interest rate paid. The denominator of the last term in (10), placed there for symmetry with earlier expressions, turns out to be equal to one on the assumption, maintained here throughout, that the capital market is cleared. With $\sum_k S_k - \sum_j I_j \equiv B$ both before and after the increment in government borrowing, it follows that $\sum_k \dfrac{\partial S_k}{\partial B} - \sum_j \dfrac{\partial I_j}{\partial B} = 1$.

When one attempts to put (9) in the framework of the formula $\sum_l D_l \dfrac{\partial \mathcal{Z}_l}{\partial B} \Delta B$, one obtains as the external reduction in social cost stemming from an increment of investment $\left(\sum_k \delta_k \dfrac{\partial S_k}{\partial i} - \sum_j \delta_j \dfrac{\partial I_j}{\partial i} \right) \dfrac{\partial i}{\partial B} \Delta B$. To express this as a fraction of the amount of incremental borrowing, we could simply divide by ΔB. Alternatively, however, we can divide by $\left(\sum_k \dfrac{\partial S_k}{\partial i} - \sum \dfrac{\partial I_j}{\partial i} \right) \dfrac{\partial i}{\partial B} \Delta B$, which under the assumption of capital-market equilibrium is equal to ΔB. Following the latter procedure eliminates $\partial i / \partial B$ from the resulting expression and yields the last term of equation (9).

[11] Except, of course, in the case where the government injects so large an amount of funds into a particular sector (for example, credit to poultry farmers) as to drive out private sector capital altogether, produce a subsidized interest rate in the affected sector, and in effect 'unhook' that sector from its former ties with the over-all capital market.

[12] It is interesting, nonetheless, to trace out the strategy that a thoroughly rational authority would adopt if it had the necessary fiscal powers to 'validate' its decisions. Obviously, it would want to obtain its funds at the lowest social cost, which entails drawing them from the incremental savings of the highest tax bracket. This in turn involves, as was indicated in the text, reducing the marginal tax rate applicable to that bracket. On the other hand, the authority would want to invest its funds in projects with the highest social yield, which means, in the context of the numerical example of Table 4.1, that it would not undertake public investments unless they yielded more than the most productive private-sector investments. Some funds would, therefore, in all likelihood be channeled to the corporate sector, and to 'validate' this allocation the corporate tax rate would have to be reduced. A continuation of this process would reduce the top personal tax rate from 50 to 40 to 30 percent, and finally to zero, and would eliminate first the corporation income tax and ultimately the property and (income-type) value-added taxes. The end result would be an undistorted capital market in which, under the assumptions of the basic model, all relevant rates would be the same. The marginal rates of productivity of capital would be equal in all sectors, as would the marginal rates of time preference of all individuals, and all of these rates would be equal to the government borrowing rate. Under more realistic assumptions the only differences in yields appearing in the market would be due to differences in riskiness of different activities, differences in risk preferences among savers, monopoly elements (including the transitory monopoly power that accrues to many innovators) and so forth. Government revenue would obviously have to be raised by other taxes. Two important and potentially high-yielding taxes that do not distort the capital market are: (1) a fully general value-added tax of the consumption type (for example, one in which capital expenditures as well as the cost of materials inputs are deductible) and (2) a tax on consumer expenditures, which could be made, à la Kaldor, as progressive as was deemed desirable.

[13] See A. C. Harberger, 'Taxation, Resource Allocation and Welfare', in National Bureau of Economic Research and The Brookings Institution, *The Role*

of Direct and Indirect Taxes in the Federal Revenue System, Princeton, N.J.: Princeton University Press, 1964, pp. 25–75, and 'The Measurement of Waste', *American Economic Review* 54 (May 1964), 58–76.

[14] In the earlier exercise it was accepted as a goal simply to have no distortions in the capital market; hence, at least implicitly, any market rate of interest that would emerge in the absence of distortions would be 'acceptable'. When a 'social rate of time preference' approach is used, on the other hand, the market interest rates that emerge under alternative nondistorting tax policies might all be too high. Suppose that the lowest equilibrium interest rate attainable by nondistorting policies is 5 percent, while the 'social rate of time preference' is 4 percent. Then the appropriate policy mix would be to eliminate corporation income, property, and (income-type) value-added taxes as before, thus driving the marginal productivity of corporate and noncorporate investment down to equality with i. But in addition to these measures, subsidies to investment would properly have to be introduced, so as to produce a situation where, for all j, $\rho_j = i(1 - s) = P$, where P is the social rate of time preference and s is the rate of subsidy to corporate and noncorporate investment. Similarly, the optimum rate of income tax would no longer be zero but would instead equal s, so that for all individual savers the net-of-tax yield of saving is $r_i = i(1 - s) = P$. As in the case previously dealt with, consumption taxes or value-added taxes of the consumption type would presumably be called upon to generate the bulk of fiscal revenues.

[15] We appropriately ignore here the mutually offsetting inframarginal transfers between the private and the public sectors which are referred to on page 97 and in note 3.

[16] This does not say that costs and benefits should be evaluated by pricing individual products and factors at the levels current at the time of evaluation. Anticipated relative price changes, as distinct from general-price-level changes, should be reflected in cost-benefit analyses. Standardizing on the current *general* price level is necessary simply in order to express the benefits and costs of various years in terms of a unit of common general purchasing power.

SELECTED BIBLIOGRAPHY

Hirshleifer, Jack, DeHaven, James C., and Milliman, Jerome W. *Water Supply: Economics, Technology, and Policy*. Chicago: University of Chicago Press, 1960.

Marglin, Stephen A. 'The Social Rate of Discount and the Optimal Rate of Saving.' *Quarterly Journal of Economics* (February 1963).

——. *Approaches to Dynamic Investment Planning*.

——. 'The Opportunity Costs of Public Investment.' *Quarterly Journal of Economics* (May 1963).

Sen, A. K. 'On Optimizing the Rate of Saving.' *Economic Journal* (September 1961).

Stockfisch, J. A. 'The Social Rate of Discount: Some Issues in the Theories of Cost and Public Finance' (mimeographed 1968).

——. 'The Interest Rate Applicable to Government Investment Projects.'

Strotz, Robert H. 'The Social Rate of Time Discount' (mimeographed, 1964).

U.S. Interagency Committee on Water Resources, *Proposed Practices for Economic Analysis of River Basin Projects*, 1950.

CHAPTER FIVE

PROFESSOR ARROW ON THE SOCIAL DISCOUNT RATE

In this section I briefly sketch an alternative conceptual framework for measuring the social rate of discount. In it, the discount rate is obtained by tracing through the effects of additional government borrowing on various classes of investment and saving. The resulting figure for the social rate of discount is a weighted average of the marginal rates of productivity of capital in the various sectors from which investment is displaced and of the marginal rates of time preference applicable to the various groups (if any) whose saving is stimulated (through higher interest rates) by the additional government borrowing.

We approach the problem indirectly, considering first the social opportunity cost of an input into a public-sector project, the private use of which is subject to tax; second, the social opportunity cost of foreign exchange under both uniform and diverse tariff treatment of various classes of imports; and only then the social opportunity cost of public funds. This indirect approach will reveal that essentially the same methodology is applicable to all three cases, thus reinforcing its credibility when it is applied to the discount rate problem.

(A) THE SOCIAL OPPORTUNITY COST OF AN INPUT

Let $S(P)$ be the total supply of the input in question, and $D[P(1+t)]$ be the total private-sector demand. The net-of-tax price is P, and t is the rate at which the use of the input by the private sector is taxed. Following the established convention of cost-benefit analysis that a competitive demand price reflects

Excerpts from 'Professor Arrow on the Social Discount Rate', G. G. Somers and W. D. Wood, eds., *Cost-Benefit Analysis of Manpower Policies* (Kingston, Ontario, Canada: Industrial Relations Centre, Queen's University, 1969), pp. 76–88.

the value of the commodity to the purchaser and a competitive supply price reflects the value of the commodity to the seller, we can say that the social opportunity cost of an additional unit of the commodity taken by the government will be a weighted average of P and $P(1+t)$, the weights depending on the relative impact of added government demand in stimulating additional production of the input on the one hand and in displacing its private-sector use on the other. The weights can be derived from the identity:

$$G \equiv S(P) - D[P(1+t)], \tag{1}$$

by differentiating with respect to G, which refers to government demand. This yields:

$$\frac{\partial S}{\partial G} = \frac{\partial S}{\partial P}\frac{\partial P}{\partial G} = \frac{S'}{S' - D'(1+t)} = \frac{\epsilon}{\epsilon - \eta(D/S)}$$

$$-\frac{\partial D}{\partial G} = \frac{-\partial D}{\partial P}\frac{\partial P}{\partial G} = \frac{-D'(1+t)}{S' - D'(1+t)} = \frac{-\eta(D/S)}{\epsilon - \eta(D/S)}, \tag{2}$$

where ϵ and η (defined as <0) are the elasticities of supply and demand for the good. The social opportunity cost of the input, P_s, is obtained using these weights.

$$P_s = \frac{\epsilon P - \eta(D/S)P(1+t)}{\epsilon - \eta(D/S)}. \tag{3}$$

(B) THE SOCIAL OPPORTUNITY COST OF FOREIGN EXCHANGE

For this case we assume the country in question to have no influence over the world prices of its exports or its imports. This permits the aggregation of heterogeneous commodities, with the common unit of account being the 'dollar's worth' at world market prices. If X represents private-sector exports, M private-sector imports, N net demand on the part of the public sector for foreign exchange, E the exchange rate, and t the uniform ad valorem duty on private-sector imports, then (1) is replaced by

$$N \equiv X(E) - M[E(1+t)], \tag{4}$$

and (3) becomes

$$E_s = \frac{\epsilon E - \eta(M/X)E(1 + t)}{\epsilon - \eta(M/X)}, \tag{5}$$

where E_s is the social opportunity cost of foreign exchange and ϵ and η here refer to the elasticities of the private sector's supply of exports and of its demand for imports, respectively.

Assuming now that there are several categories of imports, each struck by a different tariff rate t_i, (4) must be replaced by

$$\mathcal{N} \equiv X(E) - \sum_i M_i[E(1 + t_i)], \tag{4'}$$

and (5) becomes

$$E_s = \frac{\epsilon E - \sum_i \eta_i(M_i/X)E(1 + t_i)}{\epsilon - \sum_i \eta_i(M_i/X)}. \tag{5'}$$

Here the social opportunity cost of foreign exchange is a weighted average of the exchange rate governing exports, and of the internal values that a dollar's worth of foreign exchange produces when spent on imports in the various categories. The weights are the fractions in which an extra dollar of net government demand for foreign exchange will be reflected in increased exports on the one hand and in reduced imports of the various categories on the other.

(c) THE SOCIAL OPPORTUNITY COST OF CAPITAL

In most modern economies the effective weight of taxation of income from capital varies substantially among sectors. Let us assume that the rate of return i, defined to be after such taxes as corporation income and property taxes but before personal income tax, is equalized in all lines of investment, through the operation of market forces. The marginal productivity of capital will accordingly be different in the various lines of activity, being equal to $\rho_j = i/(1 - t_j)$, where t_j is the average rate at which such levies as corporation income and property taxes, taken together, strike the income from capital in sector j. At the same time, although savers by assumption all receive the same rate of return, i, before personal income taxes, their after-tax rates of return will differ as among marginal tax rate brackets. Hence we can express the marginal rate of time preference of savers in the kth tax bracket as $r_k = i(1 - t_k)$.

Using S_k to denote private saving by individuals in the kth tax bracket, I_j to denote private investment in the jth sector, and B to denote net government borrowing, we have, as the counterpart of (4′)

$$B \equiv \sum_k S_k[i(1 - t_k)] - \sum_j I_j[i/(1 - t_j)] \qquad (6)$$

and as the counterpart of (5′)

$$i_s = \frac{\sum_k \epsilon_k (S_k/S) r_k - \sum_j \eta_j (I_j/S) \rho_j}{\sum_k \epsilon_k (S_k/S) - \sum_j \eta_j (I_j/S)}. \qquad (7)$$

Here ϵ_k refers to the elasticity of supply of savings with respect to their rate of yield, by individuals in the kth tax bracket, η_j refers to the elasticity of the investment schedule of the jth sector with respect to the cost of capital, and S denotes total private savings. The savings and investment schedules are defined at the full employment level of income.

In words, (7) says that the social opportunity cost of capital will be a weighted average of the marginal rates of time preference of the various categories of savers, and of the rates of marginal productivity of capital in the various sectors. The weights are proportional to the extents to which the various types of saving increase and the various types of investment decrease when new net borrowing occurs in the capital market. In the model just sketched, which assumes that the net yield i, after other but before personal income taxes, is the same in all sectors, (7) measures not only the social opportunity cost of public borrowing, but also that of any net increment to private borrowing (such as an upward shift of any of the I_j schedules). In this case the I_j and S_k schedules should be defined not including the shift, and the shift itself, ΔI_j, replaces B in (6). By the same token, i_s as measured in (7) represents both the social yield of any autonomous increment in private savings (that is, a rightward shift in any of the S_j schedules), and also the potential social yield of any increase in taxes, as well as the social opportunity cost of any increment in government expenditures. The analogy with the foreign exchange market is useful here.

What we defined as E_s in Section (B) above is not only the social opportunity cost of public expenditures of foreign exchange, it is also the social opportunity cost of private expenditures of foreign exchange and at the same time the social opportunity yield of increments of foreign exchange, regardless of whether they are generated in the public or private sector.

(d) ADVANTAGES OF THE i_s APPROACH

The advantages of this approach, as I see them, are the following:

1. The basic data from which estimates of i_s are generated can in principle be obtained from market observations. In the case treated above, where a single interest rate i rules throughout the capital market, these observations are simply the after-personal-tax rates of return on saving r_k, in each tax bracket, and the before-tax rates of return, ρ_j, on capital in each sector. When a more complicated case is treated, in which there is a whole gamut of interest rates reflecting all kinds of variations in riskiness, in preferences concerning asset types, etc., the basic data needed are the rate of return i_g on government bonds, plus a weighted average of the distortions (taxes in our example, but monopoly profits and external effects in general can also be incorporated) prevailing in the various sectors and affecting the various income brackets.[1] Though there are unquestioned practical problems connected with the estimation of these magnitudes, there can be no question that the discount rate i_s is in principle related and responsive to market phenomena.

2. The procedures used to obtain i_s are fully consistent with the tenets that underlie cost-benefit analysis as such. I take these to be (a) competitive supply price measures marginal private opportunity cost, (b) competitive demand price measures marginal private benefit, and (c) the Hicks-Kaldor principle of potential compensation is accepted. In particular, defining i'_s as the social opportunity cost of using funds for the period between $t - 1$ and t, it can be shown that a rate of return of i'_s, on a project with costs only in $t - 1$ and benefits only in t, would be just barely sufficient to compensate all parties affected by the government's borrowing the required funds in year $t - 1$

and effectuating the corresponding compensations in year t.[2]
The principle thus developed for the case of a one-year project
can readily be extended to cover all projects.

3. The approach underlying i_s, and the measure itself, take
existing distortions amply into account. They thus seem far
more suited to the way cost-benefit problems appear in real-
world situations than do approaches (such as Professor Arrow's)
which implicitly posit optimization. Professor Arrow's treatment is one in which the government authorities actually, in
all cases but one, pursue policies that take the community to
a full optimum, and in the one remaining case they take the
community to a constrained optimum. In Section 7, Arrow
mentions that 'if, however, there are imperfections elsewhere in
the market structure, such as monopolistic price distortions,
excise taxes, or the corporate income tax . . . , then as is well
known the analysis becomes far more complicated'. I would
add that not only does the analysis become more complicated;
its nature also changes. We may not know the precise path
from an existing real-world situation characterized by numerous distortions toward an optimum, but we can be sure that
certain events will have to take place somewhere along the way.
Most import tariffs and excise taxes would be eliminated, the
corporation income tax and the property tax would disappear,
and the personal income tax would be presumably replaced by
a consumption tax (even this would not quite reach a genuine
allocative optimum, but it would not entail much of a deviation
from it). Much as many of us might like to see the sort of radical
overhaul of tax systems that pursuit of an allocative optimum
would imply, I am afraid that no one alive today will have the
pleasure of that vision.

Once it is recognized that most existing distortions are going
to be with us for some time, the task of cost-benefit analysis
must to some extent be redefined. We have to estimate the
social opportunity costs of factors and of outputs, in the presence
of the current and expected patterns of distortions. Optimization in the strict sense is not really present—not even the sort of
constrained optimization that is associated with the literature
on 'second best'. Cost-benefit analysis in this real-world context
is, in my view, a highly decentralized instrument of governmental decision-making. For a given project, the question is,

'Does this project move us up or down on the utility hill?'
Between alternative projects the question is, 'Which one takes
us farther up the hill?' At a more subtle level a sort of optimization is possible in the designing of a project, involving the choice
of that design which promises to have the highest net present
value. Operating at this mundane level the overall and constrained optima of which Professor Arrow's analysis speaks
seem hopelessly far away. One also wonders how many of the
acute insights that one obtains from such a celestial flight of
theorizing will have counterparts that will prove to be useful
in the jungle of distortions in which we live.

One may question, however, whether the i_s measure does not
build in too great a degree of rigidity in the pattern of distortions. Is it not, in a sense, too fatalistic about the possibilities
of reducing or eliminating distortions? I think that the answer
is no. In the first place, the values of i_s^t projected for future
years may embody any desired set of changes in the pattern of
distortions. The corporation income tax may be projected to
decline, the personal tax to rise, etc. No limits are in principle
imposed on the analyst—but the ultimate test is the realism of
his projections.

There is a second way in which the approach in question can
be defended against the charge of excessive rigidity or 'fatalism'
regarding distortions. For although the analysis builds in distortions, it also throws out strong signals as to the changes in
the pattern of distortions that would most improve the economy.
For example, suppose that the highest sectoral marginal productivity of capital, ρ_j, is 15 percent in the corporate sector (as
distinct from the housing and unincorporated business sectors)
of the economy, and that the lowest marginal rate of time
preference, r_k, is 3 per cent, in the highest personal income tax
bracket. The social rate of discount, i_s, must necessarily lie
between two extremes. Obviously, whether or not i_s is used, the
prospect of obtaining funds at a social cost of 3 percent, and
putting them to use with a social yield of 15 percent, is very
appealing indeed. If we leave tax rates unchanged, we cannot
accomplish this, for the market, not the borrower, dictates what
investments will be forgone and what savings will be stimulated
as a consequence of additional public borrowing. However, if
the government reduces somewhat the highest personal tax

rate, it will thereby generate a certain increment of saving by the affected group. It can then borrow these incremental savings without affecting the interest rate, and hence without influencing the saving of other income groups. By the same token, lending by the government to the private capital market would without tax rate changes affect investment in all sectors. However, if the government lowers somewhat the corporation income tax, additional investible funds will be demanded by the corporate sector at the same interest rate as before. The government can therefore under such circumstances lend the relevant amount of funds to the corporate sector, financing the additional investment there—without affecting investment in other sectors of the economy.

If policy-makers obey the implicit signals emitted by the approach underlying i_s, they will obviously at each point in time reduce the highest sectoral taxes t_j and the highest-bracket personal taxes t_k. The end result of this procedure is the complete elimination of corporate, property, and personal income taxes. What would replace them? In theory, perhaps, the proverbial head tax, with no distorting properties at all. But in practice some combination of a value-added tax of the consumption type and a progressive consumption-expenditure tax of the type advocated by Kaldor would be a more plausible alternative. Such taxes have a certain (probably very mild) distorting effect on the labor-leisure choice, but otherwise they are neutral as among goods and services and as between saving and consumption. Given that they can provide any desired degree of progression in the tax structure, economic theory leads us naturally to prefer a system based on them to the present pattern of personal income, corporate, and property taxes. Thus, when the methodology underlying i_s is used for the purpose of seeking reform, rather than sticking with given or sluggishly changing tax rates, it leads to conclusions that follow directly from economic theory. Whatever degree of fatalism may be implied by an analyst's assuming that the tax structure will not change much or rapidly over time must therefore (assuming he is right) be attributed to the realities of political life—not to the i_s methodology!

Notes

[1] Defining $\delta_k = (r_k - i)$, and $\delta_j = (\rho_j - i)$, (7) can be reexpressed as

$$i_s = i + \frac{\sum_k \epsilon_k (S_k/S)\delta_k - \sum_j \eta_j (I_j/S)\delta_j}{\sum_k \epsilon_k (S_k/S) - \sum_j \eta_j (I_j/S)}; \qquad (7')$$

when the assumption of a single interest rate, i, is dropped, the equation corresponding to (7') contains i_g in place of i. The interpretation of δ_k and δ_j also changes in this case, becoming $(r_k - i_k)$ and $(\rho_j - i_j)$ respectively, i_k being the before-personal-tax yield required to elicit the marginal unit of savings from the kth income bracket, and i_j the expected rate of return, before personal taxes but after other ones, which is required to obtain voluntary financing for the marginal unit of investment in sector j. These modifications are discussed in detail in Section II of 'On Measuring the Social Opportunity Cost of Public Funds,' in *The Discount Rate of Public Investment Evaluation* (Denver: Conference Proceedings of the Committee on the Economics of Water Resources Development), Western Agricultural Economics Research Council. The entire approach is also presented there much more fully than is possible here.

[2] The discounting in cost-benefit analysis should in principle be at a rate which can vary through time. If discounting is done to year 0 (the initiation of a project), this implies that the costs and benefits of year j should be divided by $\sum_{t=1}^{j} (1 + i_s^t)$. This also emphasizes the fact that the most important uses of cost-benefit analysis are forward-looking. Past data on observed yields on capital are relevant, but only because they provide us with experience to help us reach judgments concerning their likely trend in the future.

CHAPTER SIX

ON ESTIMATING THE RATE OF RETURN TO CAPITAL IN COLOMBIA

INTRODUCTION

The historical rate of return to capital in any country is a matter of interest both because it provides a basis for assessing the contribution of capital investment to the growth process and also because it is a key guide for estimating the opportunity cost of capital—a figure which in turn has a major role to play in the evaluation of projects by the public sector. The historical rate of return can be obtained for any year by taking the ratio of (a) that part of the national income which accrues to capital during the year to (b) the value of the national capital stock at the beginning of the year, with both (a) and (b) expressed in terms of prices of the same year. The problem is that we do not have direct information on either factor.

The national income accounts of Colombia explicitly segregate wage and salary payments, but it would be incorrect to attribute the remainder of the national income as income accruing to capital. The problem here concerns the income accruing to independent proprietors and partners in unincorporated enterprises. Some part of this income typically represents a compensation for the labor of the individual in question and possibly (especially in the cases of farms and small businesses) of his family members. Such income typically shows up as part of the profits of the enterprise, because the individuals concerned do not receive direct wage and salary payments. The problem, then, is how much of what is called *ingreso de las*

This paper was published as 'La Tasa de Rendimiento en Colombia,' Colombia, Departamento Nacional de Planeacion, *Revista de Planeacion y Desarrollo* (October, 1969).

*unidades familiares procedente de la propiedad y de empresas no con-
stituidas en sociedades de capital* should be added to the *Remuner-
ación de los asalariados* before we regard the remainder of the
national income as accruing to capital. This problem would
exist even if there were no errors of estimation in the national
accounts. It is naturally made more serious to the extent such
errors exist.

With respect to (b), the problem is still more difficult. To
my knowledge, there are no estimates of the entire capital stock
of Colombia—or even of major segments of it such as fixed
reproducible capital—for any year. And the data needed to
obtain estimates that would deserve the term 'reliable' are
simply unavailable.

Does this not render impossible the effort to estimate the
rate of return to capital in the Colombian economy? I believe
not. We obviously are not going to be able to have exact or
nearly-exact estimates of either (a) or (b), but we can probably
find plausible ranges for each of them, through judicious sifting
of the available information. Using these ranges, in turn, we
can obtain a plausible span of values for the ratio of (a) to (b),
which is the rate of return that we seek.

THE NET EARNINGS OF CAPITAL

During the years 1951–60, wage and salary payments as reported in the national income accounts averaged around 40
percent of national income, with a rising tendency beginning
about 1958. By 1962–67 this percentage appears once again to
have stabilized, this time around 44 percent. Our first task is
to estimate the imputed income generated by the labor effort
of proprietors, independent workers, and unpaid family members. Fortunately, Robert L. Slighton has made such an estimate, in his study *Relative Wages, Skill Shortages, and Changes in
Income Distribution in Colombia* (Table 2), for all sectors other
than agriculture. Slighton uses three alternative assumptions
to generate imputed labor income; for the purposes of this study,
and for reasons that will become evident later, we shall adopt
the lowest of his estimates, based on the assumption that in
each sector the average labor income generated by the typical
proprietor, independent worker, and unpaid family member is

equal to 80 percent of the average earnings of white- and blue-collar workers in that sector. On this assumption the imputed income accruing to proprietors, independent workers, and unpaid family members outside of agriculture was equal to 29·2 percent of non-agricultural wages and salaries in 1964. In Table 6.1, column 2, this percentage is applied to non-agricultural wages and salaries in each of the years 1960–67 to generate estimates of imputed non-agricultural labor income for these years.

In agriculture, the number of proprietors, independent workers, and unpaid family members exceeds the number of wage and salary earners by more than 30 percent; that is to say, these groups constitute over 55 percent of the total labor force. Their labor earnings have been estimated for 1964 using the following assumptions: the labor of the average proprietor (most of whom operate very small farms) is valued at 120 percent of the average earnings of wage and salary workers in agriculture, and the labor of the average independent worker is valued at 80 percent of this same figure.[1] For unpaid family members (many of whom are women and children who work only part of the normal agricultural work year), we imputed an average value-of-labor equal to 50 percent of the average earnings of wage and salary workers in agriculture. These assumptions combined to generate, for the three groups together in 1964, an imputed labor income equal to 110 percent of the wages and salaries paid in agriculture.

In Table 6.1, column 4, this percentage is applied to total agricultural wages and salaries to generate figures on imputed labor income within agriculture. In column 5, total labor income (including imputed income) is presented. This figure is subtracted from national income in order to produce the estimates of total income accruing to capital that are given in column 7. Finally, in column 8, the estimates of income accruing to capital are expressed as fractions of the national income.

Because our procedures for estimating the capital stock generate estimates that are expressed in pesos of 1958 purchasing power, we apply to national income in 1958 pesos the fractions derived in column 8 of Table 6.1. This is done in Column 2 of Table 6.2. At the same time, we generate in

TABLE 6.1

Estimates of Income Accruing to Capital

(In Millions of Current Pesos, Except Column 8)

Year	(1) Total wages and salaries paid outside agriculture	(2) Imputed labor income outside agriculture = (1) × ·292	(3) Total wages and salaries paid within agriculture	(4) Imputed labor income within agriculture = (3) × 1·1	(5) Total labor income = (1) + (2) + (3) + (4)	(6) National income	(7) Total income accruing to capital = (6) − (5)	(8) Fraction of national income accruing to capital (7) ÷ (6)
1960	6,533	1,908	2,669	2,936	14,046	22,104	8,058	·365
1961	7,846	2,291	3,029	3,332	16,498	25,476	8,978	·352
1962	9,459	2,762	3,357	3,693	19,271	28,819	9,548	·331
1963	12,236	3,573	4,360	4,796	24,965	36,402	11,437	·314
1964	14,345	4,189	4,979	5,477	28,990	45,356	16,366	·361
1965	16,365	4,779	5,936	6,530	33,610	51,000	17,390	·341
1966	20,194	5,897	6,560	7,216	39,867	60,360	20,493	·340
1967	23,253	6,790	7,429	8,172	45,644	68,802	23,158	·337

column 3 an alternative set of estimates of income accruing to capital, expressed in pesos of constant purchasing power. We call the first set of estimates R_a and the second set R_b.

TABLE 6.2

Estimates of Income Accruing to Capital

(in Billions of 1958 Pesos)

	(1)	*Income accruing to capital*	
		(2)	(3)
		R_a	
	National	$= (1) \times$ col. (8)	R_b
Year	*income*	*Table 6.1*	$= (1) \times \cdot 4$
1960	18·246	6·725	7·298
1961	19·131	6·734	7·652
1962	20·173	6·677	8·086
1963	20·757	6·610	8·303
1964	22·884	8·261	9·154
1965	23·491	8·010	9·396
1966	24·825	8·441	9·930
1967	25·749	8·677	10·300

The alternative set is presented because, in my own opinion and that of a number of other economists I have consulted, it is indeed unusual for labor's share in national income to be as high as 65 percent in a country at Colombia's level of development.

Many countries with income per head equal to or greater than Colombia's have labor shares ranging between 50 and 60 percent. And it is quite possible that the procedures used by Slighton and by me to estimate imputed labor income have overstated the true value of such income. We have accordingly based R_b on the assumption that 60 percent of the national income accrues to labor, and 40 percent to capital.

ESTIMATING THE STOCK OF FIXED CAPITAL ASSETS

Colombia's national income accounts distinguish four categories of gross investment in fixed assets: (a) buildings; (b) other construction and works (including roads, railways, aqueducts, sewers, telephone and telegraph investments, land clearing, irrigation works, fences, and so forth; (c) transport equipment; and (d) machinery and other equipment. For our purposes, we have aggregated (a) and (b) into one category, buildings and other construction, and (c) and (d) into another, machinery and equipment. For each of these categories a series of estimates of capital stock was generated, using the following procedure. First, an estimate was made of the capital stock at the beginning of 1952, this estimate being in part based on an assumed depreciation rate for the category. Capital stock at the beginning of 1953 was then obtained by first reducing the 1952 capital stock by the assumed depreciation rate, and then adding gross investment in that category during 1952, less one-half year's depreciation on such gross investment. The same procedure was followed for subsequent years.

When, for given assumed depreciation rates on the two major categories of investment, the procedure described above had been completed, the results were checked for plausibility in two different ways. The first check consisted of computing the total depreciation implied for each year by our procedure, and comparing it with the figures for depreciation given in the national accounts. The second check consisted of taking the ratio of estimated capital stock to GNP and to national income, in order to assess its reasonableness.

The details of the procedure will become apparent from the calculations presented below. These calculations will be based on assumed depreciation rates of 2·5 percent per year for buildings and other construction and 8 percent per year for machinery and equipment. To estimate the capital stock at the beginning of 1952, the following relationship was employed:

$$GI = (\delta + \gamma)K. \tag{1}$$

Here GI refers to gross investment, γ to the annual rate of growth of the capital stock, δ to the annual rate of depreciation, and K to the capital stock at the beginning of the year. For example, if the initial capital stock were 100, and if it were to grow by 5 percent in the following year while being subject to 10 percent annual depreciation, gross investment would have to be 15—10 to make up for the loss of capital through depreciation, and 5 to provide for the 5 percent growth of the capital stock that we have assumed. Our procedure goes through the same sort of calculation in reverse: if we are prepared to assume a depreciation rate of 10 percent and a growth rate of the capital stock equal to 5 percent, and if we observe that gross investment is equal to 15, we infer that the initial capital stock was 100.

In the years from 1950 to 1953, both gross domestic product and national income in Colombia were growing at almost exactly 5 percent per year. We shall assume here that the normal rate of growth of capital in the form of buildings and other construction was also 5 percent at that time. However, because of the likelihood that war-induced shortages of machinery and equipment were not yet completely overcome, we shall assume that the stocks of these assets had a normal growth rate of some 6 percent per year during this period.

In the first exercise to be presented, it will be assumed that buildings and other construction have a depreciation rate of 2·5 percent per year, and that machinery and equipment have a depreciation rate of 8 percent per year. These depreciation rates, as will be seen, yield estimates of total depreciation that are quite close to those given in the national accounts. In order to generate initial capital stock in 1952, 'normal' 1952 investment was estimated by taking the average gross investment for the three years 1951–53 in each of the two categories. The calculation of initial 1952 stock is shown in Table 6.3.

Tables 6.4 and 6.5 show how estimates of capital stock and

TABLE 6.3

Value of Stock in Colombia, 1952

(Columns 1 and 4, Billions of 1958 Pesos; Columns 2 and 3, Annual Rates)

	(1) Average gross investment, 1951–53	(2) Assumed depreciation rate (δ)	(3) Assumed growth rate of capital stock) (γ)	(4) Estimated initial (1952) capital stock $= (1) \div [(2) + (3)]$
Buildings and other construction	1·368	·025	·05	18·24
Machinery and equipment	1·876	·08	·06	13·40

of annual depreciation are generated on the basis of the assumptions summarized in Table 6.3. In Table 6.6, the annual amounts of depreciation implied by Tables 6.4 and 6.5 are compared with the depreciation figures given in the national accounts. As can be seen, the correspondence is very close. For no single year does the implied figure differ by as much as 10 percent from that presented in the national accounts, and the average amounts of depreciation in Columns 1 and 2 are only 1·3 percent apart.

TABLE 6.4

Estimation of Capital Stock of Buildings and other Construction

(In Billions of 1958 Pesos)

Year	(1) Entering stock = (1) + (2) − (5) of previous year	(2) Gross investment during year[a]	(3) Depreciation on stock = ·025 × (1)	(4) Depreciation on gross investment = ·0125 × (2)	(5) Total depreciation = (3) + (4)
1952	18·24[b]	1·34	·46	·02	·48
1953	19·10	1·53	·48	·02	·50
1954	20·13	1·95	·50	·02	·52
1955	21·56	2·07	·54	·03	·57
1956	23·06	2·10	·58	·03	·61
1957	24·55	2·07	·61	·03	·64
1958	25·98	1·95	·65	·02	·67
1959	27·26	2·21	·68	·03	·71
1960	28·76	2·13	·72	·02	·74
1961	30·15	2·34	·75	·03	·78
1962	31·71	2·47	·79	·03	·82
1963	33·36	2·25	·83	·03	·86
1964	34·75	2·38	·87	·03	·90
1965	36·23	2·39	·91	·03	·94
1966	37·68	2·62	·94	·03	·97
1967	39·33	3·13	·98	·04	1·02

[a] From *National Accounts of Colombia*; sum of gross investment in 'buildings' and 'other construction and works'.

[b] From Table 6.3, row 1, column 4.

In Table 6.7 the ratios of fixed capital to GNP and to national income are presented, with the estimates of fixed capital being based on the assumptions listed in Table 6.3.

TABLE 6.5

Estimation of Capital Stock of Machinery and Equipment
Including Transportation Equipment

(In Billions of 1958 Pesos)

Year	(1) Entering stock = cols. $1+2-5$ for previous year	(2) Gross investment during year[a]	(3) Depreciation on stock = ·08 × col. 1	(4) Depreciation on gross investment = ·04 × col. 2	(5) Total depreciation = cols. $3+4$
1952	13·40[b]	1·64	1·07	·07	1·14
1953	13·90	2·48	1·11	·10	1·21
1954	15·17	2·72	1·21	·11	1·32
1955	16·57	2·86	1·33	·11	1·44
1956	17·99	2·58	1·44	·10	1·54
1957	19·03	2·44	1·52	·10	1·62
1958	19·85	1·39	1·59	·06	1·65
1959	19·59	1·37	1·57	·06	1·63
1960	19·33	2·10	1·55	·08	1·63
1961	19·80	2·24	1·58	·09	1·67
1962	20·37	2·13	1·63	·09	1·72
1963	20·78	1·98	1·66	·09	1·74
1964	21·02	2·38	1·68	·10	1·78
1965	21·62	2·11	1·73	·10	1·83
1966	21·90	2·24	1·75	·11	1·86
1967	22·28	2·05	1·78	·10	1·88

[a] From *National Accounts of Colombia*; sum of gross investment in transport equipment and machinery and other equipment.
[b] From Table 3, row 2, column 4.

These estimates appear to be on the low side, when judged against data for other countries. Moreover, the implication of Table 6.5, that the stock of machinery and equipment in Colombia grew by only 66 per cent during the period 1952–67, while gross domestic product was gaining by 98 percent in real terms, and national income by 89 percent, also appears to be on the low side (although there is obviously no theoretical ground for precluding such a possibility).

The doubts expressed in the previous paragraph are not serious enough to warrant the outright rejection of the estimates generated in Tables 6.4 and 6.5, but they clearly warrant exploring the consequences of some alternative assumptions. This is particularly so in the light of the fact that many obser-

TABLE 6.6
Depreciation Check[a]
(In Billions of 1958 Pesos)

Year	(1) Depreciation implied by[b] Tables 6.4 and 6.5	(2) Depreciation from national accounts	(3) Difference
1952	1·62	1·52	+ ·10
1953	1·71	1·62	+ ·09
1954	1·84	1·81	+ ·03
1955	2·01	2·05	− ·04
1956	2·15	2·25	− ·10
1957	2·26	2·43	− ·17
1958	2·32	2·44	− ·12
1959	2·34	2·45	− ·11
1960	2·37	2·48	− ·11
1961	2·45	2·58	− ·13
1962	2·54	2·67	− ·13
1963	2·60	2·71	− ·11
1964	2·68	2·70	− ·02
1965	2·77	2·71	+ ·06
1966	2·83	2·72	+ ·11
1967	2·90	2·74	+ ·16
Total	37·39	37·88	− 0·49

[a] Based on assumptions presented in Table 6.3.
[b] Sum of total depreciation figures from Tables 6.4 and 6.5.

vers of the Colombian economic scene are of the view that the amounts of depreciation (capital consumption allowances) are overstated by the national income accounts. We have accordingly arbitrarily reduced by 20 percent the amounts of depreciation given in these accounts, and have sought a plausible set of assumptions regarding depreciation rates (in our two categories of assets) which are compatible with the national accounts depreciation figures thus adjusted. These assumptions are that buildings and other construction depreciate at 2 percent per year, while machinery and equipment depreciate at 5 percent per year. These assumptions, plus the estimates of initial stocks that they imply, are summarized in Table 6.8.

Tables 6.9 and 6.10 derive estimates of capital stock and of depreciation for the two categories of fixed assets, on the basis of the assumptions summarized in Table 6.8. In Table 6.9, the depreciation check is presented, showing that depreciation rates

TABLE 6.7
National Income Check[a]
(In Billions of 1958 Pesos)

	(1) Entering total stock of fixed capital (K_f)	(2) Gross domestic product (GDP)	(3) National income (Y)	Ratios	
Year				(4) K_f to GDP	(5) K_f to Y
1952	31·64	16·1	13·6	1·97	2·33
1953	33·00	17·1	14·8	1·93	2·23
1954	35·30	18·3	16·4	1·93	2·15
1955	38·13	19·0	16·2	2·01	2·35
1956	41·05	19·7	16·8	2·08	2·44
1957	43·58	20·2	16·7	2·16	2·61
1958	45·83	20·7	16·5	2·21	2·78
1959	46·85	22·2	17·5	2·11	2·68
1960	48·09	23·1	18·2	2·09	2·64
1961	49·95	24·3	19·1	2·06	2·61
1962	52·08	25·6	20·2	2·03	2·58
1963	54·14	26·5	20·8	2·04	2·60
1964	55·77	28·1	22·9	1·98	2·44
1965	57·85	29·1	23·5	1·99	2·46
1966	59·58	30·7	24·8	1·94	2·40
1967	61·61	31·9	25·7	1·93	2·40
				2·03	2·48

[a] Based on assumptions presented in Table 6.3.

TABLE 6.8
Estimated Value of Initial Capital Stock, 1952
(Columns 1 and 4, Billions of 1958 Pesos; Columns 2 and 3, Annual Rates)

	(1) Average gross investment 1951–53	(2) Assumed depreciation rate (δ)	(3) Assumed growth rate of capital stock (γ)	(4) Estimated initial (1952) capital stock $= col. 1 \div [cols.$ $2 + 3]$
Buildings and other construction	1·368	·02	·05	19·54
Machinery and equipment	1·876	·05	·06	17·05

of 2 percent per year on buildings and other construction, and of 5 percent per year on machinery and equipment, imply annual amounts of depreciation which are very close to the adjusted national accounts figures.[2]

TABLE 6.9

Estimation of Capital Stock of Buildings and Other Construction

(In Billions of 1958 Pesos)

Year	(1) Entering stock = cols. 1 + 2 − 5 of previous year	(2) Gross investment during year[a]	(3) Depreciation in stock = ·02 × col. 1	(4) Depreciation in gross investment = ·01 × col. 2	(5) Total depreciation = cols. 3 + 4
1952	19·54[b]	1·34	·39	·01	·40
1953	20·48	1·53	·41	·02	·43
1954	21·58	1·95	·43	·02	·45
1955	23·08	2·07	·46	·02	·48
1956	24·67	2·10	·49	·02	·51
1957	26·26	2·07	·53	·02	·55
1958	27·78	1·95	·56	·02	·58
1959	29·17	2·21	·58	·02	·60
1960	30·78	2·13	·62	·02	·64
1961	32·27	2·34	·65	·02	·67
1962	33·94	2·47	·68	·02	·70
1963	35·71	2·25	·71	·02	·73
1964	37·23	2·38	·74	·02	·76
1965	39·85	2·39	·80	·02	·82
1966	41·42	2·62	·83	·03	·86
1967	43·18	3·13	·86	·03	·89

[a] From *National Accounts of Colombia*; sum of gross investment in buildings and other construction and works.

[b] From Table 6.8, row 1, column 4.

Table 6.12 presents the national income check. On the particular points on which the results of the earlier exercise gave us pause, those of the present one are considerably superior. The ratios of fixed capital stock to GDP and to national income are more in accord with other countries' experience, and the growth of the stock of machinery and equipment (79 percent between 1952 and 1957) does not strike one as implausibly low, particularly in the light of the import restrictions that were applied with varying intensity throughout the period.

TABLE 6.10

Estimation of Capital Stock of Machinery and Equipment including Transportation Equipment

(In Billions of 1958 Pesos)

Year	(1) Entering stock = cols. 1 + 2 − 5 of previous year	(2) Gross investment during year[a]	(3) Depreciation on stock = ·05 × col. 1	(4) Depreciation on gross investment = ·025 × col. 2	(5) Total depreciation = cols. 3 + 4
1952	17·05[b]	1·64	·85	·04	·89
1953	17·80	2·48	·89	·06	·95
1954	19·33	2·72	·97	·07	1·04
1955	21·01	2·86	1·05	·07	1·12
1956	22·75	2·58	1·14	·06	1·20
1957	24·13	2·44	1·21	·06	1·27
1958	25·30	1·39	1·27	·03	1·30
1959	25·39	1·37	1·27	·03	1·30
1960	25·46	2·10	1·27	·05	1·32
1961	26·24	2·24	1·31	·05	1·36
1962	27·12	2·13	1·36	·05	1·41
1963	27·84	1·98	1·39	·05	1·44
1964	28·38	2·38	1·42	·06	1·48
1965	29·28	2·11	1·46	·05	1·51
1966	29·88	2·24	1·49	·05	1·54
1967	30·54	2·05	1·53	·05	1·58

[a] From *National Accounts of Colombia*; sum of gross investment in transport equipment and machinery and other equipment.

[b] From Table 6.8, row 2, column 4.

Another interesting feature of the results of Table 6.12 is the close correspondence between the average capital-output ratios there derived, and the marginal capital-output ratios derived from the national income accounts. Between the beginning of 1952 and the beginning of 1957, accumulated gross investment was 63·45 billion 1958 pesos. During the same period adjusted depreciation (that is, ·8 times the national accounts figures) was 28·12 billion 1958 pesos. Accumulated net investment, based on adjusted depreciation figures, was therefore 35·33 billion pesos. The change in GNP between 1952 and 1967 was 15·85 billion 1958 pesos. The implied marginal capital-output ratio of 2·23 is quite close to the 2·37 average figure emerging from Table 6.12. The correspondence is even closer when the

TABLE 6.11

Depreciation Check[a]

(In Billions of 1958 Pesos)

Year	(1) Depreciation implied by Tables 6.9 and 6.10[b]	(2) Depreciation from national accounts × 0·8	(3) Difference
1952	1·29	1·22	+ ·07
1953	1·38	1·30	+ ·08
1954	1·49	1·45	+ ·04
1955	1·60	1·64	− ·04
1956	1·71	1·80	− ·09
1957	1·82	1·94	− ·12
1958	1·88	1·95	− ·07
1959	1·90	1·96	− ·06
1960	1·96	1·98	− ·02
1961	2·03	2·06	− ·03
1962	2·11	2·14	− ·03
1963	2·17	2·17	·00
1964	2·24	2·16	+ ·08
1965	2·33	2·17	+ ·16
1966	2·40	2·18	+ ·22
1967	2·47	2·19	+ ·28
Total	30·78	30·31	+ 0·47

[a] Based on assumptions presented in Table 6.8.

[b] Sum of total depreciation figures from Tables 6.9 and 6.10.

ratio of fixed capital to adjusted national income (Y') is taken. The change in Y' between 1952 and 1967 was 12·43 billion 1958 pesos; the marginal capital-output ratio obtained by taking $\Delta K_f' / \Delta Y'$ over this period is 2·84, almost exactly the same as the 2·83 figure that we obtain for the average capital-output ratio in Table 6.12. This correspondence is reassuring, although it must be recognized that there is no theoretical necessity or presumption that the marginal capital-output ratio should be equal or close to the average.

The exercise summarized in Tables 6.8 through 6.12 thus yields results which are more plausible than those emerging from the exercise developed in Tables 6.3 through 6.7. Given this fact, it is important that readers fully understand the implications of the depreciation adjustment which is the fundamental source of the differences between the two exercises. The

TABLE 6.12

National Income Check[a]

(In Billions of 1958 Pesos)

Year	(1) Entering total stock of fixed capital (K'_f)	(2) Gross domestic product (GDP)	(3) National income (Y) + 20% of depreciation (Y')	(4) Ratios K'_f to GDP	K'_f to Y'
1952	36·59	16·1	13·9	2·27	2·63
1953	38·28	17·1	15·1	2·24	2·54
1954	40·91	18·3	16·8	2·24	2·44
1955	44·09	19·0	16·6	2·32	2·66
1956	47·42	19·7	17·3	2·41	2·74
1957	50·39	20·2	17·2	2·49	2·93
1958	53·08	20·7	16·9	2·56	3·14
1959	54·56	22·2	18·0	2·46	3·03
1960	56·24	23·1	18·7	2·43	3·01
1961	58·51	24·3	19·6	2·41	2·99
1962	61·04	25·6	20·7	2·38	2·95
1963	63·55	26·5	21·3	2·40	2·98
1964	65·61	28·1	23·4	2·33	2·80
1965	69·13	29·1	24·0	2·38	2·88
1966	71·30	30·7	25·3	2·32	2·82
1967	73·72	31·9	26·3	2·31	2·80
Average				2·37	2·83

[a] Based on assumptions presented in Table 6.8.

national accounts series on gross national product remains unaffected by the downward adjustment of the depreciation figures. However, since depreciation is one of the main elements that is subtracted from GNP to obtain national income, the downward adjustment of depreciation implies a corresponding upward adjustment of the national income. This is what was done to generate the series on Y' in column 3 of Table 6.12.

A similar adjustment is required for our series on income accruing to capital. The adjustment of depreciation does not affect the series on wage and salary payments, nor does it impinge on the procedures we used to derive imputed labor income. Since the earnings accruing to labor remain unaffected by the downward adjustment of the depreciation figures, this latter adjustment has as its direct counterpart a corresponding increase in the net income accruing to capital. This adjustment is presented in Table 6.13, columns 4 and 5.

TABLE 6.13

Revised Estimates of Net Income Accruing to Capital, Reflecting a 20 Percent Downward Adjustment of Official Depreciation Figures

(In Billions of 1958 Pesos)

	Initial estimates			Revised estimates	
	(1)	(2)	(3) Revision = 20% of national accounts depreciation	(4) = Cols. 1 + 3 (R_a)	(5) = Cols. 2 + 3 (R_b)
Year	R_a (Table 6.2, col. 2)	R_b (Table 6.2, col. 3)			
1960	6·73	7·30	·50	7·23	7·80
1961	6·73	7·65	·52	7·25	8·18
1962	6·68	8·09	·53	7·21	8·62
1963	6·61	8·30	·54	7·15	8·84
1964	8·26	9·15	·54	8·80	9·69
1965	8·01	9·40	·54	8·55	9·99
1966	8·44	9·93	·54	8·99	10·47
1967	8·68	10·30	·55	9·23	10·85

It should be noted for future reference that wherever figures from column 1 of Table 6.7 are used for fixed capital stock, the corresponding income figures should be those from Table 6.2. By the same token, wherever figures from column 1 of Table 6.12 are used for fixed capital stock, the corresponding figures on income accruing to capital should be those from Table 6.13.

INVENTORIES

From the beginning of 1952 to the beginning of 1967, net inventory accumulation in Colombia, according to the national accounts, totaled 6·87 billion 1958 pesos. During the same period the increment in gross domestic product was 15·85 billion 1958 pesos. The marginal inventory/GDP ratio was thus 0·43. If this is applied to the 1952 GDP (16·1 billion pesos) in order to estimate the inventory stock at the beginning of 1952, a figure of 6·92 billion pesos is obtained for that stock.[3]

Starting from 6·92 billion 1952 pesos as the base, annual inventory changes were accumulated to yield the inventory-stock series given in Table 6.14.

TABLE 6.14

Stocks of Inventories

(In Billions of 1958 Pesos)

Year	Inventory stock at beginning of year
1960	9·15
1961	9·70
1962	10·38
1963	10·61
1964	11·09
1965	11·68
1966	12·40
1967	13·79

LAND

Land is by far the most difficult category for which to estimate capital value. The only available Colombian data are collections of property value assessments for tax purposes. These tend to be significantly out of date, a problem made even more acute by Colombia's rapid rate of inflation. There is also the problem of how accurately the assessments reflect market values, even at the moment when they are completed. Finally, there are problems connected with the fact that the statistics generated by the official assessments in Colombia do not distinguish between land and improvements.

Rather than contend directly with all these difficulties in the Colombian data, we shall follow an alternative estimation procedure. Goldsmith, Lipsey, and Mendelson[4] have recorded the values of land, structures (residential and nonresidential), producer durables, and inventories in the United States for the years 1945–58. From these data we compute the ratios of land to the sum of structures, producer durables, and inventories on the one hand and of land to GNP on the other, for each of the fourteen years. Then, since there is not a significant trend in either of these ratios, we take their fourteen-year averages and apply them to the corresponding Colombian concepts (that is, to buildings and other construction plus machinery and equipment plus inventories, for which sum we have two alternative series, and to GDP) to obtain three sets of land value estimates for the years 1960–67. Of course, such estimates cannot be ideal. However, they do give a plausible range of land values, and, perhaps more important, the implied values are not subject to the same degree of capriciousness as would be those derived from the tax assessment data.

TABLE 6.15

Ratios of Land to the Sum of Structures, Producer Durables and Inventories, and Land to GNP, for the United States

(In Billions of Current Dollars)

	(1)	(2) Sum of structures, producer durables, and inventories[a]	(3)	(4) Land/ Sum	(5) Land/ GNP
Year	Land		GNP[b]		
1945	121·5	386·9	211·9	·314	·574
1946	142·0	472·1	208·5	·301	·681
1947	164·2	568·3	231·3	·289	·711
1948	178·9	623·1	257·6	·287	·695
1949	176·0	622·6	256·5	·281	·686
1950	201·7	713·8	284·8	·283	·707
1951	221·6	779·4	328·4	·284	·674
1952	226·7	817·6	345·5	·277	·657
1953	228·0	854·2	364·6	·267	·625
1954	238·3	887·9	364·8	·269	·653
1955	256·1	953·6	398·0	·273	·643
1956	274·1	1036·3	419·2	·264	·654
1957	295·7	1110·2	441·1	·266	·670
1958	310·8	1163·5	447·3	·267	·710
Averages				·283	·667

[a] *Studies in the National Balance Sheet of the United States*, Vol. II: *Basic Data*. National Bureau of Economic Research, Princeton University Press, 1963, pp. 42–69.

[b] *Economic Report of the President* (Washington, D.C.: U.S. Government Printing Office, 1970), p. 177.

As seen in Table 6.16, the largest land value estimates, for all eight years, are those derived from the other three components of capital stock, including the depreciation adjustments (column 5); the lowest are those derived from GDP (column 6). Consequently, in the calculations of the rate of return to capital which follow, the results of column 5 will be used with the depreciation-adjusted capital stock data and the results of column 6 will be used with the nonadjusted data. (The land value estimates in column 4 will henceforth be ignored.)

TABLE 6.16

Estimates of the Value of Land in Colombia

(In Billions of 1958 Pesos)

	Sum of buildings, construction, machinery, equipment, and inventory					
	(1)	(2) Depreciation	(3)	(4) Col. 1	(5) Col. 2	(6) Col. 3
Year	Unadjusted[a]	adjustment[b]	GDP[c]	× ·283	× ·283	× ·667
1960	57·24	65·39	23·1	16·19	18·48	15·40
1961	59·65	68·21	24·3	16·89	19·30	16·20
1962	62·46	71·44	25·6	17·68	20·21	17·08
1963	64·75	74·62	26·5	18·31	21·10	17·69
1964	66·86	76·70	28·1	18·90	21·70	18·22
1965	69·53	80·81	29·1	19·69	22·85	19·40
1966	71·98	83·70	30·7	20·38	23·70	20·47
1967	75·40	87·51	31·9	21·35	24·79	21·28

[a] From Tables 6.4, 6.5, and 6.14.
[b] From Tables 6.9, 6.10, and 6.14—contains depreciation adjustments.
[c] From Table 6.12.

ESTIMATES OF CAPITAL STOCK AND THE RATE OF
RETURN: NO DEPRECIATION ADJUSTMENT

Table 6.17 presents estimates of the total capital stock for the years 1960 through 1967 on the basis of the assumptions presented in Table 6.3 (accepting at face value the depreciation figures of the national accounts). In Table 6.18 these figures are compared with the two alternative series on income accruing to capital (R_a and R_b) which are consistent with these assumptions.

TABLE 6.17

Estimates of Capital Stock at Beginning of Year, No Depreciation Adjustment

(In Billions of 1958 Pesos)

Year	(1) Fixed capital (Table 6.7, col. 1)	(2) Inventories (Table 6.14)	(3) Land (Table 6.16, col. 6)	(4) Total capital stock (K) (cols. 1+2+3)
1960	48·09	9·15	15·40	72·64
1961	49·95	9·70	16·20	75·85
1962	52·08	10·38	17·08	79·54
1963	54·14	10·61	17·69	82·44
1964	55·77	11·09	18·22	85·08
1965	57·85	11·68	19·40	88·93
1966	59·58	12·40	20·47	92·45
1967	61·61	13·79	21·28	96·68

TABLE 6.18

Estimates of Rate of Return, No Depreciation Adjustment

(Columns 1–3: Billions of 1958 Pesos; Columns 4–5: Annual Rates)

| | (1) | Income accruing to capital | | Rates of return | |
Year	Total capital stock (K) (Table 6.17)	(2) R_a (Table 6.2, col. 2)	(3) R_b (Table 6.2, col. 3)	(4) R_a/K	(5) R_b/K
1960	72·64	6·73	7·30	·093	·101
1961	75·85	6·73	7·66	·089	·101
1962	79·54	6·68	8·09	·084	·102
1963	82·44	6·61	8·30	·080	·101
1964	85·08	8·26	9·15	·097	·107
1965	88·93	8·01	9·40	·090	·106
1966	92·45	8·44	9·93	·091	·107
1967	96·68	8·67	10·30	·090	·106
Averages				·089	·104

ESTIMATES OF CAPITAL STOCK AND THE RATE OF RETURN: 20 PERCENT DEPRECIATION ADJUSTMENT

In Tables 6.19 and 6.20, the counterparts of Tables 6.17 and 6.18 are presented. Here the calculations are based on the assumption that depreciation is over-stated by 20 percent in the national accounts, and on the series for capital stock, for income from capital, and for land values that were derived on the basis of this assumption.

TABLE 6.19

Estimates of Capital Stock and the Rate of Return, 20 Percent Depreciation Adjustment

(In Billions of 1958 Pesos)

Year	(1) Fixed capital (Table 6.12, col. 1)	(2) Inventories (Table 6.14)	(3) Land (Table 6.16, col. 5)	(4) Total capital stock (K') (cols. 1 + 2 + 3)
1960	56·24	9·15	18·48	83·87
1961	58·51	9·70	19·30	87·51
1962	61·04	10·38	20·21	91·63
1963	63·55	10·61	21·10	95·26
1964	65·61	11·09	21·70	98·40
1965	69·13	11·68	22·85	103·66
1966	71·30	12·40	23·70	107·40
1967	73·72	13·79	24·79	112·30

TABLE 6.20

Estimates of Rate of Return, 20 Percent Depreciation Adjustment

(Columns 1–3: Billions of 1958 Pesos; Columns 4–5: Annual Rates)

Year	(1) Total capital stock (K') (Table 6.19)	Income accruing to capital		Rates of return	
		(2) R'_a	(3) R'_b	(4) R'_a/K'	(5) R'_b/K'
1960	83·87	7·23	7·80	·086	·093
1961	87·51	7·25	8·18	·083	·093
1962	91·63	7·21	8·62	·079	·094
1963	95·26	7·15	8·84	·075	·093
1964	98·40	8·80	9·69	·089	·098
1965	103·66	8·55	9·99	·083	·096
1966	107·40	8·99	10·47	·084	·097
1967	112·30	9·23	10·85	·082	·097
Averages				·083	·095

THE OPPORTUNITY COST OF CAPITAL TO THE
PUBLIC SECTOR

On both sets of assumptions, the estimates of the rate of return to capital range between 8 and 10·5 percent. The differences between the results emerging with no depreciation adjustment and those that are implied by a 20 percent depreciation adjustment are surprisingly small. This stems from the fact that the depreciation adjustment increases both the numerator and the denominator of the rate-of-return ratio.

We now turn to the question of what is the opportunity cost of capital to the public sector. The figures on income accruing to capital in 1967 include only ·24 billion 1958 pesos of income received by government from public enterprises and properties. Yet during the period 1952 through 1966, the public sector accounted for 14·5 percent of total gross investment. In Table 6.21, row 2, we assign to the public sector 14·5 percent of the

TABLE 6.21

Capital, Income from Capital, and Rate of Return
by Major Sectors, 1967

(Cols. 1, 2, 4, 5: Billions of 1958 Pesos; Cols. 3, 6: Annual Rates)

	No depreciation adjustment			20% depreciation adjustment		
	Beginning of year capital stock	Income accruing to capital	Rate of return	Beginning of year capital stock	Income accruing to capital	Rate of return
	(1)	(2)	(3)	(4)	(5)	(6)
Total	96·68*a*	9·49*b*	·098	112·30*c*	10·04*d*	·089
Public sector	14·02*e*	·24*f*	·017	16·30*e*	·24*f*	·015
Private sector	82·66	9·23	·112	96·00	9·80	·102
Housing	27·71	1·94*g*	·070	27·71	1·94*g*	·070
Private sector less housing	54·95	7·29	·133	68·29	7·86	·115

a Table 6.17, column 4; Table 6.18, column 1.
b Average of R_a and R_b; Tables 6.2 and 6.18, columns 2 and 3.
c Tables 6.19, column 4; Table 6.20, column 1.
d Average of R'_a and R'_b.
e 14·5 percent of total capital stock.
f Income of government enterprises in 1967 (652 million current pesos) deflated by GNP deflator (2·674) for 1967. Both figures from national accounts.
g Net house rents in billions of 1958 pesos from national accounts.

capital stock of the nation. It can there be seen that the rate of
cash return on public sector capital is less than 2 percent. This
is only in part due to low levels of public utility tariffs; it also
stems from the fact that a lot of public investment is in areas
(roads, public buildings, and the like) where no cash return is
received even though the benefit to the economy may be
substantial.

In row 3 of Table 6.21, the capital and the income accruing
from capital in the public sector are deducted from the corresponding national totals to yield private-sector figures. Total
income from capital was taken to be the average of R_a and R_b
in column 2 and of R_a' and R_b' in column 5 of row 1. The
resulting estimates of private-sector rate of return are greater
than 10 percent under both of our alternative assumptions
regarding depreciation. This is conceptually the best estimate
of the opportunity cost of capital to the public sector in
Colombia.

Rows 4 and 5 of Table 6.21 attempt to break down the
private sector capital stock and related income into those
amounts corresponding to the provision of housing services
and the remainder. The capital stock (that is, buildings and
land) devoted to residential housing was estimated by capital-
izing the figure given in the national accounts as net rent from
housing (including the imputed rent from owner-occupied
housing) at a rate of 7 percent. This is consistent with gross
annual rents (including depreciation maintenance, and property taxes) of from 10 to 12 percent of the value of the property. When housing and house rents are taken out of the
private sector figures, as is done in row 5, it is seen that the
remaining private-sector capital stock has estimated yields of
from 11·5 to 13 percent. If the government could guarantee
that any funds that it fails to spend on public projects would
be put to use in the non-housing area of the private sector, then
11·5 to 13 percent would be an appropriate estimate of the
opportunity cost of public funds. However, it is difficult to
guarantee this. If the government raises more funds by taxation
or if it spends less on current or capital account, the end result
in all likelihood will be a reduction in the amount of public
borrowing. This in turn would permit the banking system to
augment its credit to the private sector which has as its likely

outcome the stimulation of investment throughout the private sector, including the area of housing construction. I therefore feel that it is more appropriate to consider the over-all private-sector rate of return of 10 to 11 percent as the opportunity cost of public funds.

A word of caution in closing: the opportunity cost of capital that is relevant for public decision-making is a forward-looking magnitude: what would be the yield of these private-sector investments that would additionally be undertaken this year if more capital were to be made available to the private sector? Our figures do not provide a direct answer to this question. They rather estimate what has been the historical yield of investments undertaken in the past. It can be seen in Tables 6.18 and 6.20 that the estimated rates of return based on R_a and R_a' show no perceptible trend, while those based on R_b and R_b' reveal a tendency to rise over time. This is indeed the direction in which we would expect the yield in capital to move as Colombia's economic development efforts bear increasing fruit.

Notes

[1] In this exercise, total wages and salaries are taken from the national accounts of Colombia, and the numbers of wage and salary workers, proprietors, independent workers and unpaid family workers are taken from Departamento Administrativo Nacional de Estadistica *XIII Censo Nacional de Población, Resumen general*, Table 37, pp. 134–35.

[2] They could be made still closer by taking, for example, depreciation rates of ·019 and ·049 for the two categories, respectively; we did not carry out such an exercise because it would give an exaggerated impression of the degree of accuracy of the procedure and the results. It can be stated clearly, however, that either reducing the depreciation rate on buildings and other construction from 2 to 1·5 percent, or reducing that on machinery and equipment from 5 to 4 percent per annum would result in a substantially greater difference between the depreciation figures corresponding to columns 1 and 2 of Table 6.11. In short, depreciation rates of ·02 and ·05 for the two categories provide the set of plausible 'round numbers' for which the implied depreciation is closest to the adjusted official series given in column 2 of Table 6.11.

[3] There is a possibility that the use of the 0·43 ratio might overestimate the 1952 inventory stock, because of the unprecedented buildup of inventories (1·388 billion pesos of 1958) that occurred in 1966. But even if the year 1966 is neglected in the computations, the marginal inventory/GDP ratio turns out to be ·384, and applying this to 1952 GDP yields estimated beginning-1952 inventories of 6·18 billion 1958 pesos. The absolute difference between 6·18 and 6·92 billion pesos, when compared with the probable levels of total capital stock in Colombia, did not seem

great enough to warrant making two alternative sets of inventory estimates. The 6·92 billion peso figure was therefore chosen as the base for deriving the inventory stock series.

[4] *Studies in the National Balance Sheet of the United States*, Vol. II, *Basic Data*. National Bureau of Economic Research, Princeton University Press, 1963, pp. 42–69.

CHAPTER SEVEN

ON MEASURING THE SOCIAL OPPORTUNITY COST OF LABOUR

In this paper I attempt to examine in some detail the commonly held notion that the opportunity cost of labor is represented by the product that is forgone from other activities as a consequence of being labor for a given activity. The first variant of this notion that will be treated is the idea that in some poor countries the pool of labor in the agricultural sector is so abundant, and its marginal product so low (effectively zero, according to this idea) that other sectors can expand their demand for labor without entailing any significant loss in production elsewhere. The second variant to be considered is the idea, less restrictive than the first, that the product forgone in other sectors (in this case not necessarily zero or insignificant) is the appropriate measure of the social opportunity cost of labor. I shall argue that the data seem to contradict the idea that great masses of labor can be withdrawn from the agrarian sector without a palpable loss in product. I shall also contend that the use of forgone product as a measure of opportunity cost is an oversimplification which can lead an analyst to wrong conclusions in a number of different ways. Far preferable is the concept that the supply price of marginal units of labor of given skill characteristics for given jobs in given labor-market areas is the relevant measure of social opportunity cost. But even this concept has some deficiencies, and I shall present analyses indicating that the true measure of social opportunity cost lies somewhere between the measurable supply price of labor and the market price actually paid in a given activity. In the course of this analysis, I shall discuss how to deal with

Paper presented at a Meeting of Experts on Fiscal Policies for Employment Promotion, sponsored by the International Labor Office at Geneva, Switzerland, January, 1971.

the phenomenon of unemployment (of the chronic disguised, and the cyclical varieties) in evaluating labor's social opportunity cost. Finally, I shall comment briefly on the use of macroeconomic approaches to derive measures of this opportunity cost.

I. THE IDEA OF ZERO MARGINAL PRODUCT

The idea that labor has an effectively zero marginal productivity in the agrarian sector of densely populated underdeveloped countries is widespread, and it is reflected in a number of different branches of the literature of economics. Cost-benefit analyses that take the benefits of a project to be the value of its output, and its costs to be the capital and materials outlays involved, implicitly (by failing to deduct anything in the way of labor costs) assume that labor's opportunity cost is zero. Likewise, models of economic growth (of which there are many, at varying levels of mathematical sophistication) which explain that growth solely as a function of capital accumulation fail to assign any role to increases in the labor force and hence implicitly assume that labor, in the relevant economic sense, is in oversupply. Similarly, many authors who use the term 'disguised unemployment' in describing the labor-market situation of less-developed countries have in mind the idea that workers can be drawn into 'productive employment' from the pool of 'disguisedly unemployed' with no loss in output in the sectors where they were formerly occupied.

I shall defer for the time being the detailed discussion of the phenomenon of abnormal open unemployment and confine myself to the case where open unemployment is within the limits set by normal job turnover, migration seasonal variations in demand, strikes, and the like. The terms 'frictional' and 'seasonal,' as distinct from 'chronic,' 'structural,' and 'cyclical,' are commonly used to describe the types of unemployment that can be thought of as prevailing in the economic situations that will be discussed at this point.[1] Cases where unemployment is significantly in excess of the limits dictated by frictional and seasonal considerations will be discussed later.

My discussion will be based on the general economic principle that employers do not wittingly pay workers more than they (the employers) believe the incremental contribution of each worker to the value of output to be. This principle has an automatic implication: in a market economy in which most labor consists of hired workers as distinct from family members, the marginal product of the labor actually employed will equal or exceed the wage it is paid. The wage may be set—by law, by collective bargaining, or even perhaps by custom and tradition —at a level higher than that which would cause employers to employ the full labor force, but this would lead to open unemployment above and beyond the 'normal' frictional and seasonal amount, and that in turn would present us with a case whose discussion has explicitly been deferred to a later point in this paper. Hence, if we have a market economy, with labor consisting mainly of hired workers, and without abnormal open unemployment, we can conclude that the marginal product of labor equals or exceeds its wage.

We may postulate, then, that cases where the marginal product of labor actually employed is below the going wage will be those where the marginal workers are family members, not hired hands. It is not surprising, therefore, that many of the writings based on the assumption of zero marginal product of labor in agriculture have referred to countries like India and its neighbors, where the 'extended family system' is a deep-rooted part of the culture. The extended family system in effect requires a householder to 'take in' and care for as a member of his own family any of a broad class of relatives who may appear on the scene. They, in turn, are required to behave as family members, contributing to the operation of the household either by finding an outside job or—what is most relevant in this case—by working on the family farm. If they cannot find an outside job, and do end up working on the farm, they may, of course, simply displace some hired labor that the landowner was already using. In this case their marginal product would still equal or exceed the wage. However, if their landowner-relative was originally hiring no labor, or if the number of extended family members he was called upon to take in were to exceed the number of workers he otherwise would have hired, it is possible that the marginal product of labor on his farm might fall below the wage level, and perhaps even come close to zero.

That this sort of phenomenon should be widespread in a

country like India is certainly, on the surface, plausible. After all, well over 300 million people live in the rural sector of India, and the absorption into productive employment of the able-bodied laborers in such a large mass of people certainly appears to be a staggering task. Yet, initial appearances to the contrary, the Indian rural sector seems to have been quite successful in accomplishing that feat. Not only that, but the marginal productivity of labor in rural India appears to be closely approximated by the market wage.

I have two pieces of evidence to offer in support of this contention. First and most important, successive surveys of the rural labor force in India reveal that some 25 percent are landless workers who make their living as hired workers. This is precisely the group that would tend to be most disadvantaged under the extended family system: they are the hired hands who would be displaced as relatives were absorbed on the family farm. And only after all hired workers of given skill qualifications were displaced on a given farm would the marginal productivity of that type of labor possibly be pressed below the going wage (in the case that the number of relatives that had to be absorbed exceeded the number of hired hands that were let go). The whole process by which the extended family system leads to relatives being cared for would work to the detriment of hired hands. Thus it is indeed surprising to find that the average landless agricultural laborer works some 250 full-time-equivalent man days per year, and that his annual earnings are approximately equal to the per capita income of the country.[2] Of course one must realize that annual earnings equal to a country's per capita income are likely to be well below the average level of earnings *per worker* in that country. Nonetheless, though low, these earnings levels are far from negligible. In fact, the average earnings from all sources of members of the labor force in United States agriculture are also approximately equal to that country's per capita income. No one would dream of asserting that the marginal product of labor in United States agriculture was zero—and the evidence indicates that such an assertion is equally inapplicable to India.

A second piece of evidence negating the idea of a zero marginal productivity of labor in Indian agriculture comes from Professor K. N. Raj's study of the great Bhakra Nangal Dam project.[3] In discussing the recruitment of labor for this project, Professor Raj states:

> It is a common assumption to make, on theoretical analyses, that the supply of unskilled labor in underdeveloped countries is almost infinitely elastic. This, obviously, is not always true. For instance, the additional demand for unskilled labor created by the Bhakra Nangal project, even at the peak level of activity during the construction of the canals, cannot be regarded as very large, when considered with reference to the investment under-taken or the area (and population) over which the construction work was spread. Yet the supply of unskilled labor from the areas adjoining the work proved hardly adequate. In March 1954, when the total number employed on the Bhakra Canals was around 100,000, it would appear that as much as 60 per cent of the labor required had to be imported from other States.[4]

This result was observed in spite of the fact that the wages paid were comparatively good (typically 2 rupees per day plus free housing). It is obviously hardly consistent with the notion of a large pool of labor having zero marginal productivity, which can readily be drawn upon to meet additional labor requirements.

If Indian agriculture is not characterized by zero (or negligible) marginal productivity of labor, it seems hardly likely that the phenomenon is widespread in the rest of the underdeveloped world, in which incomes tend to be substantially higher and population densities substantially less than India's. Indeed, one might say that the zero marginal product hypothesis was a 'straw man,' and that my efforts to refute it were unnecessary, if it were not for the fact, cited at the outset of this section, that the assumption is so widely made, explicitly or implicitly, in growth studies, project analyses, and other economic writings.

I conclude, then, that the best approximation to the marginal product of rural labor is the going market wage applicable to each skill category, and that the social opportunity cost of such labor, in the absence of substantial open unemployment, is also best measured by the going wage.

II. FORGONE PRODUCT AS A MEASURE OF SOCIAL OPPORTUNITY COST

The tendency for migration to flow in a more or less steady stream from rural to urban areas appears to be almost universal and it has led some observers to conclude that when new jobs are created in urban areas they are filled, directly or indirectly, by migration from rural areas. The process is direct when a recent migrant himself takes the new job and indirect when someone else takes the new job, leaving a vacancy that in turn is filled by another person, until the last vacancy in the chain is occupied by a recent migrant. The conclusion that is normally drawn is that, at least for unskilled urban jobs, the relevant measure of social opportunity cost is the marginal product of agricultural labor in rural areas. This, it is said, is what is forgone when a worker moves from the country to the city. Implicit in the reasoning, of course, is the idea that the creation of a new job has the effect of inducing additional migration.

Plausible though it sounds, I believe the above argument contains a basic flaw. This arises from the fact that urban wages are in practically all countries substantially above those for similar labor in the rural areas from which migration flows. In discussing urban wages I want to distinguish those that are held up above the market-clearing level from those that are determined freely in the market. I call the former 'protected-sector wages' and the latter 'unprotected-sector wages.' Wages can be held above the market-clearing level by minimum wage laws, by collective bargaining agreements in industries with strong unions, or (as is often the case with large international concerns operating in less-developed countries) by the policy of the hiring company itself. Protected-sector jobs can readily be identified because so many people want them. Companies paying wages higher than market levels for equivalent skills and working conditions tend to have very low labor turnover and long lists of applicants waiting for an opening to arise. 'Unprotected-sector' companies tend to have more 'normal' (that is, higher) labor turnover and shorter waiting lists of applicants, and they may frequently have to engage in active recruiting efforts in order to obtain additional labor when they need it.

My hypothesis is that the unprotected-sector wage for a given skill classification of labor and in a given labor market area is the best available measure of the social opportunity cost of that type of labor in that area. The reasoning is essentially the same as that of the forgone-agricultural-product theory, except that it stops one step short (that is, it takes the urban wage that migrants receive after they migrate as the measure of opportunity cost rather than the rural wage that they received before migrating). Before elaborating on the reasons for my preference, I shall briefly recapitulate the process involved. A large international company increases its work force in the capital city. Some of those it hires may have previously been working in unprotected-sector jobs and some in other parts of the protected sector. But these latter workers leave behind them vacancies, which in turn have to be filled. Ultimately, they are filled from the unprotected sector, including recent migrants whose alternative city employment would have been in the unprotected sector.

My argument turns around the fact that practically everywhere, wages in the *unprotected* sector in urban areas are substantially higher than the wages for comparable workers in the rural regions from which migration flows. The annual earnings of casual construction workers, household sweepers, and ricksha drivers in major Indian cities are about double those of landless agricultural workers in the rural hinterland. The wages of unskilled and low-skilled workers in the highly competitive textile industry of Santiago, Chile are also about double those of workers of comparable skill levels in rural areas. This type of wage differential (though not always so large) seems to be replicated in country after country.

Let us suppose, taking India as an example, that unprotected-sector earnings of unskilled labor in Delhi amount to 1000 rupees a year, while those of corresponding labor in the rural areas are 500 rupees per year. When a new job appears in the unprotected sector and is filled by a migrant, is there a true social benefit equal to the 500 rupees excess of his urban over his rural wage? This is what the forgone-agricultural-product approach implies, yet can it really be true? If rural workers truly can double their standard of living by migrating, why do they not come in hordes to the cities? Of course if they did

come in hordes, they would drive down the wage in the unprotected sector, perhaps, in our example, all the way to 500
rupees. Why does this not occur? Why have the differentials
between urban unprotected-sector wages and rural wages been
so persistent over time rather than being eliminated as a
consequence of more rapid migration flows? My answer is that
the differential in question is very largely an equalizing one.
In rural areas of India, most of the houses (or huts) of rural
laborers are built by the laborers themselves (with help from
family and friends) and are made of local materials; they
are very inexpensive, if not virtually free. By contrast, even
the most rudimentary urban quarters have rents amounting to
a third or more of the unprotected urban wage. Food in the
cities is also considerably more expensive than it is in the
villages, where largely local produce is consumed. Transportation to and from work also typically claims a nonnegligible
portion of the urban laborer's budget, while in the villages, the
trip to the nearby fields is usually made on foot. In my view,
1000 rupees in the cities (in my example) is attractive enough
to induce a steady stream of migration; the average migrant
probably finds it a bit better than the 500 rupees he earned in
the countryside. But it could not be substantially better, or the
stream of migration would become a flood! In my opinion, it
is far closer to the truth to say that the migrants are approximately indifferent between 500 rupees in the country and 1000
rupees in the city than it is to say that they double their real
income on making the move.

I conclude, then, that the social opportunity cost of labor to
be used on a project in a rural area is the going wage in that
area (500 rupees in my example), while that of labor to be used
in an urban project is the prevailing wage in the unprotected
sector of the labor market in that area (1000 rupees in my
example). Some readers may feel that we have here lost the
entire meaning of social opportunity cost as being distinct from
market price, but such is not the case. Many projects in the
urban area will be in the protected sector and will thus be
paying wages far higher than the 1000 rupees of my example,
and some projects in the rural area may be for factories,
electrical generating plants, and the like, and may pay wages
well above the going rural rate for farm labor (perhaps because

they are subject to minimum wage laws that do not apply to farm labour). In all such cases, the social opportunity cost of labor is lower than the wage actually paid and it, rather than the wage actually paid by the project, is the relevant price of labor to use in social decision-making.

III. THE CONCEPT OF SUPPLY PRICE

One useful way of interpreting the example just discussed is that 500 rupees is the amount for which members of the un-skilled labor force are willing voluntarily to present themselves for work at a newly created job in the rural area, and 1000 rupees is the corresponding amount for which they are willing to present themselves for work at a newly-created job in the city. In this section, I shall elaborate on the concept of voluntary supply price and show that it provides a far more technically rigorous and subtle basis for approaching the measurement of social opportunity cost than does the concept of forgone product.

The issue turns, I believe, on the quite familiar but often forgotten deficiencies of the national accounts as measures of welfare. In the frequently cited example of the man who marries his housekeeper, welfare has, we presume, been enhanced, but national income as reflected in the national accounts has gone down because the money the man gives his new wife does not appear as wages. Likewise, when a miner suffering from silicosis voluntarily gives up a $7-an-hour job in a coal mine in order to take a $2-an-hour job as a grocery clerk, we must presume, because he acted voluntarily, that he conceives his welfare to have improved (or at worst stayed the same), in spite of the fact that the national income and product aggregates would have fallen as a consequence of his move. On the other hand, the contribution to national income of the farm-to-city migrant of our earlier example was doubled as a consequence of his move, but we have seen that there are good reasons to believe that his welfare was probably only marginally affected.

Let us now ask what is the true purpose behind the use of social opportunity costs (shadow wages) in the evaluation of investment projects. I believe the answer is that where there is an excess of wages actually paid over social opportunity costs, this excess should be counted as part of the benefits of the project. Put another way, instead of counting against the project all of its wage costs, we charge it only with that part which represents the true social opportunity cost. The notion of voluntary supply price fits quite naturally and elegantly into this framework. Suppose three workers on a project are hired for identical jobs at $10 a day. The first worker might have been willing to present himself for that job for as little as $6, and the second for as little as $8, while the third might have been just barely willing to come for $10. While the wages bill actually paid by the project is $30 a day, the social opportunity cost of the labor used is only $24. When labor is valued at social opportunity cost the project is given credit for the $4 'profit' gained by the first worker and for the $2 'profit' gained by the second worker.

This is quite as it should be. If only we knew the voluntary supply prices of the workers to be hired by a project, we would surely want to use them as our measures of the social opportunity cost of each man's labor. The reason why we resort to market information is not that it gives the ideal measure, but rather because we cannot get inside the head of each worker in order to find out his voluntary supply price for a given job (nor indeed can we predict when we analyze a prospective investment project who will be employed on what job). Unprotected-sector wages serve in nearly all cases as a good proxy for supply price because they represent, in effect, what the workers who leave the unprotected sector to take jobs in the protected sector were previously willing to offer their services for. If a worker was willing to work in the unprotected sector for $10 and takes a job in the protected sector for $15, we presume that he has gained a 'profit' of $5, which should be attributed to the project in evaluating it using social criteria. Similarly, if the $15 job is filled by worker A who was previously earning $12 in another part of the protected sector, and if A is replaced by B, who was previously earning $10 in the unprotected sector, we presume that A has made a $3 gain and B a $2 gain that should be attributed to the project. Of course, we cannot in practice identify A's and B's individual gains but we know that the total presumed gain will be the difference between the newly created $15 wage and the $10 wage corresponding to workers of equivalent skill and capacity in the unprotected sector. This applies no matter how many links they may be in the vacancy-replacement chain, so we do not have to worry about how many there are or are likely to be.

The use of unprotected-sector wages as the best approximation to supply price and therefore to social opportunity costs has the added great advantage that data can be obtained on these wages classified into a wide range of occupational and skill groups. We all recognize in daily life the enormous heterogeneity of the labor factor, but we too often forget this in conducting economic analyses. I have had a long-standing complaint against most labor ministries (and the U.S.'s own Department of Labor) in that I believe they have neglected the important task of gathering good information on the wages and salaries of workers at many different skill levels, classified by labor-market area, industry, size of firm, and so forth. Such information can be of enormous usefulness for many purposes, not the least of which is in the measurement of social opportunity costs of various types of labor. Fortunately, one does not have to wait for massive studies of the entire labor market in order to obtain the information needed for this latter purpose. For normally one can easily distinguish the protected from the unprotected sector. Once the unprotected sector has been identified, a sampling from the personnel records of a number of firms drawn from within it should provide the information needed to ascertain what wages are typically being paid to workers of different skill and capacity characteristics. That this is feasible has already been demonstrated by Professor Sergio de Castro who, for a study that is as yet unpublished, has gathered detailed data on over 10,000 workers from some 600 firms in Santiago, Chile.[5]

I have argued above that unprotected-sector wages are the best available approximation to the supply price of labor. Let us now investigate the cases in which some adjustment might be called for. First, there is the obvious case of noncomparable working conditions. If our project provides better working conditions than typically prevail in the unprotected sector, the social opportunity cost of labor to it should presumably be lower than the corresponding unprotected-sector wage, and conversely if our project entails working conditions more unpleasant than normal. Second, and perhaps less obvious, is the case in which some of the workers on a project, or who are hired by other parts of the protected sector somewhere along the vacancy-replacement chain, may be newly drawn into the labor force as a consequence of the project. For example, a newly created job at $15 a day might be filled by someone who was unwilling to work in the unprotected sector at $10 a day. His supply price could be anywhere between, say, $11 and $15. The fact that a project in the protected sector can draw some of its labor from the ranks of the voluntarily unemployed (voluntarily as against working in the unprotected sector), or from outside the labor force means that the unprotected-sector wage tends to be an underestimate of the effective average supply price of the labor hired. However, the degree of under-estimation is likely to be negligible except in clearly identifiable cases where the bulk of the labor supply is obtained from the voluntarily unemployed or from outside the labor force.[6]

The concept of supply price, as applied to entry into the labor force or exit from voluntary unemployment, points up sharply another important fact, to which we shall return later. This is that supply price (and therefore social opportunity cost) is not zero even for involuntarily unemployed labor. Such labor invariably has a reservation price below which it is not willing to work, and the 'profit' that an unemployed worker gains upon getting a job is accordingly not the full wage, but the excess of that wage over his reservation price (supply price).

IV. CHRONIC URBAN UNEMPLOYMENT: THE PANAMA CASE

I shall begin the discussion of chronic urban unemployment with the case of Panama, which exhibits in extreme form characteristics that probably apply in lesser degree in a number of other less-developed countries. Panama had been a booming country during World War II, when the passage of ships through the Canal reached an all-time peak. The end of the war, however, witnessed a sharp slackening off of Canal activity and left the country with a substantial pool of unemployed in the so-called metropolitan area (principally Panama City and Colon) adjacent to the Canal Zone. What has puzzled many observers is that this pool of unemployed, though fluctuating in size over time, has remained large in spite of substantial—even spectacular—economic growth. Panama's real GNP grew at a compound annual rate of about 5·5 percent in the decade of the 1950s and of about 8 percent in the decade of the 1960s, in spite of which the urban unemployment problem remains severe.

How can this paradox be explained? I believe the answer lies in the wage regulations prevailing in the metropolitan area, together with the phenomenon of migration. In brief, minimum wage legislation is applicable to nearly all employments in the metropolitan area. What we have called the unprotected sector hardly exists for unskilled workers in Panama's metropolitan area. For clarity of exposition, I shall here assume that there is no unprotected sector for the unskilled—that is, that all jobs are covered by the minimum wage provisions.

Now let us recall what, in the analysis in Section II, was the relationship between developments in the unprotected sector and the flow of migration. It should be clear from that earlier discussion that the wage level in the unprotected sector operated as a regulator of the flow of migrants. If initially the wage level were so high as to attract floods of migrants, the forces of supply and demand would soon bring wages down to an equilibrium position in which the steady stream of migrants was more or less in balance with the growth of urban demand for such workers.

In the Panama case, with no urban unprotected sector, quite clearly the unprotected-sector wage cannot perform the function of regulating the flow of migration. Yet somehow this flow will in fact be contained. If the minimum wage is so high as to attract floods of migrants under conditions of high employment, the way in which migration will be held down to more 'normal' levels is obviously through increased unemployment.[7] Given the rate of growth of demand for unskilled labor at the minimum wage, there will be a certain 'equilibrium' rate of unemployment that will stem the potential flood of migration and hold it down to a stream that is consonant with the given rate of growth of demand. But is it important to realize that in a steady-state 'unemployment equilibrium' situation the number of migrants will regularly exceed the number of jobs created.[8]

TABLE 7.1

	Initial equilibrium situation	After creation of 100 new jobs	
		Immediate response	Ultimate equilibrium situation
Labor force	1,000	1,000	1,125
Employment	800	900	900
Unemployment	200	100	225
Unemployment rate	20%	10%	20%

Table 7.1 illustrates the way in which the equilibrating process works. In the initial situation we have an urban unskilled labor force of 1000, of whom 800 are employed at the minimum wage and 200 are unemployed. The equilibrium rate of unemployment is 20 percent. Now 100 extra jobs are created. Initially, these are filled from the ranks of the urban unemployed, and as a consequence the unemployment rate is reduced to 10 percent. But this makes movement to the city extremely attractive and sets in motion a process of migration that terminates only when the equilibrium unemployment rate of 20 percent is once again restored. Paradoxically, the creation of 100 new jobs in the end actually increases the absolute number of unemployed (though of course not the unemployment rate).[9]

One should not infer that the overall unemployment rate in the urban area measures the actual average experience of new migrants. The newly arrived migrant will almost certainly be unemployed for a time. The longer he remains in the area, the greater will be his chances of having a job at any given moment. The point is that his chance of having a job after, say, a month in the city might be 50 percent when the overall unemployment rate is 20 percent, with this chance jumping to 75 percent when the overall unemployment rate is 10 percent. We are thus using the overall unemployment rate (among unskilled workers) as a proxy for the whole spectrum of job probabilities that the typical migrant would face after different lengths of stay in the urban labor market. The important point is that when the unemployment rate is below equilibrium the typical migrant evaluates life in the city as being very much better than life in the country (which tends to produce a flood of migration), while when the unemployment rate is at its equilibrium level the typical migrant is more or less on the margin of indifference between the prospects of life in the two places (which explains why the rate of migration is constrained to that amount consistent with the rate of creation of new jobs while maintaining the equilibrium rate of unemployment).

This fact—that migrants are more or less on the margin of indifference when the equilibrium rate of unemployment prevails—enables us to reintroduce the notion of supply price, though in a somewhat more complicated context than before. When he makes his move, the migrant is in effect buying a series of lottery tickets—a 40 percent chance of a job after two months, a 60 percent chance after four, and perhaps an 80 percent chance after six months. Let us suppose that these are in fact the probabilities of employment, and let us trace in Table 7.2 the employment experience of 100 typical unskilled migrants

TABLE 7.2

	(1)	(2)	(3)	(4)	(5)
			Total wages earned	Wages earned per migrant	Wages earned per employed migrant
	Employed	Unemployed			
After 2 months	40	60	$200	$2.00	$5.00
After 4 months	60	40	300	3.00	5.00
After 6 months	80	20	400	4.00	5.00

into say, the Panama Metropolitan Area, at a time when the minimum wage is $5.00 a day. Column 4 gives the 'expected average earnings' after two, four and six months, for which the migrants were willing to come to the city. It represents, in a sense, the 'supply price of migrants' after different durations of stay. But it says nothing whatsoever about the supply price to be attached to new jobs created by an investment project. This is given in column 5, and, quite surprisingly, it turns out to be precisely equal to the minimum wage!

The paradox is quite easily explained. When the equilibrium rate of unemployment is 20 percent (and still abstracting from local demographic increase in the city) the creation of 80 new jobs will induce the migration of 100 workers. Ultimately, an average of 80 of these will be employed at the minimum wage at any one time (although of course natural labor turnover will mean that the particular individuals employed will not always be the same). Once that point (represented by row 3 of the table) is reached, the average migrant will be earning $4 a day. Nevertheless, since only 80 new jobs were created, the cost is $5 per man day actually worked. This outcome of 80 out of 100 migrants being employed at $5 per day is what is necessary to satisfy the expectations that induced them to migrate in the first place.

The same kind of analysis applies in the intervening 'period of adjustment.' After two months, 40 are employed and 60 are not, so the average earnings per migrant is only $2 a day. This is what was necessary to satisfy the overall expectations of the group after two months, but since only 40 migrants are employed at this point, the cost to the employers that just satisfies the expectations of the migrants is $5 per man day in any case.

I must apologize here for the need to introduce such a degree of precision into this discussion. It is quite clear that no individual migrant actually has in mind a precise picture of how the probability of his being employed will vary with his length of stay. Nor is it very easy to picture the whole group of 100 as being in some sense just satisfied when, after two months, 40 of them are employed at $5 a day and the remaining 60 are unemployed. (Clearly, 40 will probably be quite happy and 60 quite unhappy.) Nonetheless, I feel that this degree of abstraction is necessary to cope rigorously with the problem at hand. The essence of the notion of an equilibrium relation between the unemployment rate and migration is that typical migrants are more or less near the borderline of indifference. If the typical migrant were exceedingly happy with the way things turned out, there would be a flood of friends and relatives into the city; and if the typical migrant were very unhappy, there would be a mass reflux to the farm.

One way of putting the problem in more down-to-earth terms is to recognize that those migrants who are employed within a month or two are very happy—in a sense, they have gained a benefit that they did not fully expect. They will probably be writing home telling their friends and relatives how good life in the city is, and some additional migration will be induced. On the other hand, some of those who fail to find employment in three, four, or five months will probably give up in despair and go home, thus counterbalancing the inflow of the friends and relatives of the lucky ones. Those who stay in the city may very well perceive benefits beyond what they expected, but those who return home disappointed have suffered costs that in principle should be counterbalanced against the extra benefits of the lucky ones. The abstraction that the typical migrant is more or less indifferent is really a shorthand way of recognizing this offsetting effect.

V. CHRONIC URBAN UNEMPLOYMENT: THE GENERAL CASE

In the analysis of sections II and III we concluded that in the absence of abnormal open unemployment, the relevant social opportunity cost of labor was best measured by the wage rates paid in the unprotected sector. In section IV we concluded that in the absence of an unprotected sector, migration to the cities would be held in check by the equilibrium level of unemployment and that at that level, the social opportunity cost of unskilled labor was best measured by the minimum wage, which was assumed to be effective for nearly all unskilled jobs. We now consider the possible case where, even in the presence of an unprotected sector of reasonable size, chronic unemployment in excess of normal seasonal and frictional levels persists. I will continue to assume, because the phenomenon is so widespread, that migration into the urban labor market continues in spite of the existence of relatively high unemployment. The easiest way to depict this case is as a sort of combination of the previous two, with the introduction of a new element into the argument—namely, the costs of searching for a job. It is well also to think of the protected sector of the labor market as having several different levels—very high wage rates in international companies, quite high ones in local companies with strong unions, moderately high wage rates in government employment, and minimum wage rates that are somewhat higher for unskilled workers (in the areas covered by the minimum wage law) than those they can obtain in the unprotected market.

Consider now the case of an unskilled migrant entering this market. His options may include taking a job in the unprotected sector, but this will interfere with his looking for a job at higher wages in the protected sector. If he chooses to spend his time searching for a high-paying job rather than working at a low-paying job, his supply price lies above the unprotected-sector wage. And I am sure that cases in which this happens are quite common. The migrant may have brought with him some accumulated savings that may last for a few months of search, or he may have friends who are willing to put him up for a certain period of time, but not indefinitely. If he uses this time to search for a high-paying job, we can say that during this period his supply price lies above the unprotected-sector wage; when his funds (or his welcome) run out, he takes a job in the unprotected sector, at which point his effective supply price to the protected sector falls to the level of the unprotected-sector wage.

The existence of search costs can thus lead to a situation of chronic unemployment even in the presence of an ample unprotected market. But now the rate of migration is a function of two things—the rate of unemployment and the wage structure (including the unprotected-sector wage). The higher the fraction of jobs located in the protected sector, and the higher their wage rates, the higher will be the fraction of people willing to bear the costs of search and the higher will be the equilibrium level of unemployment. And while we cannot be quite as specific about the social opportunity cost of labor in this case as in the Panama case, two important statements can be made. *First*, the supply price that is relevant for measuring the social opportunity cost of labor for jobs in the protected sector is at least equal to the wage of corresponding labor in the unprotected sector. *Second*, the excess of this supply price over the unprotected-sector wage will be greater, the greater is the fraction of the labor force that chooses to be unemployed while engaging in search. This is in close correspondence to the Panama case, treated earlier. If, with a minimum wage of $5, the equilibrium level of unemployment was 20 percent, we can be sure that this equilibrium level would be lower if the minimum wage were $4.50 and higher if it were $5.50. Since in the Panama case the minimum wage itself turned out to be the relevant measure of social opportunity cost, we have in that case the same relationship as in the case presently being discussed: higher equilibrium levels of unemployment are associated with higher social opportunity costs of labor. The emphasis here, of course, must be on the word *equilibrium*: The more attractive the opportunities in the protected sector, the higher will be the rates of unemployment that migrants will be willing to suffer and still come to the city. The social opportunity cost of labor in a sense includes the cost of this unemployment, and hence must go up if more attractive wages or an increased fraction of jobs in the protected sector induce a rise in the equilibrium level of unemployment.

VI. A NOTE ON DISGUISED UNEMPLOYMENT

Much has been written about the phenomenon of 'disguised unemployment,' especially with reference to less-developed countries. It is often contended that this phenomenon gives rise to a situation where the social opportunity cost of labor will lie below the market wage, and may even be zero. There are some real elements of truth in this connection, but most expositions of the argument fail to put it in proper perspective. Some treatments associate disguised unemployment simply with all low-wage, low-skill jobs—sweepers, gardeners, casual construction workers, ricksha drivers, truck loaders, and the like, in the case of India. This variant simply says that the disguisedly unemployed earn wages substantially below the average wage of unskilled workers in a given labor market. Obviously there is virtually no distinction between this definition of disguised unemployment and what I would call the employment of labor in the unprotected sector. And if one considers the case where new jobs are created in the protected sector, my analysis, which would take as the first approximation to social opportunity cost the wage prevailing in the unprotected sector, would, like that of the proponents of this variant of disguised unemployment, apply to a protected-sector project a shadow wage below that which the project actually paid.

The second variant associates disguised unemployment not just with low wages, but with situations in which the marginal productivity of labor lies below the wages actually earned

This is clearly a quite different concept, which among other things could apply to high-wage as well as to low-wage workers. There are a variety of activities to which this argument applies. A classic example is that of fishermen on a lake. The addition of fishermen increases the total catch, but not proportionately, yet the last fisherman has as good a chance of making a given catch as has the first: The expected catch is the same for all and is equal to the *average* productivity of all. But because the total catch does not increase in proportion to the number of fishermen, the marginal productivity of a fisherman is less than what he earns. More frequently cited in the economic development literature are the shoeshine boys in a given square (where the presence of the last boy does not proportionately increase the number of shines) and the hawkers and vendors in the streets of less-developed countries (where the addition of another man selling a given product does not proportionately increase the amount sold, but has the effect of somewhat reducing the average amount received by each).[10]

Several points are relevant to the connection between this type of disguised unemployment and the measurement of the social opportunity cost of unskilled labor. First, activities with the characteristic of marginal product less than earnings generally represent only a small part of the unprotected sector of the market for unskilled labor. The necessary conditions do not, in general, apply to hired laborers whether they are sweepers, construction workers, runners, loaders, or whatever. Here the presumption remains that their marginal product is at least equal to the wage. Second, when new jobs are created in the protected sector, in the absence of migration, the workers to fill them would normally come from all parts of the unprotected sector with only a relatively small fraction coming from activities in which labor's marginal product lies below its earnings. (In this case, a small downward adjustment of the social opportunity cost of labor below the unprotected-sector wage would be justified, reflecting the fact that product has not gone down by the full amount that, say, the coathanger-hawker who took a job in the protected sector had previously been earning. But the adjustment would be small because only a small fraction of the jobs created would be filled by hawkers, vendors, shoeshine men, and so forth.)

Third, just as the creation of new jobs in the protected sector can result in an increase in the number of openly unemployed, so also can it lead to an increase in the number of disguisedly unemployed in the sense now under discussion. If the hawkers and vendors taking protected-sector jobs are not fully replaced, there would be, as just indicated, a downward adjustment of the social opportunity cost of unskilled labor below the figure it would otherwise have; if migration just managed to replace those that left, no adjustment would be warranted, and if migration more than fully replaced the vendors and hawkers who left for protected-sector jobs, this would warrant an upward adjustment in the social opportunity cost of unskilled labor, over and above the level that it otherwise would have.

In my judgment, the number of people who would abandon jobs with marginal product less than earnings would be so small in relation to the number of new jobs per hundred created in the protected sector and the likelihood of their being substantially replaced by migration so high that any adjustment on account of disguised-unemployment effects would probably be negligible.

VII. THE CASE OF CYCLICAL UNEMPLOYMENT

In a sense, the key question with respect to cyclical unemployment has already been answered, in the sense that the relevant social opportunity cost of a given unemployed worker is his voluntary supply price. In this section I shall further develop this idea, and indicate conditions under which further adjustments would be indicated. In the first place, it is important to note that cyclical unemployment rates tend to differ substantially for different classes and grades of labor, the unskilled tending to suffer far wider swings in employment than do the skilled, and skilled blue-collar workers in turn tending to have somewhat sharper variations in employment than do white-collar workers. This being the case, the setting of a shadow wage below the market wage in cases of cyclical variation would very likely apply only to certain types of labor.

In the second place, it is important to note that it is quite possible to have substantial amounts of cyclical unemployment even when a well-developed unprotected sector exists. This is so because even in the best of labor markets the adjustment of wages to equilibrate supply and demand is generally sluggish, particularly when the pressure on wages is in the downward direction. This observation carries with it the consequence that for categories of labor suffering from substantial cyclical unemployment, the social opportunity cost of labor can for the period of such unemployment lie significantly below even the unprotected-sector wage (it could not be zero, however, being limited to the reservation price below which such labor would not accept employment).

In the third place, while for most cases of cyclical unemployment the estimated reservation price of the unemployed would be an appropriate measure of their opportunity cost, special further downward adjustment from the market wage is warranted in cases of massive cyclical unemployment extending to all or nearly all categories of workers (such as in the Great Depression). The reason for this is the 'multiplier effect' that applies in such cases. If unemployed workers are given jobs, and the increase in their spending has the effect of absorbing still more unemployed, this effect, plus subsequent multiplier rounds, should be taken as an external benefit associated with their employment and should therefore reduce still further the social cost charged against the project hiring them. The magnitude of the adjustment should not be exaggerated, however, for several reasons:

a. The multiplier effect comes into being from the increase in total (first round) spending generated by the worker's gaining employment. Since he was already spending something even while unemployed, the increase in spending is not likely to equal the wage that he is paid even if he spends it all.

b. Since one of the effects of unemployment is to deplete the savings of the unemployed and their relatives, some considerable effort is likely to be made, when they become employed, to replenish the depleted family coffers. This means that they will not be spending their entire wage, but possibly saving a significant fraction of their income.

c. Not all the extra spending will result in the employment

of unemployed labor. Very likely, a substantial fraction of it will accrue to capital or categories of labor that are fully employed, and in some countries a large part will go for imports.

d. The extra benefit to be assigned to the employment of extra workers is not equal to the full amount of wages paid to the labor newly employed as a multiplier effect of the first group's increase in spending. Once again, it is the excess of the wages paid to the second group over and above their individual reservation prices.

All these reasons suggest that even when unemployment is extremely widespread—say 25 or 30 percent of the labor force —the downward adjustment of the social opportunity cost of labor in order to take into account its multiplier effect would probably not exceed 10 or at most 20 percent of its wage. The same reasons indicate that for moderate recessions, when only a limited number of categories of labor is seriously affected by unemployment, the adjustments of the social opportunity cost of labor to account for multiplier effects are small enough to be neglected.

Finally, a caveat concerning the making of adjustments for cyclical unemployment in the course of preparing evaluations of investment projects. If cyclical unemployment is present in the economy and the project is to be initiated soon, it is by all means correct to adjust for cyclical unemployment in estimating the social opportunity cost of labor during the first year or so of the project's life. But it would be a serious mistake to apply the same adjustment to the labor cost that will apply over the whole ten- or twenty- or fifty-year-life of the project. Beyond the immediately foreseeable future, the best assumption that we can make is that any given year will be one neither of cyclical boom nor of cyclical recession, and we should therefore project the social opportunity cost of labor on the basis of the normal employment situation that we expect to prevail. Such an employment situation can quite easily include substantial amounts of chronic unemployment of the migration-regulating type, but not cyclical unemployment as such. As we have seen, the adjustment of the social opportunity cost of labor for the influence of migration-regulating unemployment is actually in the opposite direction from the adjustment that is indicated in the cyclical case.

VIII. CONCLUDING COMMENTS

I have attempted to present the case for using prevailing wage levels in what I have called the unprotected sector as the point of departure for estimating the social opportunity cost of labor in a given labor market area.

In section II, this was shown to be the appropriate value for the simple case of a full-employment economy, abstracting from the presence of people not currently employed, but with reservation prices above the unprotected sector wage.

In section III the concept of supply price was introduced and it was shown that in the presence of people with higher reservation prices, the unprotected-sector wage somewhat underestimates the true social opportunity cost. In section IV, a rigorous model was presented showing how, in the absence of an unprotected sector and in the presence of a relatively high minimum wage, the phenomenon of migration can lead to an equilibrium level of chronic unemployment in the urban sector. In that model, the relevant social opportunity cost of unskilled labor was shown to be the minimum wage itself. In section V, the model of section IV was adapted to a more general situation where both the phenomenon of migration and an unprotected sector were present. Here there once again turned out to be an equilibrium level of chronic unemployment, and the relevant social opportunity cost of labor turned out to exceed the unprotected-sector wage by an amount which was greater, the greater the level of chronic unemployment. In section VI the concept of disguised unemployment was discussed. It was there shown that one variant of that concept coincided closely with my own line of analysis—especially in the form presented in section II. The second variant—quite different—was shown to give rise to modest downward adjustments of the social opportunity cost of labor below the unprotected-sector wage in the absence of migration, but in its presence the adjustment was shown to be indeterminate in sign and probably negligible in magnitude. In section VII, the phenomenon of cyclical unemployment was discussed. It was shown that even with the existence of an ample unprotected market, cyclical unemployment could cause the social opportunity cost of labor to fall below the unprotected-sector wage—the relevant measure of opportunity cost here being the reservation price of the affected labor. But it was emphasized that, particularly for the social evaluation of projects, adjustments of social opportunity costs on the basis of cyclical unemployment was strictly a near-term phenomenon. Looking ahead for three or more years, one can make no better assumption than that the economy will be at a 'normal' level of activity, giving rise to no adjustment for cyclical unemployment for the great bulk of most prospective projects' lives.

All this means that with modest qualifications and occasional adjustments (usually upward) the unprotected-sector wage stands as the basic measure of social opportunity cost. As against alternative measures, most of which are based on macro-economic analyses of one form or other, it has the great advantage of being readily capable of reflecting the complexity and subtlety of labor-market phenomena. This measure can reflect that the social opportunity cost of the same type of labor might be 500 rupees in the countryside, 750 rupees in Hyderabad, and 1000 rupees in Calcutta. It can easily branch out to take separate account of an indefinite number of skill and capacity classifications of labor. It subtly reflects these differences of location and skill, as well as the tastes of workers (even, with an adjustment, the tastes that lead to chronic unemployment).

By contrast, the estimation of the social opportunity cost of labor by macroeconomic approaches seems crude indeed. Rarely do programming approaches distinguish more than two skill categories of labor, and equally rarely do they distinguish more than one labor market area (the whole economy or a single part thereof). And it is difficult if not impossible to imagine more than a modest additional amount of disaggregation under a programming approach. The data requirements are far too severe, and the computational requirements astronomical. Similar comments can be made about global econometric models of the economy. These models can serve many useful purposes, but among them the task of estimating the social opportunity costs of twenty classes of labor in six major labor markets of a country simply cannot be counted. The approach here advocated takes the infinitely complex machinery of the economy itself as its computer and finds in the data generated by that machinery—in the form of unprotected-sector wages—the best approach to measuring the social opportunity cost of labour—by type, skill, and location.

Notes

[1] Seasonal and frictional unemployment are generally considered to average about 4 percent of the labor force in the United States, and may amount to as much as 6 or 7 percent of the labor force in the urban labor markets of some less-developed countries.

[2] See Government of India: The Cabinet Secretariat, *The National Sample Survey, No. 33: Wages, Employment, Income and Indebtedness of Agricultural Labor Households in Rural Areas*, Delhi, 1960, pp. 18, 23, 61.

[3] K. N. Raj, *Economic Aspects of the Bhakra Nangal Project*, Bombay: Asia Publishing House, 1960.

[4] *Ibid.*, pp. 77–78.

[5] One minor clarification is perhaps in order. It should be borne in mind that some firms may be in the protected sector with respect to certain skill categories of labor and in the unprotected sector with respect to others. A firm without a strong union might be in the protected sector with respect to its lowest-skill workers (because the minimum wage is effective for them) but not for other workers, whose market price is above the minimum in any case. Similarly, a firm might be in the protected sector for its blue-collar workers (who have a strong union) but not with respect to its white-collar workers (who are not unionized). In this case, data on the salaries of white-collar workers would be useful for estimating social opportunity cost, even though the information on blue-collar wages would not be useful for this purpose.

[6] A characteristic case of this kind is the establishment of a canning factory in an agricultural region. These are often staffed by married women or students on summer vacation who enter the labor force only for the brief canning season.

[7] This conclusion was independently arrived at by Michael Todaro on the basis of an analysis quite similar to my own. See his 'A Model of Labor Migration and Urban Employment in Less Developed Countries,' *American Economic Review* (March, 1969).

[8] Actually, the growth of the urban labor force stems both from the natural increase of the urban population and the flow of migration from outside the urban area, but for simplicity, I am here abstracting from the natural demographic growth of the urban labor force. This enables me to directly compare new job creation in the urban area with the flow of migration. No generality is lost in this simplification, however. When I speak of an equilibrium relationship between new job creation and migration, readers can interpret this as meaning an equilibrium relationship between the number of new jobs and the net increase of the urban labor force from both sources. Since the natural growth from within the area is overwhelmingly governed by demographic considerations, the element which responds significantly to changes in the unemployment rate will in any case be the flow of migration.

[9] This of course has to happen if the unemployment rate remains constant. Rarely, however, is it possible to check the process in detail because the rate of

growth of new jobs is relatively small (compared to the labor force) and steady, as is the rate of immigration. However, Professor Frederick Harbison reports on a case where the number of jobs in the urban sector of Nairobi was increased rapidly by nearly 15 percent in 1964. 'This acted like a magnet attracting new workers into the urban labor markets. . . . In the end, the volume of unemployment, as a consequence of the expansion of the modern labor force . . . was probably increased rather than decreased.' Michael P. Todaro, *op. cit.*, pp. 140–41.

[10] Even in these cases, the discrepancy between earnings and marginal productivity arises only when, as is sometimes the case, the market price (of shoeshines or, say, of coathangers sold on street corners) is a 'conventional' price that does not adjust downward to clear the market. With full price adjustment the 'last' worker would in fact earn his marginal product, which consists in part of the value of the net increment to output due to his presence and in part of the alternative earnings of the labor displaced by the downward price adjustment that his presence brought about.

CHAPTER EIGHT

INVESTMENT IN MEN VERSUS
INVESTMENT IN MACHINES:
THE CASE OF INDIA

This chapter attempts to evaluate the economic rate of return
to society as a whole of investment in physical capital, on one
hand, and of investment in secondary and higher education, on
the other. The chapter deals exclusively with data from India.
It goes into considerable methodological detail in an effort to
indicate ways of making as good use as possible of data that are
far from ideal. Poor data are characteristic of underdeveloped
countries—indeed, the Indian data are probably better than
those for the overwhelming bulk of poor countries. Part of my
purpose in presenting this study is to help 'break the ice' by
suggesting a variety of ways of overcoming potential inadequa-
cies in the data. The other part of my purpose is to draw some
inferences about the Indian situation.

Part I of the chapter is devoted to measuring the rate of
return to physical capital investment in the private sector of
Indian industry. Part II attempts to measure the rate of return
to investment in education. The measures of the rate of return
to investment in physical capital were consciously biased downward in the choice of procedures; the measures of the rate of
return to investment in education were consciously biased upward. In spite of these biases, the 'best' estimates resulting from

Reprinted from C. Arnold Anderson and Mary Jean Bowman, eds., *Education and
Economic Development* (Chicago: Aldine Publishing Company, 1965), copyright
© 1965 by Aldine Publishing Company. Reprinted by permission of Aldine·
Atherton Publishing Company. The bulk of the research underlying Part I of this
chapter was done while the author was a member of MIT Center for International
Studies at New Delhi. Professor Harberger acknowledges his indebtedness to
Gary S. Becker, Mary Jean Bowman, and H. Gregg Lewis for helpful discussions
during the preparation of Part II, but warns that no share of such deficiencies
as remain should be imputed to them.

the computations suggest that the economic rate of return to investment in physical capital is higher (and may be substantially higher) than the economic rate of return to investment in secondary and higher education. This does not, of course, say that investment in education is a bad idea, for it has other than purely economic advantages. Part III of the paper attempts to interpret the results of Parts I and II, and to mention some qualifications that seem appropriate.

I. THE RATE OF RETURN TO CAPITAL IN INDIAN INDUSTRY

It is almost tautological to say that the contribution of a given investment to economic development is measured by the annual net increment of national output attributable to that investment. If this year's net investment amounts to 10 percent of the national income, and it yields a rate of return of 15 percent, next year's national income should on this account be 1·5 percent greater than this year's income. Obviously, the rate of return is likely to differ from sector to sector, and among individual projects within sectors. Undoubtedly it would be better to know the rate of return to be expected from each individual project than to have estimates of the rate of return to investment in rather broad sectors of the economy. But we have to start somewhere, and broad sectoral averages seem to be as good a starting place as any, particularly when the issue under discussion is itself as broad as 'investment in men versus investment in machines.' We begin, then, with an attempt to estimate the rate of return to physical capital in private industry in India.

I shall devote a good deal of space to measuring the return to physical capital because (a) it is on this half of the 'men versus machines' issues that the greater amount of relevant and reliable data are available, and (b) this is an area in which very little work has been done relating to underdeveloped countries. I feel that investigators have been reluctant to work in this field —with data from underdeveloped countries—because of uncertainty as to the size and importance of a number of possible biases. In the first place, it is well known that in any country with substantial taxes on company income there is a strong incentive for firms to claim as rapid depreciation as possible on their assets. In this way they postpone the taxation of the income accruing from any given set of assets, obtaining, in effect, an interest-free loan from the government. Under these circumstances the rate of return measured on the basis of net income and net assets appearing on the books of a company may be quite different from the rate of return that we would get if we calculated net income and net assets using the 'true economic depreciation' of existing assets in each year. In the second place, companies usually keep their accounts in current prices; changes in the price level may lead to a situation in which the accounts give a false picture of the 'real rate of return' on capital assets. In the third place, company accounts measure the private and not the social return to capital, and it is the latter which is of greatest interest to those concerned with promoting economic development.

I propose to show that these potential biases are probably not as serious as one might at first suppose. However, first I should like to discuss a device for dealing with the data that is probably more important than any other single device in coping with problems of this type. In brief, a good underestimate or overestimate is likely to be more useful than a bad estimate. As we move from 'raw' to 'corrected' estimates, many rather arbitrary decisions have to be taken. If, at each crossroad, we consciously take a course which will bias our final result in a given direction (say, downward), we know where we stand at the end. If we do not try to overcorrect in this way, we will probably come out with an objectively better result, but one which will be less convincing to others.

In this study, I have tried to obtain a good underestimate of the rate of return to physical capital in private sector industry in India. The data are based on a survey conducted by the Reserve Bank of India, covering 1,001 companies in virtually all branches of industry. The great bulk of 'modern' large enterprises are directly represented in the sample. The Reserve Bank of India presents each year a consolidated balance sheet and a consolidated income statement for the 1,001 companies as a group, and for subgroups of the 1,001 broken down by industrial classification. We shall here be dealing with the consolidated data for the 1,001 companies taken together.

We are interested here in measuring the social net productivity of physical capital. Because it is net productivity with which we are concerned, we want to exclude from the companies' income a provision for depreciation. But because it is the social rather than the private rate of return to capital which interests us, we must define 'net income' to be inclusive of corporation income tax payments. Thus we are at the outset taking into account one of the most important sources of divergence between the social and the private productivity of capital.

Being suspicious of the data in a number of ways, I decided to explore a number of alternative methods of measuring the rate of return to capital. Five essentially different methods were followed:

Method I takes as its starting point the ratio of 'net income', as defined above, to the net book value of physical assets as shown on the companies' records.

Method II doubts the validity of net book value as representative of the current replacement cost of assets. It uses instead an estimate consisting of the current market value of the firms' shares plus the (book) value of the firms' borrowings minus the (book) value of the firms' net financial assets. This method thus uses the stock market's estimate of the value of the firm as the basis on which to derive the estimated current value of physical assets. The 'net income' figures used in Method II are the same as those used in Method I.

Method III doubts the accuracy of the firms' depreciation accounting procedures. It uses the ratio of gross income to gross assets as a device for estimating the ratio of the firms' 'true net income' to their 'true net assets'. This method will be explained in detail at the appropriate place; suffice it to say here that the method consciously aims at understating the ratio of true net income to true net assets.

Method IV also doubts the depreciation accounting procedures, and instead uses the 'cash flow' method of modern capital budgeting to estimate the net rate of return to physical capital. For each of a series of years, the expenditures of the firms on physical capital are deducted from the gross income from this form of capital, yielding a net cash inflow (or outflow) for each year. In Method IV the initial cash outflow is taken to be the net book value of the physical assets carried into the first year for which flows are measured, and the final cash inflow is taken to be the net book value of the physical assets carried out of the last year for which flows are measured. The estimated net rate of return is that which yields a zero present value for the pattern of flows thus generated.

Method V recognizes that depreciation accounting procedures still have some influence in Method IV because they affect the net book values used to estimate the initial outflow and the final inflow. Under Method V the extreme assumption is made that all depreciation charges are fictitious; therefore gross book values are taken as the measures of the initial outflow and the final inflow. The net rate of return is then calculated as in Method IV.

Under each method, an estimate based on the raw data (estimate A) was first made; this estimate was then subjected to three successive adjustments (B, C, and D).

Adjustment B takes into account the fact that some of the observed income of the firms may have been due to financial rather than physical assets. Under this adjustment the net financial assets of the firms are estimated, and a rate of return of 10 per cent is arbitrarily imputed to these assets. The resulting imputed income from financial assets is then deducted from the raw income figures to obtain the adjusted income series. As the actual rate of return on net financial assets is likely to be less than 10 percent, this adjustment probably yields an understatement of the income attributable to physical assets.

Adjustment C begins with the figures emerging from Adjustment B, and modifies them to take account of price level changes.

Adjustment D begins with the figures emerging from Adjustment C, and modifies them to take account of excise taxes. This adjustment recognizes that in cases where excise taxes apply, the value to consumers of the product of a taxed industry is measured by the price of the product gross of tax. Under Adjustment D a fraction (equal to capital's share in value added) of the excise taxes paid by the firms was imputed as part of the marginal product of capital.

The estimated rates of return to capital obtained under these alternative methods and adjustments are summarized in Table 8.1. (The computations are presented in detail in the appendix to this paper.)

Table 8.1

Estimated Rate of Return to Capital in Indian Industry, 1955–59

(In percentages)

Method	Adjustment			
	A	*B*	*C*	*D*
I	12·8	11·7	11·4	14·4
II[a]	15·5	14·7	—[b]	19·3
III	12·1	11·3	11·1	13·1
IV	13·4	12·4	10·0	13·6
V	12·6	11·4	10·4	13·0

[a] Method II measures the rate of return for 1959 only, as this was the only year for which an adequate estimate of the market value of the firms' shares could be obtained.

[b] Since the market value of the assets of the firms is measured for the same year as the corresponding income, there is no need for a price-level correction when Method II is used.

An Adjustment for Market Imperfections

So far we have implicitly assumed that the wages paid to labor by the 1,001 companies in the Reserve Bank survey accurately reflect the alternative productivity of the workers employed. There are, however, some grounds for doubting the validity of this assumption. Large companies in many countries appear to pay higher wages to similar labor than do small companies: even more striking are the disparities between the earnings of comparable labor in big companies, on the one hand, and agricultural employment, on the other. In 1956–57 the average annual *wages* paid *per worker* in factory establishments in India was more than 1200 rupees[1] while the average annual *income per household* was only 385 rupees,[2] for agricultural laboring households. Even within urban areas, the factory worker appears to have a substantially better-than-average economic position. More than half of all urban households in India had, in 1957–58, monthly per capita expenditures of less than 24 rupees[3]—and it should be borne in mind that many Indian households have more than one earner.

The idea that factory workers probably receive more than they could get elsewhere is also borne out by the fact that most factories have long lists of applicants who are ready and willing to work at the prevailing wage, but for whom posts are not available. This is not the place to explore the possible reasons why factory wages do not fall. Both union pressure and special wage legislation applicable to factory employment must certainly play an important role, and there may be other additional explanatory factors.

Some economists are prone to assume, when dealing with countries like India, that the alternative productivity of labor is zero. This means that the social marginal product of capital is not what capital gets, but the entire value added of the operation in question. The wages paid to labor in this case are, from the economic point of view, not a necessary cost but simply a sort of transfer payment out of the marginal product of the really scarce factor, capital.

I am not a member of the 'zero alternative productivity' school. There is a large and growing body of evidence, and an increasing degree of consensus among Indian economists, against this extreme position. But this does not say that the Indian labor market is a perfectly functioning mechanism, with the value of the marginal product of equivalent labor exactly the same in all employments. Granted that modern industry is recognized to be a high-wage sector, some allowance should be made for this fact in estimating the social marginal productivity of capital. I believe it is reasonable to assume that the wage bill paid by modern industry in India exceeds the alternative earnings of the workers involved by some 25 percent. That is, the same physical investments that in 1959 produced a return to capital of 2·0 billion rupees, while paying a wage bill of 3·4 rupees, could have yielded a return of 2·68 billion rupees while operating in exactly the same way, simply by paying the same workers 20 percent less. Once it is assumed that the alternative productivity of the labor employed in a given operation is less than the wages actually paid to that labor, it follows automatically that the accounting profits of that enterprise understate the true social benefit attributable to the capital investment involved.

In the accompanying diagram (Figure 8.1) *OCDH* represents the wages bill actually paid by a given enterprise, while *OFEH* represents the alternative productivity, or 'social cost', of the labor employed by that enterprise. Our procedure takes as the social return to the capital involved in the enterprise its accounting profits *BCD*, plus *CDEF*, the excess of the wages actually paid to the labor employed in the enterprise over the alternative productivity of that same labor. Obviously, this measure understates what would be the social return to the capital already invested in the project if its managers faced a market wage equal to the alternative product of labor. In this last case, *OJ* of labor could be employed, and profits of *BFG* would be produced.

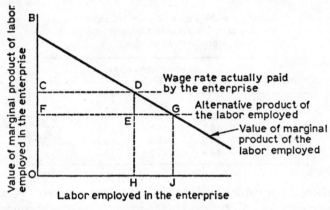

Figure 8.1

Thus, in making an adjustment for market imperfections, we augment the accounting figures on income from capital by an amount equal to 20 percent of the wage bill paid by the companies in question in each respective year. Unfortunately, I do not have the data to support the particular numerical value (20 percent) chosen for this exercise, and as a consequence I fully expect that some readers will not place much weight upon the calculations that follow. But I am certain that the majority of professional observers of the Indian scene would consider my assumption as reasonable or even conservative, and I shall proceed on that basis, anticipating disagreement on the part of some readers and hoping that most will be prepared to go along with my assumption.[4]

Table 8.2 shows estimates of the rate of marginal productivity of capital in Indian industry, obtained using the same methods and adjustments that were discussed in detail above. The only difference is that, before these computations were begun, the income from capital used in the previous calculations was augmented by an amount equal to 20 percent of the wage bill of the 1,001 companies.

TABLE 8.2

Estimated Rate of Marginal Productivity of Capital in Indian Industry, 1955–59

(In percentages)

(Assuming that 20 percent of wage bill represents the excess of actual wages over alternative marginal productivity of labor)

Method	Adjustment			
	A	*B*	*C*	*D*
I	17·5	16·4	16·0	20·1
II	20·4	20·0	—	26·1
III	15·5	14·7	14·3	17·2
IV	19·6	18·5	15·7	21·3
V	16·9	15·7	14·3	18·3

Whereas our earlier analysis yielded results between 13·0 and 19·3 percent for adjustment D (the most 'refined' adjustment), we here get figures between 17·2 and 26·1 percent under the same adjustment. Bearing in mind that the procedures used to obtain these figures create a presumption of downward bias in the final results, I certainly think that it is fair to conclude that physical capital is highly productive in the industrial sector of the Indian economy.

II. THE RATE OF RETURN TO INVESTMENT IN EDUCATION IN INDIA

For a long time I looked without success for a body of data from which it would be possible to estimate the rate of return to investment in education in India. I had about given up the search when I came across a table in C. Arnold Anderson's paper for this conference (see my table 8.3). This is certainly not the best set of data that one could imagine for estimating the rate of return to investment in education, but it is, to my

knowledge, the best that is presently available for India. The
rest of this section will be devoted to an attempt to squeeze as
much juice as possible out of this 'lemon'.

TABLE 8.3

Distribution of Monthly Male Earnings by Schooling,
Hyderabad[a]

Earnings (Rupees)	Illiterate	Primary	Secondary	Lower Professional & Technical
– 25	658	264	220	14
26 –	912	541	308	15
51 –	376	407	510	44
101 –	68	190	417	66
201 –	6	15	158	55
501 –		3	21	18
1001 –			8	3
2501 –			3	1
5000+			1	2
Total	2020	1420	1646	218

Earnings (Rupees)	Under-graduate	Graduate-Postgraduate	Higher Professional & Technical	Total
– 25	4	2	2	1164
26 –	18	1	4	1799
51 –	59	22	25	1443
101 –	51	56	42	890
201 –	49	117	54	454
501 –	8	36	9	95
1001 –	4	5	11	31
2501 –		2		6
5000+				3
Total	193	241	147	5885

[a] Indian Institute of Economics. *A Socio-Economic Survey of Hyderabad*, Hyderabad: Government Press, 1957.

The first problem was to decide what to measure. I had some
difficulty in interpreting the results for 'lower professional and
technical' and 'higher professional and technical' education,
and accordingly decided to leave them out of consideration. In

the case of primary education, there was not much difficulty in interpretation, but I felt hard put to estimate the forgone earnings of students at this early a stage. Since forgone earnings are the most important 'cost' of education at higher levels, and since I found it easier to estimate forgone earnings than the associated direct costs of education, I decided not to estimate the rate of return to primary education. Within higher education there were two categories—undergraduate and graduate-postgraduate. I decided not to split higher education into two pieces, and instead to measure the rate of return involved in higher education all the way up to the graduate-postgraduate stage.

Three types of 'investments' will be dealt with here:

1. An investment in four years of secondary schooling, as compared with a person's entering the labor force after completing primary schooling.
2. An investment in six years of college and university training, as compared with a person's entering the labor force after completing secondary schooling.
3. An investment in ten years of secondary plus college and university training, as compared with a person's entering the labor force after completing primary schooling.

In all these cases we are comparing the situation of a person who completes a later stage of schooling with one who completes an earlier stage. Unfortunately, the data of the sample survey refer to people who have had 'some' primary, 'some' secondary, 'some' undergraduate training, etc. They do not refer to those who have completed the stage in question. We must therefore first estimate the average incomes of 'completers' of the various stages.

This was done by the following procedure. First, the mean income in each educational class was estimated from the Hyderabad survey table (Table 8.3). These are shown in column 1 of Table 8.4. Second, on the basis of consultation with Indian colleagues, an effort was made to establish the probable duration of each successive stage of the educational process. Since educational practices vary among places and institutions in India, we cannot be certain about these figures. I present the

results in the hope that these assumptions are accurate; in the
event that readers want to explore some modification of these
assumptions, the general method presented and described in
this paper can be readily applied using alternative assumptions.
Column 2 of Table 8.4 shows the estimated total schooling a
typical person has had on completion of each stage. Column 3
shows the estimated average years of education completed by
the persons sampled in each category. Column 4 shows the
compound rate of increase that would carry a person from the
income associated with the prior stage to the income associated
with the given stage, in the number of years' difference between
the estimated average years completed for the two stages. For
example, average earnings of 65·04 rupees are associated with
an estimated average of four years of schooling completed for
the primary category; average earnings of 132·57 rupees are
associated with an estimated average of ten years of schooling
completed for the secondary category. The compound rate of
increase that will make 65·04 grow to 132·57 in six years is
12·4 percent.

TABLE 8.4

Estimated Average Earnings and Years of Schooling by
Education Class

Level of Education	(1) Estimated Average Earnings from Hyderabad Sample (Rupees per month)	(2) Estimated Total Years of Schooling to Completion	(3) Estimated Average Years Completed	(4) Percentage Rate of Increase of Average Earnings from Prior Educational Class
Illiterate	43·72	—	—	—
Primary	65·04	8	4	10·5
Secondary	132·57	12	10	12·4
Undergraduate	222·74	16	15	11·0
Graduate and postgraduate	391·40	18	17	32·6

At this early stage I had to decide whether I would aim for
an underestimate or an overestimate of the rate of return to
education, and I opted for an overestimate. There are two ways
in which the estimates in Table 8.4 reflect this decision. The

first is the estimate that the average of the sample group at each stage was halfway to completing that stage; the second is the decision to treat the undergraduate stage as occupying the fifteenth and sixteenth years of total education. How these assumptions work to produce an overestimate of the rate of return will be indicated presently. First, however, I shall present estimates of the average incomes of 'completers' of each stage.

Estimated Average Incomes of Completers:

	Rupees per Month	
Primary	100·49	$[=65·04 \times (1·115)^4]$
Secondary	160·49	$[=132·57 \times (1·11)^2]$
Graduate and postgraduate	519·00	$[=391·40 \times (1·326)]$

The estimated average monthly earnings of a person with four years of primary education are 65·04 rupees. How do we estimate the average earnings of someone with eight years? We observe that the average rate of increase of earnings associated with the first four years of education was 10·5 percent per year, and the average rate of increase associated with the next six years was 12·4 percent. I was in doubt as to which of these rates to apply to the last four years of primary education, and settled on a rough average of the two—11·5 percent. In the case of secondary education, the rate of increase from the secondary to the undergraduate stage (11·0 percent) was used to project the earnings of secondary completers from the average earnings of the secondary category. In the case of graduate and postgraduate education, the earnings of completers were projected from the average earnings of the class on the basis of the rate of increase (32·6 percent) from the undergraduate to the graduate-postgraduate stage.

Turning now to why these assumptions are likely to produce overestimates of the rate of return to education, consider first the assumption that the average years of education in each stage represent half-completion of that stage. This assumption is likely to overstate the average, probably particularly so in the primary category. If 65·04 rupees represent only three years of average education, we would end up projecting higher average earnings than 100·49 rupees for primary completers. Since the earnings of primary completers are the forgone earnings of people at higher educational stages, and represent a large part of the total costs of investment in education, our procedure, by tending to understate forgone earnings, tends to overestimate the rate of return. Since the later educational stages are much shorter than the primary stage, a tendency for the average years completed to be somewhat less than half-completion of the stage would have far less impact than in the primary stage.

My informants were not sure how to treat the undergraduate stage. Apparently some undergraduates begin with two years of prior training at the lower professional and technical level, and spend only two years as undergraduates; others may enter undergraduate school direct from secondary school and spend four years as undergraduates. If the former group dominate in the sample, the average years completed for the under-graduate group is likely to be close to 15; if the latter group predominate, the average years completed is likely to be close to 14. Probably the truth lies in between, and, if this is so, my decision to use the 15-year figure as the average for the group operates to magnify the estimated rate of return to investment in education through the graduate-postgraduate level. If I had set the average years completed of undergraduates at 14 years, the percentage rate of increase between the undergraduate average and the graduate-postgraduate average would have been 20·9 percent rather than 32·6 percent; and the average earnings of graduate-postgraduate completers would have been projected at 473 rupees rather than 519 rupees per month. The choice of the procedure leading to the latter figure is thus likely to introduce an upward bias in the estimated rate of return to higher education.

The next step in my procedure was to recognize that the sample was heavily weighted with younger people. We do not have data on the age distribution of the people included in the earnings-by-schooling table, but the Hyderabad survey does present a breakdown by age and education of a larger group of which the earnings-by-education sample was a subset. I assumed that the earnings-by-education group had essentially the same age distribution as the broader group for which data were available.

The age-by-education data were classified by very broad age groups, and I thought that further refinement would be desirable so as to reflect the three main forces that determined the age distribution of each educational class. For the very old, mortality and retirement are the principal reasons why older cohorts have fewer earners than younger ones. For the middle age groups, the relationship between adjacent cohorts would tend to reflect the pace at which the output of given educational levels had been expanding in the period before Indian independence. For the very young, this relationship will reflect the postwar rate of growth of the output of the relevant class of educational institutions. Table 8.5 presents some relevant statistics.

TABLE 8.5

Average Annual Rates of Growth of Number of Male Students

(In percentages)

Years	Primary	Secondary	University
1916–39[a]	2·6	3·3	3·7
1950–57[b]	4·9	7·0	10·4

[a] Source: *Statistical Abstracts, British India.*
[b] Source: *Statistical Abstracts, India.*

In estimating the age distributions in Table 8.6, I tried to bear in mind the data given above, as well as the information about the broad age distribution of the Hyderabad survey itself. In the graduate-postgraduate class, I assumed a recent rate of increase of completers considerably lower than the 10·4 percent figure in Table 8.5, because of the substantial lag between entry into higher education and completion of this final stage and also because, even apart from the lag, I would anticipate a slower rate of growth of this 'final product' than of the population of university students as a whole. Table 8.6 presents a comparison between the percentage distributions of males by age and education as shown by the Hyderabad survey, on the one hand, and my allocation, on the other.

Table 8.7 presents the detailed age distribution resulting from my allocation. The next step in my procedure was to

TABLE 8.6

Distribution of Males by Age and Education

(In percentages)

Age		Primary[a]	Secondary[b]	Graduate and Postgraduate[b]
13–21	Hyderabad sample	36·4	——	——
	My allocation	36·5	——	——
22–40	Hyderabad sample	43·5	69·0	70·7
	My allocation	43·5	68·5	70·4
41–55	Hyderabad sample	15·5	23·2	23·2
	My allocation	15·4	24·0	23·5
56–70	Hyderabad sample	4·6	7·8	6·1
	My allocation	4·6	7·7	6·1

[a] As percentages of total from age 13 through age 70.
[b] As percentages of total from age 22 through age 70.

assume age-earnings profiles for the different educational groups. I assumed that these had the form of a steady upward rise of income with age, until a peak (or, better, plateau) was reached, with income staying at this peak level all the way to age 65. The following requirements were borne in mind in estimating these profiles:

1. The average earnings of each education class, weighted by its assumed age distribution, had to be approximately equal to the average earnings estimated above for completers of that stage of education.
2. The peak in earnings had to be reached at a later age for each successively higher educational stage.
3. The peak earnings had to be a higher fraction of average earnings at each successively higher educational stage. This was to be true both when the average was weighted by the assumed age distribution of each class, and when the average was an unweighted one covering all the years from entry into the labor force to retirement at 65.

Table 8.8 presents some of the key features of the assumed age-earnings profiles. Here, once again, I have consciously tried to bias my assumptions in the direction that will produce high estimated rates of return to investment in education. The steeper the age-earnings profile of a given mean earnings, the

Project Evaluation

TABLE 8.7

Assumed Age Distribution by Education Class

(Each figure shows assumed number of males of the given age for every 10
males aged 65 in the specified education class)

Age	Primary	Secondary	Graduate & Postgraduate	Age	Primary	Secondary	Graduate & Postgraduate
13	215	—	—	40	68	60	80
14	205	—	—	41	65	58	76
15	196	—	—	42	62	56	73
16	187	—	—	43	59	54	70
17	179	—	—	44	56	52	67
18	171	200	—	45	53	50	64
19	164	187	—	46	50	48	61
20	157	175	—	47	47	46	59
21	151	164	—	48	44	44	56
22	145	154	201	49	42	42	53
23	139	145	190	50	40	40	50
24	133	137	180	51	38	38	47
25	127	130	171	52	36	36	44
26	122	123	162	53	34	34	41
27	117	117	154	54	32	32	38
28	112	111	146	55	30	30	35
29	108	105	139	56	28	28	32
30	104	100	132	57	26	26	29
31	100	95	126	58	24	24	26
32	96	90	120	59	22	22	23
33	92	85	114	60	20	20	20
34	88	81	108	61	18	18	18
35	84	77	103	62	16	16	16
36	80	73	98	63	14	14	14
37	77	69	93	64	12	12	12
38	74	66	88	65	10	10	10
39	71	63	84	66–70	16	16	16

greater the fraction of total income received late in life, and
hence the smaller the present value of a given total income.
Now it is universally recognized that age-earnings profiles are
steeper with higher educational levels. But I made them only
slightly steeper. The ratio of peak earnings to average earnings
was 1·11 for primary completers, 1·14 for secondary completers,
and 1·20 for graduate-postgraduate completers; I am sure that
these figures understate the relative steepening of the profile as
one moves up the educational ladder. By the same token, they
tend to produce an overstatement of the rate of return to
investment in education.

TABLE 8.8
Characteristics of Assumed Age-Earnings Profiles

	Primary	Secondary	Graduate & Postgraduate
Age at which peak earnings reached	30	35	40
Ratio of peak earnings to earnings at age 21	1·55	2·11	——
Ratio of peak earnings to earnings at age 26	1·19	1·51	3·00
Ratio of peak earnings to average over lifetime	1·11	1·14	1·20
Ratio of peak earnings to weighted average earnings	1·27	1·33	1·42
	(Rupees per month)		
Average earnings over lifetime	113·92	187·50	611·90
Weighted average earnings	100·15	160·68	519·30
Weighted average earnings computed from sample	100·49	160·41	519·00

TABLE 8.9
Assumed Age-Earnings Profiles

Age	Earnings (Rupees per month) Primary	Secondary	Graduate & Postgraduate	Age	Earnings (Rupees per month) Primary	Secondary	Graduate & Postgraduate
14	47	—	—	28	117	157	315
15	52	—	—	29	122	165	350
16	57	—	—	30	127	173	385
17	62	—	—	31	127	181	420
18	67	77	—	32	127	189	455
19	72	85	—	33	127	197	490
20	77	93	—	34	127	205	525
21	82	101	—	35	127	213	560
22	87	109	—	36	127	213	595
23	92	117	—	37	127	213	630
24	97	125	175	38	127	213	665
25	102	133	210	39	127	213	700
26	107	141	245	40–65	127	213	735
27	112	149	280				

The profiles given in Table 8.9 permit us to estimate part of the cost of education—the earnings that a person would have been making if he had stopped on completion of primary schooling or, alternatively, on completion of secondary schooling. But they do not include any part of the direct costs of schooling, whether these are borne by the individual or his family, by the institution he attends, or by the government. These direct costs are surely part of the social 'investment' in education, and should be incorporated in our analysis. Unfortunately, I had not encountered adequate estimates of them at the time this paper was prepared. The Indian government does publish data labeled 'direct costs of education' by educational category. These were, in 1956–57, 440 rupees per year per student at the university level, 61 rupees per student at the secondary level, and 24 rupees per student at the primary level.[5] I find it difficult, however, to believe that these represent total outlays. Twenty-four rupees represents about \$5·00 a year per student at the primary level, and 61 rupees about \$18.00 a year per student at the secondary level. These seem very low indeed as estimates of total direct costs.

For the United States, Becker estimates that university students bear about two-thirds of the total cost of their education.[6] Since what they bear includes fairly substantial outlays for tuition and the like, in addition to forgone earnings, it may well be that total costs are something like twice forgone earnings. In the light of this figure, it seems conservative to assume that in India the direct costs of education amount to 50 percent of forgone earnings. I make this assumption as Assumption II of Table 8.10. Assumption I is even more conservative. It takes direct costs of the first year of secondary school to be 12 percent of the earnings of a primary school graduate aged 14; of the second year of secondary school, to be 16 percent of the earnings of a primary school graduate aged 15; of the third year, to be 20 per cent of the earnings of a primary school graduate aged 16; and of the fourth year, to be 24 percent of the earnings of a primary school graduate aged 17. For the successive years of higher education, the direct costs are taken to be 30, 35, 40, 45, 50, and 50 percent of the earnings of a secondary school graduate aged 18, 19, 20, 21, 22, and 23, respectively. This latter assumption produces an estimate of direct costs at the university level which is very close to the government figure of 440 rupees per student per year, if we assume that each higher cohort at the university level contains 10–12 percent fewer students than the immediately preceding cohort.

TABLE 8.10

Assumed Schooling Costs by Age

(Rupees per month)

Age	Assumption I		Assumption II	
	Secondary	Higher	Secondary	Higher
14	6	—	23	—
15	8	—	26	—
16	11	—	28	—
17	15	—	31	—
18	—	23	—	33
19	—	30	—	42
20	—	37	—	46
21	—	45	—	50
22	—	54	—	54
23	—	58	—	58

Table 8.11 presents an illustration of the way in which the rate of return to education was calculated. An iterative procedure had to be followed, the iteration being carried to the point where there was a negligible difference between the present value of the capital-at-charge at age 39, and the present value at the same age of the extra income which the better-educated individual in the comparison would earn during the remainder of his working lifetime (to age 65). In the case illustrated, a rate of 16·3 percent per annum led to such a negligible difference.

Calculations similar to those in Table 8.11 were carried out for five other comparisons. The final results are given in Table 8.12.

After the forgoing estimates were prepared, I had the benefit of numerous comments and suggestions, many of which came from Jacob Mincer's excellent critique of my paper at the conference. Moreover, my attention was called to an unpublished paper by G. S. Sahota, 'Returns on Education in India' (University of Chicago, Asian Workshop, Paper No. 61–11 [1962]), in which he developed independent estimates of the direct costs of education per pupil at various educational stages. These costs, according to Sahota, ranged from approximately 20 rupees per student per month in the ninth and tenth years of education, to roughly 70 rupees per student per month at the university level.

I have accordingly reestimated the rate of return to secondary

TABLE 8.11

An Illustrative Calculation of the Rate of Return to Investment in Education

(Graduate-Postgraduate Compared with Secondary)

(1) Age	(2) Earnings of Second- ary School Product (Rupees per month)	(3) Earnings of Grad- uate-Post- graduate Product (Rupees per month)	(4) Schooling Costs of Graduate- Postgrad- uate Product (Rupees per month) Assump- tion II	(5) Net Excess of Income (+) or Net Cost (−) of Grad- uate as Com- pared with Secondary Product [(3)−(2)−(4)]	(6) Last Year's Capital at Charge Accum- ulated at 16·3%[a] [(7)t₋₁ × 1·163)]	(7) Capital at Charge at Given Age ÷ (−12)[a] [(5)+(6)]
18	77	—	33	−110	—	−110
19	85	—	42	−127	−128	−255
20	93	—	46	−139	−297	−436
21	101	—	50	−151	−507	−658
22	109	—	54	−163	−765	−928
23	117	—	58	−175	−1079	−1254
24	125	175	—	50	−1458	−1408
25	133	210	—	77	−1638	−1561
26	141	245	—	104	−1815	−1711
27	149	280	—	131	−1990	−1859
28	157	315	—	158	−2162	−2004
29	165	350	—	185	−2331	−2146
30	173	385	—	212	−2496	−2284
31	181	420	—	239	−2656	−2417
32	189	455	—	266	−2811	−2545
33	197	490	—	293	−2960	−2667
34	205	525	—	320	−3102	−2782
35	213	560	—	347	−3235	−2888
36	213	595	—	382	−3359	−2977
37	213	630	—	417	−3462	−3045
38	213	665	—	452	−3451	−3089
39	213	700	—	487	−3593	−3106
40–65	213	735	—	522		

Present value at age 39 of 522 per year at 16·3 percent per annum =

$$\frac{522}{\cdot 163}\left[1 - \frac{1}{(1\cdot163)^{26}}\right] = 3138$$

Net present value at age 39 = 3138 − 3106 = + 32

(Net present value at age 39 obtained using a 16·4 percent rate is − 142.)

[a] Columns 6 and 7 represent one-twelfth of the actual capital at charge. If all columns were multiplied by 12, we would have annual earnings, annual costs, and actual capital at charge in the respective columns. I carry capital at charge as a negative figure for convenience of reference. This figure represents what the graduate-postgraduate has yet to recover (in terms of present value) before the investment in his education will have paid off at 16·3 percent.

TABLE 8.12

Estimated Rates of Return to Investment in
Education in India

	Assumption I	*Assumption II*
Graduate-postgraduate compared with primary	15·0	14·1
Secondary compared with primary	11·9	10·0
Graduate-postgraduate compared with secondary	16·9	16·3

and university education combined, taking into account both
the suggestions made by readers and Sahota's direct cost figures.
The principal changes made were:

(a) The earnings figure of 391·40 rupees per month, given in
the Hyderabad sample as the average earnings of persons with
graduate and postgraduate education, was taken in this exercise to reflect the average earnings of those with 16 total years
of education. This assumption obviously will lead toward an
overstatement of the rate of return to higher education. The
earnings profile of persons with 16 years of education was then
estimated so as to produce an age-weighted average income of
391·40 rupees for this group and so as to have other reasonable
properties. The estimated pattern begins with earnings of 180
rupees per month at age 22, and proceeds by annual steps of
20 rupees per month to a maximum of 540 rupees per month
at age 40. The ratio of peak earnings to earnings at age 26 for
this group was thus estimated at 2·08; and the ratio of peak earnings to weighted average earnings at 1·38. As in the example
previously cited, this allocation of observed earnings by age
groups probably tends to overstate the rate of return to education, as the 'true' allocation is likely to be steeper than the one
assumed.

(b) Secondary students were assumed to earn, while in school,
average incomes equal to one-third of the estimated incomes of
primary school graduates of the same age working full time.
Likewise, university students were assumed to earn, while in
school, average incomes equal to one-third of the estimated
incomes of secondary school graduates of the same age working
full time. Thus an ample allowance was made for the possibility of part-time earnings of students.

(c) It was assumed that mortality and ill health caused the withdrawal from the labor force, annually, of a certain fraction of workers at ages from 40 onward. This fraction averaged approximately 2 percent for primary school graduates and approximately 1 per cent for university graduates. The result of this assumption is that only some 60 percent of primary school graduates are taken to be still working at age 65, while some 80 percent of university graduates are taken to be in the labor force at age 65. I believe that this assumption allows for a substantial difference in the health and mortality experience of the two groups.

(d) It was assumed that 6 percent of the primary school graduates in each age bracket were unemployed, while there was no unemployment among the university graduates. The 6 percent figure should really be interpreted as the assumed differential between the unemployment rates of the two groups. The fact that 0 per cent unemployment was assumed for the university group operates once again to bias the results in favor of a high estimated rate of return to education at the secondary and university level; for the estimated net gain to secondary and higher education would be lower if we had assumed, say, 6 percent unemployment of university graduates and 12 percent unemployment of primary graduates, rather than the 0 and 6 percent figures used.

In calculating the implied rate of return to investment in sixteen years as against eight years of education, the age-income profiles were thus modified to take account of reduced labor force participation, mortality, and unemployment, in all cases using assumptions that would tend to overestimate the rate of return. Moreover, ample provisions were made for possible part-time earnings of secondary and university students; and the income that persons with sixteen years of education were assumed to earn was overstated by imputing to this group the average income observed in the Hyderabad sample for a group with seventeen, or possibly even more, average years of education. The net result of this exercise was an estimated rate of return to university education (sixteen years) compared with primary education (eight years), that was just barely 16 percent.

III. INTERPRETATION OF THE RESULTS AND
SOME QUALIFICATIONS

With all adjustments (including an imputation of 20 percent of the wage bill to capital), the marginal productivity of physical capital equipment was estimated to be between 17·2 percent and 26·1 percent. These figures should be compared with our original estimates of 10–12 percent for investment in secondary education, of 16–17 percent for higher education, of 14–15 percent for ten years of secondary and higher education taken together, and with our more refined estimate of 16 percent for eight years of secondary and higher education. When it is recognized that the estimates for physical capital were 'designed' to be underestimates, while those for investment in education were 'designed' to be overestimates, a very strong presumption is created that the economic productivity of investment in physical capital exceeds the economic productivity of investment in education in India. This presumption is reinforced by the fact that differences in natural abilities certainly explain part of the extra earnings of more highly educated groups. That is to say, the forgone earnings of those in secondary school are likely to be higher than the average earnings of those who stop upon completion of primary school, and the forgone earnings of college and university students are likely to be higher than the average earnings of secondary school completers of the same age, purely because of differences in natural ability. If we could take this into account, we would come out with still lower estimates of the economic rate of return to investment in education.

There remain some questions, however, concerning the range of applicability of the results obtained, and it is to questions of this nature that we turn in this section. We consider first the representativeness of the Hyderabad sample. We have really measured the rate of return to investment in education as reflected in that sample; it is by no means clear that this rate of return would apply to all India. In Table 8.13 certain key features of the distribution of persons by monthly per capita expenditure classes are compared for Andhra Pradesh (the state in which Hyderabad is situated) and India as a whole.

On the whole, I would interpret the figures in Table 8.13 as showing Andhra Pradesh to be reasonably representative of all

TABLE 8.13

Distribution of Persons by Monthly Per Capita Expenditure Classes

(Rupees per month)

	Urban		Rural	
	Andhra Pradesh	All India	Andhra Pradesh	All India
First quartile	13·7	13·3	9·5	10·3
Median	21·9	20·1	13·3	15·1
Third quartile	26·8	31·2	21·0	22·4
Top decile	41·4	49·7	29·6	32·6

Source: *National Sample Survey, No. 80* (Thirteenth Round, Sept. 1957–May 1958), pp. 6–7, 117–18.

India. The median expenditure per capita is higher in urban areas in Andhra Pradesh, but lower in rural areas. The distribution is less skewed for Andhra than for all India, but that is to be expected, since Andhra does not contain any of India's great metropolitan centers. Moreover, the sample did not cover Andhra Pradesh as a whole, but only the Hyderabad area; and the distribution of male earnings in the Hyderabad sample (see Table 8.3) is considerably more skewed than the distribution of per capita expenditures for all urban areas in India, the top decile in the Hyderabad sample being about twice the third quartile, and the third quartile about twice the median. The distribution of male earnings in the Hyderabad sample is also more skewed than the distribution of households by per household expenditure in all India. For this latter distribution, the third quartile is about two-thirds higher than the median, and the top decile about six-sevenths higher than the third quartile.[7] It is likely that, the greater the skewness in the distribution of earnings in the sample, the higher will be the estimated rate of return to investment in education. Hence on this criterion we have no good grounds for suspecting that the sample has led us to underestimate the rate of return to investment in education in India as a whole.

I now inquire into the representativeness of the sample of 1,001 companies represented in the Reserve Bank survey. As already indicated, these companies constitute a large part of 'modern' industry in India. Their total value amounted to about 4 percent of the national income, while all mines and factory establishments taken together accounted for less than 10 percent of the national income during the period surveyed. Moreover, they accounted for more than two-thirds of all gross capital formation in the corporate sector in India (see Table 8.14).

TABLE 8.14

Gross Capital Formation in India, 1956–59

(Crores of current rupees)

Year	1,001 companies, RBI survey[a]	Total corporate sector[b]
1956	238	330
1957	236	327
1958	159	220
1959	130	188

[a] 'Estimated Outlay on Physical Assets', as derived in Section I of this paper, under Method IV.
[b] Government of India, Central Statistical Organization, *Estimates of Gross Capital Formation in India for 1948–49 to 1960–61* (Delhi, 1962), p. 43.

The 1,001 companies clearly do reflect the corporate sector rather well, but this does not mean that they are representative of all investment in physical capital. Total physical capital formation in India has been about ten times corporate capital formation in recent years, the remainder being accounted for by the household sector and the public sector. I believe, however, that the rate of marginal productivity of capital in the corporate sector is something of legitimate interest in its own right, and also one of the elements needed to determine a wise allocation of the community's investible resources.

Some readers may be disturbed by the fact that I included capital's share of the excise duties paid by the 1,001 companies in my measure of the marginal product of capital, while I made no similar allowance in estimating the rate of return to investment in education. The main reason behind this procedure is that so long as primary school graduates, secondary school graduates, and university graduates are similarly distributed among industries, and adjustment for excise taxes would have no effect on our calculations of the rate of return to investment in education, since that adjustment would be proportional across the board. A subsidiary reason is that excise taxes are disproportionately concentrated in the corporate sector, the 1,001 companies alone paying between 40 and 50 percent of all excise duties. Under these circumstances it is quite important to recognize excise taxes explicitly when treating the 1,001 companies; while in the case of labor, where only disproportionalities of distribution would affect our calculations, the results would be only slightly affected.

Probably the most serious defect of the measures of the rate of marginal productivity of capital presented in Section I is their failure to take account of some important divergences between actual and 'shadow' prices. Such a divergence was taken into account in the case of wages, but there are, in addition, a number of other areas in which actual prices do not reflect the true economic scarcity of the items in question. Without a doubt the most important of these cases is foreign exchange, of which the supply and demand are brought into balance only through a very rigid system of licensing, allocation, import prohibitions, etc. But it is clear also that railway transport and electricity are sold by public enterprises at prices below their current scarcity values, and also below the levels that would be dictated by the cost of expanding these services.

It is difficult to assess the net effect of these factors on the profitability of the 1,001 companies. Looking at the cost side, it would appear at first glance that the maintenance of low prices for foreign exchange, electricity, and rail transport would add to the profitability of the corporate sector as a whole. But this effect is at least partly offset by the fact that none of the above-named items is freely available at the prevailing low price. Company profits are not helped when the firms have to generate their own high-cost electricity to supplement an inadequate allocation, or when production lines are closed down while waiting for an allocation of foreign exchange for essential raw materials; or when very high-cost, domestically produced substitutes are used in place of imported goods.

Looking at the receipt side, there can be no doubt that a 'realistic' price of foreign exchange would greatly enhance the profitability of the Indian corporate sector as a whole, even though not all the products of the corporate sector would experience price increases. I have no way of guessing whether an appropriate allowance for the effects of existing distortions in the fields of foreign exchange, electricity, and rail transport on costs and receipts, taken together, would result in an increase or a decrease in our estimates of the rate of marginal productivity of capital. As I know of no way to deal with this problem empirically, with the data that are available, I must leave the question open, as something that might lead to a significant revision of the estimates of Section I.

There are other considerations that may cast some doubt on the validity of the conclusions suggested by the estimates of the rate of return to physical capital. First, the 1,001 companies in the Reserve Bank of India survey probably include some with significant monopoly power. Even though it is quite proper to include monopoly profits in the estimated social return to a given investment, it is likely that there would be a lower incidence of potential monopoly profits on new investments to be made than on the total of existing investments in the companies surveyed. For this reason, and possibly for others as well, the marginal social rate of return to capital (that is, the rate to be expected on new investments) may be lower than the average rate of return estimated in this chapter. Second, the period for which data were available was a period of rising price levels. We were able to correct for this, in a sense, by the deflation procedure used in adjustments C and D, but even this procedure does not correct for the tendency for real profits to be higher than normal in inflationary periods. Finally, there is the fact that the 1,001 companies are, in general, large and successful firms, whose profitability is likely to be greater than that for the average of all firms in the modern industrial sector of the Indian economy.

These considerations, which were raised by Mincer in his commentary on my original paper, make somewhat uncertain my assertion that the methodology used operates to understate the social rate of return to capital invested in modern industry in India. I personally believe that they are not sufficiently weighty to counterbalance the many downward biases that were consciously introduced into the estimative procedure. However, I cannot expect that all readers will agree with this judgment.

I do not want to conclude on the note that investment in

physical capital appears, from the evidence, to be economically more beneficial to India than investment in education. This is indeed what is suggested by the data that I have examined, but I prefer to regard this study as suggesting future research rather than as indicating particular alterations of existing investment patterns. We have dealt here with very broad aggregates, within each of which there is almost certain to be a great deal of diversity. For individual industries, the Reserve Bank survey data themselves show crude rates of return (Method 1 A) ranging from less than 10 percent to more than 25 percent. I have no doubt that an analysis of the rate of return to different types of education (broken down by subject matter, level, type of school, and so forth) would also produce a wide variety of results. It seems to me that a number of detailed surveys, yielding age-income profiles of various types and levels of education, would surely be worth their cost. Their results would be exceedingly useful in the process of educational planning in India, even though it is recognized that the goals and rewards of education are not exclusively economic.

In a similar vein, I would suggest follow-up studies of the graduates of different types of institutions in the same general field. Educational techniques surely differ from institution to institution, and with careful follow-up studies it should be possible to discover some determinants of later economic success about which educators can do something. I suspect that it will turn out that many actions can be taken by educators to raise the economic productivity of their students without in any way detracting from the cultural and other advantages of the educational process. The key, I think, is to recognize that education *is* an investment. When corporations contemplate particular projects, they do the best they can to assess their prospective profitability. Economic considerations influence not only the general nature of investments but also the detailed ways in which they are carried out. I am sure that educators do take economic considerations into account, in a vague way, in planning their programs. But I am also sure that a really serious effort to understand the economic consequences of different detailed types and classes of investment in education would help greatly to improve the contribution that education can make to economic progress.

APPENDIX

PROCEDURES USED IN MEASURING THE RATE OF RE-
TURN TO PHYSICAL CAPITAL INVESTED IN 1,001 COM-
PANIES IN INDIA

The income series, with adjustments

The concept of income from capital. As a first approximation, I
take the net income from capital of the 1,001 firms to be:

> Profits before tax
> + Interest paid
> + Managing agents' remuneration

Profits are taken before tax because the economic productivity
of capital includes that part of the proceeds which goes to the
government as well as that which is retained by the private
owners of the capital instruments. Interest is included because
it represents a prior claim on the earnings of capital, even
though for accounting purposes it is treated as an expense. I
follow common Indian practice in counting managing agents'
remuneration as part of the economic return to capital, since
this remuneration is largely in the nature of a participation in
the profits of the company.

The basic series. Net income, as I have defined it above for
the purpose of this study, is obtained as follows from the
Reserve Bank Survey data.

	1955	1956	1957	1958	1959
	(Crores of rupees)[a]				
Profits before tax	117·7	130·9	107·8	120·9	161·5
Managing agents' remuneration[b]	14·7	11·9	8·4	8·9	11·0
Interest	12·9	16·0	23·4	27·5	29·7
Net income (Y_a)	145·3	158·8	139·6	157·3	202·2

[a] A crore of rupees is worth $2,100,000 at the present exchange rate.

[b] Managing agents' remuneration arises out of a relationship by which the
shareholders of Company A arrange for Company B to manage Company A for
them. For tax purposes in India, the remuneration paid by Company A for Company B is deductible in obtaining the taxable income of Company A, but is taxable as part of the income of Company B. Our procedure recognizes that this
income was generated by the operations of Company A.

Adjustment for earnings of financial assets

	1955	1956	1957	1958	1959
			(Crores of rupees)		
Receivables	210·4	253·3	273·7	284·7	296·1
Investments	103·6	104·3	105·4	107·6	114·1
Other assets	22·4	23·4	20·5	20·3	19·9
Cash and bank balances	90·0	80·6	71·9	73·8	88·8
Total	436·4	461·6	471·5	486·4	518·9

Before computing the possible return to these financial assets, we deduct certain offsetting financial liabilities.

	1955	1956	1957	1958	1959
			(Crores of rupees)		
Trade dues, etc.	251·3	296·0	336·5	357·9	383·4
Miscellaneous noncurrent liabilities	13·8	15·8	16·4	17·7	18·2
Total	265·1	311·8	352·9	375·6	401·6

The reason for deducting these liabilities (principally trade dues) is that if we impute a return to receivables, etc., we must impute a corresponding cost to 'payables' of the same type.[8]

The 'net financial asset' position of the 1,001 companies is the differences between the two series just presented.

	1955	1956	1957	1958	1959
			(Crores of rupees)		
Net financial assets	171·3	149·8	118·6	110·8	117·3

In order not to overstate the amount of income to be attributed to physical assets, we impute a fairly high rate of return on net financial assets. This rate is taken to be 10 percent, which substantially exceeds the rates actually obtainable on the government and industrial securities that comprise the bulk of the 'investments' of the 1,001 companies and that are the financial assets that can most reasonably be considered 'earning assets'. We obtain net income adjusted for the earnings of financial assets by deducting these imputed earnings on net financial assets from the basic 'net income' series (Υ_a).

	1955	1956	1957	1958	1959
			(Crores of rupees)		
Net income (Υ_a)	145·3	158·8	139·6	157·3	202·2
Imputed income from net financial assets	17·1	15·0	11·9	11·1	11·7
Adjusted net income (Υ_b)	128·2	143·8	127·7	146·2	190·5

Adjustment for price level changes. To deflate the net income figures, I have chosen the index of wholesale prices of manufactured goods. This is the index that appears to correspond most closely to the output composition of the 1,001 firms in the survey. To deflate the earnings of 1956, I have taken the 1956–1957 index, since, in point of fact, the earnings carried in the survey as belonging to 1956 actually correspond to company financial years ending anywhere between June 1956 and June 1957. The index is given below, adjusted to make 1955 = 100.

	1955	1956	1957	1958	1959
		(Index points)			
Price index of manufacturers	100	106	108	108	111
		(Crores of rupees)			
Adjusted net income (Y_b)	128·2	143·8	127·7	146·2	190·5
		(Crores of 1955 rupees)			
Deflated adjusted net income (Y_c)	128·2	135·5	118·3	135·4	171·6

Adjustment for excise taxes. The price that consumers pay for a product includes whatever excise taxes apply to that product or its components. In this sense, therefore, one can defend including excise taxes in the 'value added' by a process of manufacture or transformation. Naturally, such excise taxes which are included in the value added by any process should be those taxes which become applicable as a result of that process, not those which may have been paid at a much earlier stage (for example, on raw materials before they entered the process of manufacture). When excise taxes are included in measuring the productivity of a process of transformation or manufacture, the question arises as to how those taxes should be allocated among factors of production. There is no universally valid answer to this question; but a rule that is likely to be appropriate in most cases is to allocate the excise taxes between labor and capital in proportion to their contributions to value added net of excise tax. This method is appropriate when there is a fixed input-output relationship between inputs of materials and the output of the final product, and when there is at the same time some degree of substitutability between capital and labor in the process of elaborating the materials into the final product. The relevant calculations are presented below:

	1955	1956	1957	1958	1959
	(Crores of current rupees)				
Net income of capital (Y_a)	145·3	158·8	139·6	157·3	202·2
Salaries, wages, welfare expenses	250·0	280·6	300·5	315·1	342·0
Value added net of excise tax (V)	395·3	439·4	440·1	472·4	544·2
Ratio Y_a/V	·37	·36	·32	·32	·37
Excise taxes (Rs. crores)	67·2	84·4	120·4	149·2	159·1
Capital's share of excise taxes (Rs. crores)	24·9	30·4	38·5	49·2	58·9
Price index	100	106	108	108	111
	(Crores of 1955 rupees)				
Capital's share deflated	24·9	28·7	35·6	45·5	53·0
Net income, adjusted and deflated (Y_e)	128·2	135·5	118·3	135·4	171·6
Net income, adjusted, deflated, and including capital's share of excise tax (Y_d)	153·1	164·2	153·9	180·9	224·6

The series on gross income can be obtained by adding the income figures. The gross-income counterparts to the two first net-income series (Y_a and Y_b) are obtained by adding the 'depreciation provision' figures in current rupees to Y_a and Y_b. The gross-income counterparts to the last net-income series (Y_c and Y_d) are obtained by adding to these series the 'depreciation provision' expressed in 1955 rupees.

	1955	1956	1957	1958	1959
	(Crores of rupees)				
Depreciation provision (D_a)	42·6	46·8	52·8	56·8	65·4
$(G_a) = (Y_a + D_a)$	187·9	205·6	192·4	214·1	276·6
Adjusted gross income $(G_b = Y_b + D_a)$	170·8	190·6	180·5	203·0	255·9
	(Index points)				
Price index of manufactures	100	106	108	108	111
	(Crores of 1955 rupees)				
Deflated depreciation provision (D_c)	42·6	44·2	48·9	52·6	58·9
Deflated, adjusted gross income $(G_c) = (Y_c + D_c)$	170·8	179·7	167·2	188·0	230·5
Gross income, adjusted, deflated, and including capital's share of excise tax $(G_d) = (Y_d + D_c)$	195·7	208·4	202·8	233·5	283·5

Estimates of capital stock and of the rate of return

The basis and derivation of the data used for capital stock are presented below, in conjunction with the calculations of estimated rates of return.

Method I: Using ratio of net income to net fixed assets plus stocks and stores.[9] Under this method, we use either the value

(K_1) of net fixed assets plus stocks and stores as it appears on the combined balance sheet of the 1,001 firms (adjustments A and B); or this value (K_2) expressed in 1955 prices (adjustments C and D). There is no difficulty in obtaining the figures for the K_1 series. In obtaining K_2, the deflation of the figure for stocks and stores is not troublesome, but difficulties arise in the deflation of net fixed assets. The net fixed assets figure represents a cumulation of gross asset acquisitions, less an accumulated depreciation figure. A 'correct' procedure for deflating net assets would entail isolating each year's acquisition of gross assets (starting substantially earlier than 1955), deflating this figure by an appropriate price index, accumulating a fixed asset series expressed in constant prices, and applying in each year an appropriate rate of depreciation to the 'real' fixed assets at the beginning of that year.

The difficulties of applying this procedure are (*a*) the gross annual acquisitions of assets in the years prior to 1955 cannot be calculated from the data of the Reserve Bank survey, and (*b*) available price indices do not appear to be very suitable for the purpose of deflating asset acquisitions. I have chosen not to deflate the net fixed asset figures shown on the combined balance sheet of the 1,001 companies. My defense for this choice is that it almost certainly leads to an overstatement of the 'real' capital stock and hence to an understatement of the rate of return.

To elaborate on the reasons why this procedure overstates the value of fixed assets in 1955 prices, let me consider first the situation in 1959, the end of the period being considered. The gross acquisitions of fixed assets between 1955 and 1959 exceeded the total of net fixed assets held in 1955; as virtually all prices in India were rising somewhat in the 1955–59 period, this large component of 1959 fixed assets should be deflated by price indices greater than 100 in order to convert it to 1955 prices. Consider now the fixed assets in existence in 1955. It is likely that more than half of these represent assets acquired between 1950 and 1955; and for these it is likely that the book values as of 1955 overstate value in 1955 prices. This is so because the principal price indices that come closest to being relevant for the deflation of expenditures on fixed capital goods were falling during the 1950–55 period. Thus we have:

	1950	1951	1952	1953	1954	1955
Import prices	97	199	130	129	114	116
Wholesale prices (general)	110	120	102	104	100	92
Manufactures	100	119	104	99	100	99
Intermediate products	106	125	104	98	98	98
Raw materials	124	147	106	107	104	97

Only for assets that were more (and perhaps substantially more) than five years old in 1955 can one presume that acquisition prices were less than 1955 prices; such assets would be represented by no more than half of the book value of fixed assets at the beginning of the period surveyed, and by no more than 20 per cent or so of the book value of fixed assets at the end of this period. With the remaining 50–80 percent of assets having acquisition prices almost certainly in excess of 1955 prices, there seems little doubt that book values overstate the values that would be produced by an appropriate deflation procedure.

In the derivation of the K_2 series, the stocks and stores figures are deflated by the simple average of the price index for manufactured goods (which includes intermediate products) and the price index of industrial raw materials. The details of the computation are given below:

	1955	1956	1957	1958	1959
		(Crores of rupees)			
Stocks and stores	421·1	512·4	564·7	569·8	585·2
		(Index points)			
Deflating index	100	110·4	111·6	111·3	117·0
		(Crores of 1955 rupees)			
Stocks and stores, deflated	421·1	464·1	506·0	512·0	500·2
Net fixed assets	534·5	634·7	765·8	862·5	911·6
Net assets deflated (K_2)	955·6	1098·8	1271·8	1374·5	1411·8
		(Crores of rupees)			
Net assets undeflated (K_1)	955·6	1147·1	1330·4	1432·2	1496·8

We can now proceed to derive the estimated rates of return to capital, based on Method I, with the four successive adjustments indicated earlier.

RATES OF RETURN ON CAPITAL (METHOD I)

	1955	1956	1957	1958	1959	Average
I A (Y_a/K_1)	15·2	13·8	10·5	11·0	13·5	12·8
I B (Y_b/K_1)	13·4	12·5	9·6	10·2	12·7	11·7
I C (Y_c/K_2)	13·4	12·3	9·3	9·9	12·1	11·4
I D (Y_d/K_2)	16·0	14·9	12·1	13·2	15·9	14·4

Method II: Using ratio of net income to 'market value of the enterprise'. The market value of the enterprise—the total market value of its shares plus its borrowings—is taken in this method as an alternative measure of net fixed assets plus stocks and stores. This measure has the advantage of tending to reflect price level changes more or less automatically. Also, it is not likely to be as strongly influenced by arbitrary accounting procedures as the 'book values' of assets. While the 'market' is not perfectly informed about the procedures adopted and decisions taken within a company, it is likely to be aware of situations in which the true economic value of a company's assets differs substantially from their book value, and to price the shares of the enterprise somewhat closer to 'true' value than to book value. While probably being superior to book value as far as price level errors or accounting procedure errors are concerned, the market value of the enterprise has its own flaws and peculiarities. It is sensitive to waves of optimism and pessimism in the market for shares; one can hardly hold that all movements in share prices neatly reflect variations in the true economic value of a company's assets. Second, some of the value that the market places on a company may stem from its management and know-how rather than simply its assets. This second type of error is more likely to lead to an overstatement than to an understatement of the true economic value of a company's assets; the first (expectational) type of error can easily work in either direction.

To measure the market value of the shares of the 1,001 companies in the Reserve Bank survey, we start with the tax-free yields on industrial securities. These are measured by the Reserve Bank of India on the basis of a different sample of companies, but one broadly similar in industrial coverage to the 1,001-companies survey. For the financial year 1959–60, the tax-free yield of preference shares was 5·44 percent, and that of variable dividend industrial securities was 5·27 percent. These tax-free yields are obtained after deducting a 30 percent income tax-*cum*-surcharge from the dividends paid by the respective companies. The ratios of dividends to stock prices without deducation for personal income tax were accordingly 7·77 and 7·53 percent, for preference and regular shares respectively. Actual dividends paid in 1959 by the 1,001 companies in the

Reserve Bank survey were 64·06 crores of rupees. We do not have a breakdown as to what fraction of this total was paid on preference and what fraction was paid on ordinary shares, but we roughly estimate that 14 per cent (or 8·97 crores of rupees) was paid on preference shares and 86 percent (or 55·09 crores of rupees) was paid on ordinary shares.[10] Dividing these amounts by the respective rates of return, we estimate the total market value of the shares (ordinary and preference) of the 1,001 companies to have been 847 crores of rupees in 1959. To this we add borrowing of 563 crores of rupees. These are taken at the values shown on the combined balance sheet.[11] Thus the 'Market value of the enterprise' is estimated to have been 1,410 crores of rupees in 1959 for the 1,001 companies. Since these companies had a 117·3 crores of rupees excess of financial assets over short-term financial liabilities in this year, we reduce the 1,410 crores of rupees figure by this amount, obtaining an estimate of 1,292·7 crores of rupees as the value which the market placed on the firms' physical assets in 1959. This is the value (K_2) of capital stock, used in calculating rates of return under Method II.

Estimated rates of return using K_2 are presented below:

$$\text{II A } (Y_a/K_3) \ldots \ldots 15\text{·}5 \text{ percent}$$
$$\text{II B } (Y_b/K_3) \ldots \ldots 14\text{·}7 \text{ percent}$$

Both these estimates are implicitly corrected for price level movements, as they refer to the ratio of 1959 income to the market value of the companies' assets in 1959. There is thus no need for an adjustment corresponding to I C above. In making an adjustment for excise taxes, we simply add capital's share of these tax payments in 1959 (58·9 crores of rupees) to the adjusted net income Y_b (190·5 crores of rupees) for 1959, without attempting to convert the result to 1955 prices. In this way we estimate II D $249\text{·}4/K_3 = 19\text{·}3$ percent.

Method III: Using the ratio of gross income to gross fixed assets plus stocks and stores as a device for estimating the rate of net return on net assets. It is important to realize that the ratio of gross income to gross assets is not being measured for its own sake, but as a device to enable us to say something about the economically much more meaningful ratio of net income to net assets. The method here presented is important because it provides a way of correcting for possible errors and biases in the depreciation accounting procedures used. Let me begin with two identities:

Gross income = True net income + true depreciation allowance

Gross assets = True net assets + true accumulated depreciation

By 'true depreciation allowance' I mean that (unknown) amount which truly reflects the fall in economic value of existing assets during an accounting year. I mean by 'true accumulated depreciation' that amount which would appear on the books of the companies if 'true depreciation allowances' had been made in past years. Now, using the obvious initials for notation, we have:

$$TNI = GI - TDA$$

$$TNI = \frac{GI}{GA} [TNA + TAD] - TDA$$

$$\frac{TNI}{TNA} = \frac{GI}{GA} + \left[\frac{GI}{GA} \cdot \frac{TAD}{TNA} - \frac{TDA}{TNA} \right]$$

$$\frac{TNI}{TNA} = \frac{GI}{GA} + \frac{TAD}{TNA} \left[\frac{GI}{GA} - \frac{TDA}{TAD} \right]$$

Thus the ratio of true net income to the true net assets can be expressed as the ratio of gross income to gross assets, plus an adjustment factor. The sign of this adjustment factor will be determined by whether the ratio of gross income to gross assets is greater or less than the ratio of true depreciation allowance to true accumulated depreciation.

Now we do not know the ratio of true depreciation allowance to true accumulated depreciation, but—and this is the 'trick' of the method here discussed—the ratio of book depreciation allowance to book accumulated depreciation is likely to be a relatively good estimate of the 'true' ratio. If a company's depreciation procedures always charge an allowance which is 20 percent too great, then book accumulated depreciation will also tend to exceed true accumulated depreciation by something like 20 percent.

We may now turn to the actual procedure of estimating the

ratio of true net income to true net assets under Method III. The ratio of gross income to gross assets is taken as the first approximation. Then, taking the book ratio of annual to accumulated depreciation as an estimate of the true ratio, we inquire whether this first approximation should be adjusted upward or downward. If the indicated adjustment is upward we do *not* make it, once again following the principle of biasing our estimates downward. Where the indicated adjustment is downward, however, we *do* make it, and we use a procedure likely to exaggerate the magnitude of the required adjustment. The procedure tends to exaggerate the downward adjustment because the ratio of book accumulated depreciation to book net assets is almost certain to be greater than the corresponding 'true' ratio. Accepting that company taxes create a clear incentive toward overdepreciation, we presume that book accumulated depreciation will be larger than the true figure. This in turn implies that book net assets will be smaller than the true figure, their values having been written down at an excessive rate. So our use of the book ratio of accumulated depreciation to net assets, in cases where a downward adjustment is necessary, operates to overstate the magnitude of the adjustment and to underestimate the true ratio of net income to net assets.

Table 8.15 illustrates the calculations under Method III. To obtain estimates III B, the same procedure is followed, but

TABLE 8.15

Line		1955	1956	1957	1958	1959
(1)	Income gross of depreciation (G_a)	187·9	205·6	192·4	214·1	267·4
(2)	Gross fixed assets plus stocks and stores (W_1)	1360	1587	1817	1970	2091
(3)	Ratio (G_a/W_1)	13·8	12·9	10·6	10·8	12·7
(4)	Annual depreciation allowance (D_1)	42·6	46·8	52·8	56·8	65·4
(5)	Accumulated depreciation (F_1)	404·4	441·1	487·2	538·2	593·8
(6)	Ratio (D_1/F_1)	10·5	10·6	10·8	10·4	11·0
(7)	Difference [(3) – (6)]	3·3	2·3	– 0·2	0·4	1·7
(8)	Accumulated depreciation/net fixed assets plus stocks and stores (F_1/K_1)	——	——	·37	——	——
(9)	Adjustment [(7) × (8), if (7) is negative]	——	——	– 0·1	——	——
(10)	Estimated net rate of return to capital [(3) + (9)] III A	13·8	12·9	10·5	10·8	12·7

TABLE 8.16

Line		1955	1956	1957	1958	1959
(1)	Ratio of gross income to gross fixed assets plus stocks and stores (G_b/W_1)	12·6	12·0	9·9	10·3	12·2
(2)	Ratio of annual depreciation allowance to accumulated depreciation (D_1/F_1)	10·5	10·6	10·8	10·4	11·0
(3)	Difference $[(1) - (2)]$	2·1	1·4	−0·9	−0·1	1·2
(4)	Accumulated depreciation/net fixed assets plus stocks and stores (F_1/K_1)	———	———	·37	·38	———
(5)	Adjustment $[(4) \times (3)$, if (3) is negative]	———	———	−·3	−·00	———
(6)	Estimated net rate of return to capital $[(1) + (5)]$ III B	12·6	12·0	9·6	10·3	12·2

income series C_b is used in place of C_a. Results are shown in Table 8.16.

To obtain estimates III C and III D we require a series on gross fixed assets plus stocks and stores, expressed in 1955 prices. Here, for similar reasons, I adopt the same procedure used in deriving the K_2 series for 'net fixed assets plus stocks and stores'. That is, the figures for stocks and stores are deflated by an index covering manufactured products and industrial raw materials, while the book figures on gross fixed assets are left undeflated, on the ground that this procedure is likely if anything to over-state their value in 1955 prices. Table 8.17 presents the derivation of estimates III C.

When capital's share of excise tax payments is included in gross income (series G_d) we obtain the estimates (III D), given in line 1 of Table 8.18. Since line 1 exceeds line 2 for every year, our procedure calls for no adjustment to the figures in line 1.

Readers will note that in obtaining estimates III C and III D, I used the same figure for the ratio of annual depreciation allowance to accumulated depreciation as was used previously to obtain estimates III A and III B. I made no attempt to deflate the annual and accumulated depreciation figures because (a) the appropriate deflating indexes would be complicated weighted averages of past price levels, for which neither good component indexes nor adequate data on weights were

TABLE 8.17

Line		1955	1956	1957	1958	1959
(1)	Gross income, adjusted and deflated (G_c)	170·8	179·7	167·2	188·0	230·5
(2)	Gross fixed assets plus stocks and stores, deflated (W_2)	1360	1540	1759	1913	2006
(3)	Ratio (G_c/W_2)	12·6	12·8	9·5	9·8	11·5
(4)	Rate of annual depreciation allowance to accumulated depreciation (D_1/F_1)	10·5	10·6	10·8	10·4	11·0
(5)	Difference $[(3) - (4)]$	2·1	2·2	− 1·3	− 0·6	0·5
(6)	Accumulated depreciation/net fixed assets plus stocks and stores	——	——	·37	·38	——
(7)	Adjustment $[(6) \times (5),$ if (5) is negative]	——	——	− 0·5	− 0·2	——
(8)	Estimated net rate of return to capital $[(3) + (7)]$ III C	12·6	12·8	9·0	9·6	11·5

TABLE 8.18

Line		1955	1956	1957	1958	1959
(1)	Ratio of gross income, including capital's share of excise tax to gross fixed assets plus stocks and stores (G_d/W_2) III D	14·4	13·5	11·5	12·2	14·1
(2)	Ratio of annual depreciation allowance to accumulated depreciation (D_1/F_1)	10·5	10·6	10·8	10·4	11·0

available, and (*b*) the procedure already adopted of carrying gross fixed assets and net fixed assets at their book value in the deflated capital stock indices W_2 and K_2, seemed to dictate a corresponding treatment of the depreciation associated with these assets.

The following tabulation summarizes the results obtained using Method III, giving averages of the five annual estimates obtained under each successive adjustment.

Estimates of Ratio of Net Income to Net Assets

III A	12·1 percent	III C	11·1 percent
III B	11·3 percent	III D	13·1 percent

Method IV: Using cash flows plus 1955–59 changes in net fixed assets plus stocks and stores to obtain an implicit rate of return. Modern techniques of project analysis do not place the same weight of reliance on the depreciation concept, nor on attempts to measure depreciation, as standard accounting procedure does. For determining the worthwhileness of a particular project, it suffices to know the expected time path of outlays and receipts. In the years of a project's gestation, outlays exceed receipts; later on receipts exceed outlays for most of a project's life. If one knows the time pattern of net outlays and/or net receipts, one need not inquire into whether outlays are on current or on capital account, nor what is the appropriate pattern of depreciation. The worth of the project can be determined on the basis of the net-outlays–net-receipts pattern alone. If one knows the rate of return required for acceptance of the project, one simply accumulates and discounts the time pattern of outlays and receipts at this rate to see if it has a positive net present value at a given point in time. If so, the project is worth while undertaking. If one does not know the rate of return to be used as a criterion, one may calculate the project's internal rate of return—the rate at which its outlay-receipt pattern has zero present value—and utilize this rate for comparison with those of alternative investments.

While the 'internal rate of return' is used mainly for individual projects, it may also be computed for a going concern as a whole, or even for large aggregates of companies. In these cases one must recognize that the entity of which the internal rate of return is being measured does not have a definite expected life span; one must measure the internal rate for some arbitrary period, counting as an 'outlay' the value of assets carried into this period and counting as a 'receipt' the value of assets carried out of this period. This is precisely what Methods IV and V attempt to do for the 1,001 companies in the Reserve Bank survey.

We take as 'receipts' for estimate IV A the value of net fixed assets plus stocks and stores (K_1) at the end of 1959, and the gross income G_a for 1956, 1957, 1958, 1959. We take as 'outlays' the value of K_1 at the end of 1955, and the amount spent on acquisition of physical assets during 1956, 1957, 1958 and 1959. These last amounts are estimated to a first approximation by the annual increments in book value of gross fixed assets plus stocks and stores. But actual cash outlays on physical assets are likely to exceed the change in gross book value of such assets, because of the retirement of some fixed assets in each year. If gross value of fixed assets goes up in a given year by 1,000 rupees and assets are retired in that year which were carried on the banks at 200 rupees, actual expenditure on new fixed assets would be 1,200, not 1,000 rupees.

We can estimate the amount of retirements of assets in any one year with considerable accuracy by looking at the depreciation accounts of a company. Suppose in a given year depreciation allowance of 500 rupees was made on the books, but the accumulated depreciation account rose by only 400 rupees. This reveals that 100 rupees of accumulated depreciation 'disappeared' during the year—that is, was written off, reflecting retirement of assets. Since assets are generally fully depreciated before they are retired, we can estimate that expenditure on new assets exceeded the growth in the book value of gross assets by the same amount (here 100 rupees) by which depreciation allowances exceeded the change in accumulated depreciation during the year. Results for the 1,001 companies are shown in Table 8.19.

TABLE 8.19

		1956	1957	1958	1959
			(*Crores of rupees*)		
(1)	Depreciation allowance	46·8	52·8	56·8	65·4
(2)	Increase in accumulated depreciation	36·7	46·1	51·0	55·6
(3)	Difference [(1) – (2)]	10·1	6·7	5·8	9·8
(4)	Increase in gross fixed assets plus stocks and stores	228·2	229·1	152·8	120·2
(5)	Estimated outlay on physical assets	238·3	236·1	158·6	130·0
(6)	Gross income (G_a)	205·6	192·4	214·4	267·6
(7)	Net cash inflow on account of physical assets [(6) – (5)]	– 32·7	– 43·7	55·5	137·6

In computing the implicit rate of return, one must be specific about the timing of the respective net inflows. I have arbitrarily 'dated' the capital stock at the beginning of the period at December 1955, all annual flows at June of the corresponding year, and the capital stock at the end of the period, December 1959.

To obtain the implicit rate of return, one must use an iterative procedure, trying out alternative rates of return until one is sufficiently close to a rate which yields a present value of inflows and outflows equal to zero. I have not attempted to carry this iteration process to extremes of accuracy; I have instead been content to stop with a rate of return that yielded a relatively small positive present value. As the rate yielding zero present value is higher than rates yielding small positive present values, the procedure adopted again introduces a slight downward bias into my estimates.

The rate of return estimated under Method IV A is 13·4 percent. I have accumulated net inflows at this rate in Table 8.20, and the resulting present value (as of December 1959) is 13·5 crores of rupees.

TABLE 8.20

	(1)	(2)	(3)	(4)
				Accumulated net inflow carried into
		Accumulated		*next period*
	Net inflow	*net inflow*	*Accumulation*	*(Rs. crores)*
	(Rs. crores)	*(Rs. crores)*	*factor*	
Dec. 1955	− 955·6	− 955·6	1·067	− 1019·6
June 1956	− 32·7	− 1052·3	1·134	− 1193·3
June 1957	− 43·7	− 1237·0	1·134	− 1402·8
June 1958	55·5	− 1347·3	1·124	− 1527·8
June 1959	137·6	− 1390·2	1·067	− 1483·3
Dec. 1959	1496·8	13·5		

To obtain estimate IV B, we sunstitute G_b for G_a as the gross income figure. The estimated outlay on physical assets remains the same as before. The estimated rate in this case is 12·4 percent; it yields a net present value of only 6·5 crores of rupees at the end of the period. (See Table 8.21.)

We now turn to estimating the implicit rate of return by Methods IV C and IV D. Here I have adopted a different procedure for obtaining the deflated value of the capital stock than was used under Method I C and I D. The procedure

TABLE 8.21

	(1) Net inflow (Rs. crores)	(2) Accumulated net inflow (Rs. crores)	(3) Accumulation factor	(4) Accumulated net inflow carried into next period (Rs. crores)
Dec. 1955	− 955·6	− 955·6	1·062	− 1014·8
June 1956	− 47·7	− 1062·5	1·124	− 1194·3
June 1957	− 55·6	− 1249·9	1·124	− 1404·9
June 1958	44·4	− 1360·5	1·124	− 1529·2
June 1959	125·9	− 1403·3	1·062	− 1490·3
Dec. 1959	1496·8	6·5		

adopted in measuring K_2 was designed to overstate the value
of capital goods in 1955 prices. Since K_2 appeared in the denominator of the expression for the rate of return, this meant
biasing our estimate of the rate of return downward. In the
implicit-rate-of-return method, however, the higher the terminal capital stock, the higher the estimated rate of return.
Hence, in order to bias our estimate of the rate of return in a
downward direction, we must avoid using a method which
exaggerates the terminal year's capital stock. I have accordingly
chosen an alternative method of measuring capital stock in
1955 prices, which is designed, if anything, to understate the
1959 stock.

TABLE 8.22

Net fixed assets, 1955			Rs. 534·5 crores	
	(1) Expenditure on new fixed assets (change in gross fixed assets plus estimated retirements) (crores of rupees)	(2) Deflating index (price index of manufactures) (index points)	(3) Expenditure on fixed new assets in 1955 prices [(1) ÷ (2)] (crores of 1955 rupees)	(4) Depreciation allowance
1956	147·0	106	138·7	46·8
1957	183·9	108	170·3	52·8
1958	153·5	108	142·1	56·8
1959	114·5	111	103·1	65·4
			554·2 total	221·8 total

The relevant calculations appear in Table 8.22. In column 1 there appears for each year a figure giving the change in gross fixed assets, plus the amount of retirements estimated earlier. This reflects the expenditures made on acquiring new fixed assets in each year. These expenditures are then deflated so as to express them in 1955 prices. The price index of manufactures, which I used for deflation, is not ideal for deflating capital goods expenditures, but I have encountered no superior alternative index. The deflated gross additions to assets are then summed for the four years 1956 through 1959; they yield a total of 554·2 crores of rupees at 1955 prices. To obtain the 1959 level of net fixed assets in 1955 prices, we must add this figure to the 1955 level of net fixed assets, and subtract the depreciation which accrued during the intervening years. I did *not* deflate the depreciation allowances, partly because of the difficulties of obtaining an appropriate index, but mainly because the failure to deflate depreciation allowances leads to an understatement of the 1959 capital stock, and therefore to a downward bias in the estimated implicit rate to return. To the figure for deflated net fixed assets in 1959 (866·9 crores of rupees, at 1955 prices) we add the estimate (used earlier in the construction of the K_2 figure) for the 1959 level of deflated stocks and stores (500·2 crores of rupees at 1955 prices), obtaining 1367·1 crores of rupees as our estimate of the 1959 level of net fixed assets plus stocks and stores, expressed in 1955 prices.

Estimated net fixed assets, 1959
in 1955 prices = 534·5 + 554·2 − 221·8   = 866·9
Stocks and stores, 1959, in 1955 prices   = 500·2
Net fixed assets plus stocks and stores, 1959,
in 1955 prices   = 1367·1

In the case of the net inflows in each of the years 1956 through 1959, the deflation procedure is straightforward. The net inflows used in obtaining estimate IV B are simply deflated by the price index of manufactured goods for the corresponding year, as shown in Table 8.23.

The implicit rate of return based on Method IV C is 10 per cent. The computation verifying this result is given in Table 8.24.

TABLE 8.23

	(1) *Net inflow* *undeflated*	(2) *Deflating* *index*	(3) *Net inflows in* *1955 prices*
1956	− 47·7	106	− 45·0
1957	− 55·6	108	− 51·5
1958	44·4	108	41·1
1959	125·9	111	114·4

TABLE 8.24

	(1) *Net inflow* *(crores of* *rupees* *at 1955* *prices)*	(2) *Accumulated* *net inflow* *(crores of* *rupees* *at 1955* *prices)*	(3) *Accumulation* *factor*	(4) *Accumulated* *net inflow* *carried into* *next period* *(crores of* *rupees at* *1955 prices)*
Dec. 1955	− 955·6	− 955·6	1·05	− 1003·4
June 1956	− 45·0	− 1048·4	1·10	− 1153·2
June 1957	− 51·5	− 1240·7	1·10	− 1325·2
June 1958	41·1	− 1284·1	1·10	− 1412·5
June 1959	113·4	− 1299·1	1·05	− 1364·1
Dec. 1959	1367·1	3·0		

TABLE 8.25

	(1) *Net inflow* *including* *capital's share* *of excise taxes* *(crores of* *rupees at* *1955 prices)*	(2) *Accumulated* *net inflow* *(crores of* *rupees at* *1955 prices)*	(3) *Accumulation* *factor*	(4) *Accumulated* *net inflow* *carried into* *next period* *(crores of* *rupees at* *1955 prices)*
Dec. 1955	− 955·6	− 955·6	1·068	− 1020·6
June 1956	− 16·3	− 1036·9	1·136	− 1177·9
June 1957	− 15·9	− 1193·8	1·136	− 1356·2
June 1958	86·6	− 1269·6	1·136	− 1442·3
June 1959	166·4	− 1275·9	1·068	− 1362·7
Dec. 1959	1367·1	4·4		

In order to compute the implicit rate of return by Method
IV D, we make no alteration in the initial and final capital
stock figures used for the IV C estimate. The annual net inflows

for 1956 through 1959 do change, however. Here we must add capital's share of excise tax payments (expressed in 1955 prices) to the net inflows used in the IV C computation. These figures were given earlier in the derivation of the Y_d income series. The net inflow series, adjusted for capital's share of excise taxes, is presented in Table 6.25, together with the computations supporting the estimate of 13·6 percent as the implicit rate of return under Method IV D.

Method V: Using cash flows plus 1955–59 changes in gross fixed assets plus stocks and stores to obtain an implicit rate of return. Here we recognize that depreciation accounting procedures may have led to a bias in the computations under Method IV, through their influence on the figures used for net assets carried into and out of the period for which the computations were made. In order to allow for this possible bias, we here make the extreme assumption that true depreciation is zero—that is, that the gross book value of fixed assets plus stocks and stores reflects their true economic value. The gross value of fixed assets plus stocks and stores was 1,360 crores of rupees at the end of 1955, and Rs. 2,090·6 crores at the end of 1959. These are, respectively, the figures for initial 'outlay' and final 'receipt' under Methods V A and V B. The figures for the intervening annual inflows are the same as those used under Methods IV A and IV B, respectively. The implicit rate of return estimated under Method V A was 12·6 percent, and that obtained under Method V B was 11·4 percent.

Methods V C and V D use the deflated 1955 and 1959 values of gross fixed assets plus stocks and stores as the initial 'outlay' and final 'receipt' figures. The 1959 value here is obtained by a procedure similar to that used in obtaining the 1959 stock figure under Methods IV A and IV B, except that no deduction of depreciation allowance is made. We accordingly estimate the increment in gross fixed assets between 1955 and 1959 to be 554·2 crores of rupees (expressed in 1955 prices). Since the 1955 level of gross fixed assets was 938·9 crores of rupees, we estimate deflated gross fixed assets in 1959 to be 1493·1 crores. Adding deflated stocks and stores of 500·2 crores of rupees, we have a final 1959 figure of 1993·3 crores of rupees for gross fixed assets plus stocks and stores, expressed in prices of 1955. The inflow figures (apart from initial and terminal values) are the same under Methods V C and V D as they were under Methods IV C and IV D, respectively. The implicit rate of return is calculated to be 10·4 percent under Method V C, and 13·0 percent under Method V D.

Notes

[1] *Statistical Abstract, India, 1957–58*, Delhi, 1961, p. 570.

[2] Government of India, Cabinet Secretariat, *National Sample Survey*, No. 33 (Eleventh and Twelfth Rounds, August, 1956—August, 1957), Delhi, 1961, p. 61.

[3] *National Sample Survey*, No. 80 (Thirteenth Round, September, 1957—May, 1958, Delhi, 1961, p. 115.

[4] The data needed to test this assumption are fantastically hard to come by. What is needed are not only the earnings of narrowly defined classes of workers, classified by occupation, industry, size of establishment, and probably region, but also a determination of what classes of workers in industry Y, region II, firm size B are 'equivalent' in capcity to the workers in occupation 23, industry X, firm size A, and region I. The first efforts to do anything at all of this kind on a substantial scale are now just getting under way, and even these efforts are concerned only with the labor markets of a particular metropolitan area. I refer to a study of the Chicago labor market, directed by Professors Albert Rees and George P. Shultz of the University of Chicago, and to a study of the Santiago (Chile) labor market directed by Professor Sergio de Castro of the Catholic University of Chile (Santiago).

[5] Ministry of Information and Broadcasting, *India, 1961* Delhi, 1961, pp. 93, 94, 98.

[6] Gary S. Becker, 'Underinvestment in College Education?' *American Economic Review 50* (May, 1961), p. 348.

[7] *India, 1961*, p. 178.

[8] No account is taken of the asset category 'Advance of income tax'. since it is invariably exceeded by the corresponding liability category 'Taxation reserve'. I did not choose to consider the excess of taxation reserve over advance of income tax as a liability to be offset against the other financial assets because (a) it is not a liability on which interest should appropriately be imputed; and (b) the size of taxation reserves is in part a matter of arbitrary accounting decisions.

[9] 'Stocks and Stores' is the term used in the Reserve Bank survey to represent 'Inventories'.

[10] Preference share capital is 17·6 per cent of the total paid-up capital of the 1,001 companies, and 10·5 per cent of total paid-up capital plus free reserves and surpluses. The 14 per cent figure chosen lies midway between these two limits. I did not consider that a more refined weighting procedure was worthwhile attempting, in view of the near-equality of the dividend rates on the two classes of shares.

[11] Most of the borrowings of these companies were not marketed, and those which were marketed did not, in this period, sell at prices far from their par values.

CHAPTER NINE

MARGINAL COST PRICING AND SOCIAL INVESTMENT CRITERIA FOR ELECTRICITY UNDERTAKINGS

Marginal cost pricing—which for many years appeared to be something of a theoretician's toy, with little application to reality—has been the subject of revived interest in recent years, largely as the result of the efforts by Electricité de France to put the precept into practice. In this paper, we will review the basic principles governing the marginal cost pricing of electricity, and shall attempt to elaborate upon them at a few critical points.

The reason why marginal cost pricing remained removed from practical policy-making for so long is not hard to discern: basically, it appeared that for electricity, for transport, and for other relevant industries and activities, marginal cost pricing would entail a substantial financial loss to the enterprises attempting to apply it. What is the cost of carrying an extra passenger in an empty seat? What is the cost of additional electrical energy, when the system is not using its capacity to the fullest? In both cases the answer is a figure far lower than that which would cover 'full cost'; hence the dilemma between marginal cost pricing with deficits on the one hand and budgetary solvency with suboptimal pricing on the other. Probably the greatest contribution of the French economists in this area has been to show that this dilemma can often be more apparent

This paper was published as 'Criterios Para la Fijacion de Precios de Costo Marginal y Para Las Inversiones Sociales en las Empresas de Electricidad', Ministerio de Obras Publicas (Spain), *Boletin de Informacion*, No. 120 (1968). Reprinted as 'Custo marginal e investimento social-criterio aplicavel a energia eletrica,' *Revista de teoria e Pesquisa Economica* (São Paulo, Brazil), Vol. 1, No. 2 (1970), pp. 15–21.

than real, that solvency and optimality need not be inconsistent or contradictory goals.

I

The problem of electricity pricing can best be approached by assuming a hydroelectric system of the run-of-the-stream type. The output of such a system will be governed by nature and capacity alone—being dependent on the flow of the stream at volumes less than that associated with full-capacity use of the generating equipment, and on the capacity limitation for flows at higher volumes. It will, moreover, entail virtually zero operating costs; and indeed, a casual attempt to apply marginal cost pricing in this situation might well come up with the prescription to price all the electricity produced by the system at (virtually) zero. This prescription is only half correct, however; the proper one is to price electricity at (virtually) zero if the demand for the system's output is below the level determined by water flow or generating capacity and charge that price necessary to ration the available power among demanders whenever demand at a near-zero price would exceed this level. Since demand for electricity varies widely among the hours of the day, the likelihood emerges that during some hours electricity would be virtually a free good, but during others would command a relatively high price. Moreover, the price would presumably have to vary through the period when it was higher than marginal running cost, because it would have to serve the function of making quantity demanded the same for all such hours. (A run-of-the-stream operation will have significant seasonal variations in water flow, but not within-the-day variations.)

The excess of the price above marginal running costs is in the nature of an economic rent; it is attributable to the scarcity of water in those hours in which the system's output is limited by the water flow and attributable to the limitation of generating capacity for those periods in which capacity is the factor limiting output. This economic rent can be considered as a component of the short-run marginal cost of providing electricity to any given user since, given that the system is operating at capacity, the only way to satisfy an increase in the demand for electricity by one consumer is to take it away from somebody else, presumably via that small increase in price which would once again limit demand to capacity. And it is in this sense that the charging of a price higher than marginal running cost is consistent with the overall principle of marginal cost pricing.

II

The above analysis was based on the assumption of given capacity, but the end-product of that analysis—the economic rents generated because of capacity limitations—turn out to be the key element governing decisions about changes in capacity. For example, an addition to the generating capacity of an existing run-of-the-stream hydro system will add to electricity output only in those hours of the year when, in the absence of this addition, capacity would have been the limiting factor. The value of each kwh of output thus attributable to the new capacity will be the price corresponding to the hour in which it is generated; and the income flow assignable as a return on the investment in added capacity will be the excess of the price over marginal running cost—that is, precisely the economic rent referred to in the preceding paragraph. Depending on the size of the economic rent embodied in the price of electricity for the relevant hours of the year, investment in an expansion of capacity will prove to be warranted (for a given criterion rate of return on capital) or not.

In practice, it is obviously impossible to have electricity prices that vary with each hour in the year, so as to perform *fully* the function of rationing the available capacity among demanders at all times. However, it is possible to approximate this objective by setting different prices for 'peak' and 'off-peak' use of electricity. The 'peak' is determined in large measure by the demand characteristics of the system—being concentrated in the daytime hours on weekdays when industrial demand is dominant, and in the evening hours when residential demand is dominant. Let us assume that a system is made up of identical thermal plants, and facing a growing overall demand for electricity, with a peak of, say, 2500 hours per year, concentrated in the daytime on weekdays. If we are operating with a given capacity, our objective would be to charge marginal running cost for electricity in the off-peak hours and to set a surcharge for daytime use of electricity sufficiently high so as just to contain demand within the capacity limits of the system. But if we are operating in a dynamic context, being able to vary capacity via investment, we need not worry directly about the rationing of available capacity, but instead should set the peak-time surcharge so as to yield the required rate of return on new additions to capacity. Thus, if new capacity cost were $250 per kilowatt installed and the required rate of return were 7 percent, plus 3 percent for depreciation, we would want to get an economic rent of $25 per year per kilowatt installed, which could be achieved via a one cent per kwh surcharge on all kwh sold during the 2500 hours of peaktime operation in the year. If capacity were regularly expanded to meet anticipated demand under this rule, we would be (a) charging marginal running cost at off-peak times, and in this sense pricing at marginal cost; (b) charging marginal running cost plus an economic rent sufficient to hold demand down to system capacity at peak times; and (c) earning the required rate of return on invested capital.

The secular increase in the demand for electricity, together with the gradual reduction in the number of unexploited hydroelectric sites and the increasing tendency for electricity generating systems to be combined into large grids or networks, has produced a situation in which thermal costs are the dominant factor governing optimal pricing decisions. Let us suppose, in the example above, that marginal running costs in the thermal plants were one cent per kwh. Then the optimal prices would be two cents per kwh for the 2,500 'peak' hours, and $·01 per kwh for the 6,260 'off-peak' hours in the year. In terms of those prices, the worthwhileness of any given hydro project can be judged. A run-of-the-stream project costing $1,000 per kilowatt of installed capacity would have a potential maximum yield of $62.60 per year for 'off-peak' hours plus $50.00 per year for 'peak' hours, and an actual yield quite a bit less than that because of the periods when the rate of water flow rather than installed capacity is the limitational factor. Assuming running costs to be negligible, and using 7 percent as the required rate of return plus 2 per cent for depreciation in this case, the worthwhileness of the project would depend upon whether the average expected degree of utilization of the generating capacity was greater or less than 80 percent ($112.60× ·8 = $90.08). This type of calculation, based on thermal costs, continues to be valid as long as some thermal plants remain in use at all times. If sufficient run-of-the-stream capacity were available to displace totally thermal operations for, say, the 2,000 hours of lowest system demand during the year, then the optimal pricing policy would be to charge (virtually) zero for power sold during these 2,000 hours, to charge $·02 per kwh for power sold during the 2,500 hours of peaktime operation, and to charge $·01 (the marginal running cost of thermal plants) during the remaining 4,260 hours of the year. As long as all thermal plants are identical, and as long as some expansion of thermal capacity is always needed to cover at least part of the secular increase in demand, no more than these three rates will ever be called for in an optimal pricing scheme.

III

In this section we shall indicate, still under the assumption of homogeneous thermal capacity, how the benefits of types of hydroelectric projects other than run-of-the-stream can be measured. For simplicity we shall assume that only two rates are relevant—an off-peak rate of 1¢ per kwh, and a peaktime rate of $·02 per kwh. Similarly, where it is necessary to specify the number of peaktime hours, we shall continue to assume it to be 2,500 per year.

Daily reservoirs

The principal benefit from daily reservoirs is essentially the conversion of off-peak power into peaktime power; a secondary benefit is the utilization of water that otherwise would go to waste. Consider first the conversion function in a run-of-the-stream project; by definition, the volume and timing of power generation is governed by the volume and timing of the stream-flow that is being harnessed. It is a virtual necessity that most of this power will come during off-peak hours. If, however, a small dam were built immediately upstream from the project, and if sufficient additional penstock and turbine capacity were built to carry an entire day's streamflow just during the peak-time hours, then all 24 hours worth of streamflow could be used for peaking purposes.

The second type of benefit stemming from adding a daily reservoir and the associated generating equipment to an existing run-of-the-stream project is the likely reduction in the amount of water that is 'wasted.' Clearly, it is never (or hardly ever) going to be worthwhile to build into a run-of-the-stream project enough capacity to process the maximum expected streamflow. But when the project is expanded via a daily reservoir, it is likely to be able to process virtually the full annual streamflow—in periods of relatively moderate streamflow it is likely that all the water can be used at peaktime, while when the streamflow approaches its annual highs, the full generating capacity of the project will likely be in use during the peaktime hours, and some water will be used in off-peak periods.

Pump storage

Pump storage probably represents the most exciting frontier in power engineering today. Although its principles have been known for many years, it has become more economic with the advent of nuclear power and with the development of large fossil-fuel thermal plants that for all practical purposes require continuous operation. In a sense, pump storage is simply an extension of the daily reservoir idea. But instead of merely storing the day's streamflow behind a small dam for use at peak hours, a pump-storage project would store perhaps a month's or two months' streamflow behind two much larger dams— one upstream and the other downstream from the actual generating facilities. During peak hours the water is passed from the upstream dam through the turbines to the downstream dam to generate peaktime power; during off-peak hours cheap thermal or nuclear power is used to pump the water back up from the downstream dam to the upstream dam. Needless to say, it takes more than 1 kwh of power to pump back the amount of water needed to generate one kwh; but if the pumping is done with $.01-per-kwh electricity, and if the water is used to generate $.02-per-kwh power, there is ample margin to make economically valid an operation that in purely physical terms has negative net output (that is, uses more power than it produces).

Seasonal storage

Seasonal storage is the function fulfilled by massive dams that accumulate water in the wet season(s) and use it to produce power over much of the year. In order to evaluate a seasonal storage project we must know how much of the electricity will be generated at peak hours, and how much at off-peak hours. To answer this question, let us examine two alternative methods of organizing a system containing both fossil-fuel thermal and seasonal-storage hydroelectric capacity. For simplicity, assume that the seasonal-storage capacity is given (that is, the dam has already been built) and that the dam has been so designed that it is easy to increase its instantaneous generating capacity by installing additional turbines. Figures 9.1 and 9.2 show the two

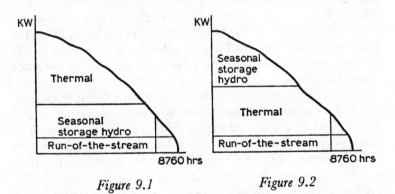

Figure 9.1   Figure 9.2

alternative strategies of using a given amount of seasonal-storage capacity in a mixed hydro-thermal system. Both diagrams show the 'load curve' of a hypothetical system. In this curve, the various hours of the year are arrayed in descending order of electricity demand (under a given rate structure). Figure 9.1 depicts a strategy of system operation, according to which only run-of-the-stream capacity is used in the hours of lowest demand, seasonal-storage hydro is introduced only when run-of-the- stream capacity is fully occupied, and thermal power is used only when both types of hydro generating-plants are operating at capacity. In Figure 9.2, run-of-the-stream capacity continues to occupy the baseload of the system, but the roles of thermal and seasonal-storage hydro capacity are inverted, with hydro storage now assigned the task of meeting peak demand. The figures are so constructed that the total number of kwh generated by each type of capacity is the same on both graphs—that is, the area in the triangle represented by thermal in Figure 9.1 is the same as that of the trapezoid representing thermal in Figure 9.2, and similarly for seasonal storage and run-of-the-stream capacities respectively. The rationale for this is as follows: the existing run-of-the-stream capacity, having the lowest opportunity cost of any of the three types, will be used up to the limits provided by either water or generating equipment under either strategy of system management; therefore, the number of kwh generated by this source should be the same in both cases. Similarly, the output of the seasonal reservoir, being determined by its storage capacity, likewise will be essentially the same under both strategies of system management.[1] Hence the amount of thermal power required, being the total area under the load curve minus that accounted for by the two types of hydroelectric power, should also be the same in the two cases.

Given the fact that the amounts of power taken from each of the three sources are the same in both cases, one must inquire into the relative costs associated with the two strategies. The strategy represented by Figure 9.1 has more thermal capacity and less turbine capacity installed in the seasonal dam(s) than is the case for the strategy depicted in Figure 9.2. Since hydro turbine capacity is substantially cheaper per KW than is fossil-fuel thermal, it follows that the strategy of Figure 9.2 is to be preferred. This holds a fortiori when differences in running cost are considered, for when thermal is used for peaking the plants have to be started up and turned down much more frequently than when thermal occupies the middle position in the load curve. Start-up and shutdown costs are thus minimized under the second strategy, for these costs are essentially nil for the peaking power obtained from the seasonal reservoir.

Thus the 'natural' location of seasonal storage hydro is at the top of the load curve, and its natural function is to provide peaktime power.[2] As a consequence, the relevant price at which to value the output of a hydro-storage project is the peaktime price of elasticity. A new element enters the picture, however, when substantial amounts of seasonal-storage capacity are available. This element is that the number of hours in the year that is relevant for the setting of the peaktime surcharge now becomes the number of hours of 'thermal peak' rather than the number of hours of the 'system peak.' In Figure 9.3, the initial load curve *ABCDE* is drawn with an exaggeratedly sharp

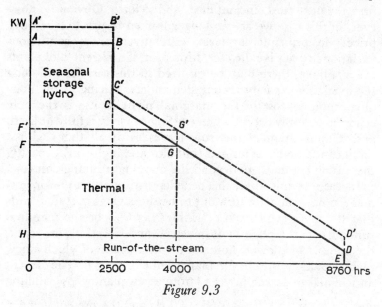

Figure 9.3

system peak so as to highlight the main issues involved. If, with a given seasonal-hydro-storage capacity, the demand for power increases to *A'B'C'D'E*, the normal response of the system would be to increase thermal capacity from *HF* to *HF'*. The new capacity, here assumed to be homogeneous with the old, would be used 4,000 hours in the year rather than the 2,500 that would be the case in the absence of seasonal storage, the extra kWh it produces being represented by the rectangle *FF'G'G*. If then, as in the example of section II, a *KW* of thermal capacity has a required annual economic rent of $25.00, this would now be reflected in a peaktime surcharge of 0.6¢ per kWh, stretching over 4,000 hours of thermal peak.

The situation changes drastically when variations in the efficiency of thermal plants are taken into account. Now the optimum price to charge at any hour is the marginal running cost of the oldest (least efficient) thermal plant that is in operation during that hour. This assumes, of course, that, as thermal power is required, the most efficient thermal plants are employed first, the next most efficient next, and so forth. Obviously, however, in this case we are no longer limited to just two or three prices; in principle, at least, a relatively more continuous variation in price is called for. Moreover, if sufficient 'old' plants are available, there may be no need in this case for rationing the available capacity among demanders. Pricing at the marginal running cost of the marginal plant in use is the only criterion to apply except when existing capacity is fully utilized, and if application of this rule leaves us at all times with a significant amount of unused (but old- and high-cost) capacity, there is no reason to go beyond the marginal-running-cost rule.

In cases of this kind, the benefits attributable to an investment in new capacity turn out to be the savings in system costs that the investment makes possible. Let $C(k)$ be the marginal running cost of a plant built in year k, and $H(k, t)$ be, for year t, the number of kilowatt-hours in the production of which a new plant would substitute for plants built in year k. The benefit anticipated to accrue in year t from a new plant whose running cost is $C(j)$ is $\sum_{k=1}^{j-1} H(k, t)[C(k) - C(j)]$; and the present value of expected benefits is

$$\sum_{t=j+1}^{\infty} \sum_{k=1}^{j-1} H(k, t)[C(k) - C(j)](1 + r)^{j-t}.$$

Investment in a plant with costs $C(j)$ should be undertaken wherever this expression exceeds the capital cost of the plant (accumulated to year j); this assumes that later investments will be governed by the same rule.

The derivation of $H(k, t)$ is illustrated in Figure 9.4. The upper curve there traced (ABC) represents the load curve expected to prevail in the first year of the new project's potential operation. The numbers 1, 2, 3, 4 indicate the positions

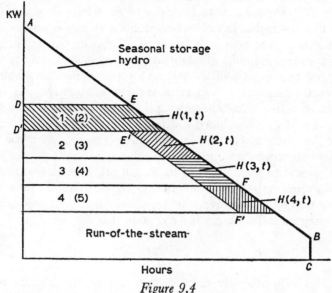

Figure 9.4

that thermal plants of different vintages (plant 1 being the oldest and least efficient, plant 4 the newest and most efficient) would occupy in the load curve in the absence of plant 5 (the one whose construction is being contemplated). The numbers (2), (3), (4), and (5) represent the positions that the respective plants would occupy if plant 5 is in fact built. What happens in that case is that plant 5, now the most efficient, occupies the base of the thermal structure, with plant 4 moving up to the next higher position, and so forth. In the case illustrated, plant 1 would be displaced entirely in the presence of plant 5. The shaded areas represent the number of kilowatt hours, $H(k, t)$ in the production of which plant 5 would, if constructed, be effectively substituting for plants 4, 3, 2, and 1 respectively (the line $D'E'F'$ lying below DEF by the amount of capacity of the new plant).

The benefits associated with a new plant are likely to decline through time. As newer and still more efficient plants are constructed, they will take over the base load of the system, and leave the plant with costs $C(j)$ to be introduced only at such times as system demand exceeds the combined capacities of all newer plants. Benefits attributable to the investment in the plant $C(j)$ appear only as the price of electricity rises above its running costs; that is, only when plants with higher costs would be the marginal ones in its absence. When the plant is new, it is generating benefits all the time, but as it ages, and is supplanted at the base of the system by more efficient plants, it generates benefits only part of the time. Moreover, as time passes, it is likely that the oldest plants that were in existence in year j will be abandoned entirely $[H(k, t)$ then would equal zero for such a $k]$, thus accentuating the tendency for the benefit stream to decline through time.

The precise time paths of price, output, investment, and so forth, represent the solution to a complex dynamic programming problem. However, the key investment criterion can be represented quite simply if we assume that the function

$$B(j, t) = \sum_{k=1}^{j-1} H(k, t)[C(k) - C(j)]$$

declines exponentially through time at the annual rate of γ. We then can write the present value of the benefits of an investment made at time j as being

$$\frac{B_{j+1}}{1+r} + \frac{B_{j+1}(1-\gamma)}{(1+r)^2} + \frac{B_{j+1}(1-\gamma)^2}{(1+r)^3} + \cdots,$$

an infinite series which is equal to $B_{j+1}/(r+\gamma)$. From this follows the requirement that anticipated benefits, in the first full year of operation of a project, should be at least $(r+\gamma)$ times the capital cost of the project [at least, since the formulation above assumes an infinite life for the project, and does not make any direct allowance for depreciation or 'mortality'].

v

Situations can emerge in which, over one range of outputs, the price of electricity should equal the marginal running cost of the marginal plant at each output, but in which over another range of output, a surcharge should be levied over and above this marginal running cost. Such situations occur when, and only when, the present value of benefits attributable to an expansion of thermal capacity under the marginal running cost rule derived in the previous section is less than the capital cost of that expansion *and* when the marginal running cost rule would lead to the system's operating at capacity at least some of the time. The common sense of this condition is clear: if the present value of benefits exceeds the capital cost of a new project, when benefits are measured by the differences between running costs of older plants and those of the new one, that is, by the formula

$$\sum_{t=1}^{\infty} \sum_{k=1}^{j-1} H(k, t)[C(k) - C(j)](1 + r)^{j-t},$$

then the new plant should be constructed, even if existing capacity is not now nor is expected in the future to be fully utilized. The lack of full utilization of existing capacity in this case is attributable to the fact that it is cheaper to incur marginal running costs plus capital charges on the new plant than to incur just the marginal running costs of some very old plants that may be in existence. The very old plants in this case remain submarginal at all times. However, should the present value of benefits from the new plant fall short of its capital cost, it is preferable to incur marginal running cost on additional (currently unutilized) older plants, rather than invest in new generating equipment.

But if all current generating capacity is now used at least at some times during the year, and if benefits (calculated on the basis of marginal running costs of existing facilities) fall short of the capital costs of new equipment, the indicated procedure is to hold off on new investments, and to use price to ration electricity during those hours when the system is being used to capacity. In a situation in which demand is growing, the price necessary to ration existing capacity will increase over time, and the number of hours during which the oldest plants are the marginal plants in use will also increase. Thus the formula for measuring the first year's benefits of investment in an expansion of capacity

$$\sum_{k=1}^{-1} H(k)[C(k) - C(j)]$$

changes through time, (a) because now we replace $C(1)$ by $R(1)$, the price which will ration existing capacity among demanders at the system peak, a price which itself increases with time; and (b) because, as time passes and demand grows, $H(k)$ will increase for the older existing plants with large cost differentials $[C(k) - C(j)]$, and will decline for the newer plants with smaller cost differentials.

As time passes, therefore, a point will be reached when it becomes worthwhile to invest in new capacity, and in the case under consideration the structure of rates at this point will consist of marginal running costs of the marginal plant at all points short of system capacity, and of the marginal running cost of the least efficient plant plus a peaktime surcharge at times when the entire capacity of the system is being utilized.

VI

Practical considerations prevent the full implementation of marginal cost pricing rules, but fairly close approximations are feasible. Electricité de France operates with five basic rates— a summer 'slack hour' rate, a winter 'slack hour' rate, a summer 'full use hour' rate, a winter 'full use hour' rate, and a winter 'peak hour' rate. This last and highest rate is more than three times the lowest rate, indicating that the degree of variation is indeed substantial.

Another compromise which is necessary in practice is the allowance for a certain amount of reserve capacity, even at the system peak. Thus peaktime charges can come into play when the system is operating at 85 to 90 percent of its physical capacity, and under the expectation that the actual level of operation will rarely exceed, say, 95 percent of physical capacity. This margin for error is necessary because of the fact that physical capacity cannot be exceeded significantly (small excess demands on the system can be accommodated with minor reductions in voltage), and because cutoffs of power to particular groups of consumers entail high real costs to them. Thus, in order to be able to meet an unexpected surge in peak demand, or to be able to accommodate an unexpected reduction in peak capacity (because of breakdowns or of abnormally low water supplies to hydro facilities), the point at which peaktime rates enter into force is set at a certain margin below the absolute capacity level of the system.

Where electricity networks extend over substantial areas (in many cases over entire countries), marginal cost pricing dictates regional variations in rates to take into account variations in marginal production costs and also to cover transmission costs in cases where electricity is sent substantial distances from low-cost producing centers. The regional pattern of rates in the French electricity system has been worked out on this basis.

Finally, it should be noted that the prices referred to so far in this paper are, in effect, 'wholesale prices' of high-voltage electricity. Differential 'retail' rates are justified to cover differential distribution costs, including in distribution costs the losses that are incurred in transforming high-voltage power to lower voltages, and the actual direct costs of distribution.

Notes

[1] One minor qualification is that when the dam is full it may in effect become a run-of-the-stream project; if this occurs *and* the instantaneous generating capacity involved in the case of Figure 9.1 is insufficient to use the full streamflow at that time, then the total amount of power generated by the second strategy, will somewhat exceed that obtainable under the first.

[2] Exceptions can occur in various ways; for example, (i) the seasonal peak demand for power may come in the rainy season when the dam is full and is functioning essentially on a run-of-the-stream basis, (ii) the water may be released at times not optimal from the standpoint of power-generation alone (because the dam is multipurpose and must attend, for example, to irrigation needs as well).

SELECTED BIBLIOGRAPHY

Harberger, A. C. and N. Andreatta. 'A Note on the Economic Principles of Electricity Pricing'. *Applied Economics Papers*, March, 1963.

Marschak, Thomas. 'Capital Budgeting and Pricing in the French Nationalized Industries'. *Journal of Business*, April, 1960.

Meek, Ronald L. 'An Application of Marginal Cost Pricing: The "Green Tariff" in Theory and Practice'. *Journal of Industrial Economics*, July and November, 1963.

——. 'The Bulk Supply Tariff For Electricity'. *Oxford Economic Papers*, July, 1963.

Nelson, J. R. Ed. *Marginal Cost Pricing in Practice*. Prentice-Hall, 1964.

Organization for European Economic Cooperation. *The Theory of Marginal Cost and Electricity Rates*. Paris: OEEC, 1958.

Steiner, Peter O. 'Peak Loads and Efficient Pricing'. *Quarterly Journal of Economics*, November, 1957

Turvey, Ralph. 'On Investment Choices in Electricity Generation'. *Oxford Economic Papers*, November, 1963.

CHAPTER TEN

COST-BENEFIT ANALYSIS OF TRANSPORTATION PROJECTS

I. INTRODUCTION

This paper will focus on the problems of evaluating transportation projects in the context of the less-developed countries. Emphasis will be placed on highway projects, because these account for the bulk of transport investments in the developing parts of the world, railroad projects being largely limited to the modernization of existing facilities, and air transport and port projects, even when they are basically new, being of small magnitude relative to road investments.

Road projects also carry a special interest as compared to other types of transport investments, because of the fact that they only rarely can be justified on strictly commercial considerations. Rail and air fares and port and landing charges constitute direct devices by which the costs of the relevant facilities can, over time, be recouped from the beneficiaries. To a first approximation, therefore, the worthwhileness of such projects can be judged by the strictly commercial criterion of prospective profitability. No such short cut is possible with respect to most road investments, whose benefits are generally freely available to their users. User charges are, of course, present in the road transport field, in the form of gasoline taxes, motor vehicle licenses and taxes, and the like. But these charges are functions of the general tax structure of the country in question, and do not vary depending on whether vehicles are used on one highway or another. They are related neither to the benefits which the users of a particular project may be expected to enjoy, nor to the costs of constructing that project.

Paper prepared for a conference on 'Engineering and the Building of Nations' held at Estes Park, Colorado, August 27–September 1, 1967.

This means that whereas for most other types of transport projects user charges can be taken as the first-approximation measure of benefits, for road projects we must confront the problem of estimating benefits essentially from scratch. This may be difficult or easy, depending upon the circumstances of the case. By and large, the great bulk of road projects entail improvements of existing roads or, what amounts to much the same thing, linking by a shorter and/or better road population centers that were already linked by the pre-existing network. In these cases we can in general have access to two key pieces of information of great value in estimating project benefits: (a) the actual volume of traffic now flowing between the points to be served by the road improvement, and (b) the probable reduction in costs of travel per vehicle-mile that will occur as a consequence of the improvement. It will be seen below that with the aid of these two types of facts, reasonably accurate measurements of the prospective benefits of road-improvement projects can normally be made.

Such is not the case with respect to totally new roads that penetrate areas not yet served by the highway network. For these roads, the prospective volume of traffic is much more of an unknown than in the case of road improvements, and the benefit per user, which for the road improvement can be measured quite accurately in terms of cost-reduction per vehicle-mile, now presents more formidable problems of estimation.

II. THE CASE OF ROAD IMPROVEMENTS

It is of the nature of the case that projects of road improvement do not bring into being possibilities of vehicular transport which did not exist before. They may generate new traffic owing to the fact that they reduce costs of travel, but the bulk of the traffic to be served by the improved road is likely already to have been travelling on the existing one. This means that the bulk of the benefits stemming from the improvement are likely to accrue to traffic that would in any case have passed over the road in its unimproved state.

The direct benefits of a road improvement all involve savings of costs. The better the road, in general, the lower will be the consumption of gasoline and oil, the less the wear-and-tear on tires, the lower the incidence of repair and maintenance expenses, and the longer the useful life of the vehicles using it. Jan de Weille, in a recent World Bank study, has drawn together the available data to provide a most useful reference document for estimating these cost savings.[1] In this study, one can see how, for example, fuel consumption varies with the type of road (earth, gravel, paved) for three sizes of automobiles and four types and sizes of trucks. The data are broken down by speed of vehicle, by the rate of rise or fall of the road, and by the degree of curvature of the road. Similar data are presented showing how, for each type of vehicle, engine oil consumption, tire wear, maintenance costs and depreciation of vehicles vary with the type of road and the speed of travel. De Weille's data are presented in physical terms (liters of gasoline or oil, hours of maintenance labor, percentage of total depreciation per 1,000 kilometers of travel), so that they can be readily adapted to the price and cost situations of different countries.

Thus, for example, if one anticipates that as a consequence of improving a given stretch of road from earth to gravel, average speed of traffic will increase from 25 to 40 miles per hour, one can ascertain savings of the above types of costs that the improvement will bring about per vehicle-kilometer of existing traffic of each vehicle type by simply consulting the relevant tables in De Weille's book.

Additional savings beyond those connected directly with vehicle costs include the saving of time for occupants of the vehicles, the savings of maintenance expenditures on the road itself, and the possible reduction in the costs of accidents as a result of the road improvement. Of these, the first two are by far the most important. If the time of the occupants of a vehicle is valued at $3 per hour, this amounts to $.12 per vehicle-mile at 25 mph and $.075 per vehicle-mile at 40 mph—the saving of $.045 per vehicle-mile is clearly large in comparison with the likely reduction in direct vehicle costs associated with an improvement from earth to gravel. Of course, the value of this saving is tied to the value placed on the hour of occupants' time, and is therefore sensitive to the level of living in the country. In a very low-income country such as India, the time-saving aspect of road improvements is likely to contribute little to the overall estimate of their benefits, but even at relatively modest income levels it has an important effect—a saving of $.01 per vehicle-mile arising from the above-assumed increase in speed at a value of $.67 per vehicle-hour.[2]

With respect to road maintenance costs, it is clear that improvement can often generate substantial savings. A recent study based on Venezuelan data estimated that the maintenance costs of a gravel road were equal to those of an earth road at an average daily traffic level of 100 vehicles per day; beyond this traffic level there was a saving of over $.02 per vehicle kilometer involved in having gravel. Similarly, the maintenance costs of paved and gravel roads were estimated to be equal at an average daily traffic of 300 vehicles per day, beyond which there was a saving of over $.02 per vehicle kilometer entailed in having a paved as against a gravel road.[3]

We now turn to the basic procedure for evaluating the direct benefits of a particular road improvement. First, we estimate, on the basis of current observed traffic volume, its past trend, and the likely rate of growth of the economy in the area, a projected time-path for the traffic volume of vehicles of each type, assuming that the improvement is not made. This will generate i time-series, V_{it}, where V stands for traffic volume, i for type of vehicle, and t for time. We sum these for each year to obtain $V_t (= \sum_i V_{it})$, the volume of traffic that we expect for each year.

On the basis of the expected volume, we then project the estimated average speed of traffic on the road in year t. This can be done either by using direct observations on the relationship between average speed and traffic volume on the road in question, or, if those are not available, by using functional relationships between speed and traffic volume for the particular type of road. Such relationships have been estimated for many years by the U.S. Bureau of Public Roads and other highway authorities. We thus obtain $S_{it} = f(V_t)$, where S_{it} is the average speed of the ith vehicle type.

The estimates of average speed, together with the characteristics of the road (such as gradient and curvature) enable us to estimate, using De Weille's data, what will be the average cost, c_{it}, per vehicle mile at time t for vehicles of class i on the unimproved road.

We next must estimate corresponding figures for the improved road. If traffic volumes are not expected to be different regardless of whether the road is improved or not, this is an easy task. It simply entails inserting the estimated V_t into the equation setting out the relationship between average speed and traffic volume for roads of the type (such as two-lane gravel) being planned. The estimated speeds s_{it}' thus obtained, along with the gradient and curvature characteristics of the proposed improved road, enable us to estimate the prospective average costs c_{it}' of travel on that road for each vehicle class.

Included in c_{it} and c_{it}' should be all costs perceived by the owners and occupants of the vehicles—including fuel, oil, maintenance, repair, depreciation, and the time costs of the occupants. The benefits accruing in year t to the owners and occupants as a consequence of the proposed improvement are therefore estimated as $\sum_i (c_{it} - c_{it}') V_{it}$, and the present value of this class of benefits is $\sum_t (1 + r)^{-t} \sum_i (c_{it} - c_{it}') V_{it}$, where r is the rate of discount used for purposes of cost-benefit analysis and the current year is taken as the origin for the purpose of measuring time. To these benefits we must then add the prospective savings in maintenance costs, $M_t - M_t'$, where M_t refers to maintenance costs on the unimproved road and M_t' to those on the improved road. These will be functions of the prospective traffic volumes V_t, and should be estimated on the basis of them. The expression for the present value of total direct benefits (I am here treating accident prevention as a negligible component of total benefits) is therefore:

$$\sum_t (1 + r)^{-t} \sum_i (c_{it} - c_{it}') V_{it} + \sum_t (1 + r)^{-t}(M_t - M_t'). \tag{1}$$

When it is anticipated that the traffic volume at time t will increase as a direct consequence of the improvement, the analysis becomes slightly more complicated. First, one must estimate the expected increase in traffic $(V_{it}' - V_{it})$ of different types. Then on the basis of $(V_t' (= \sum V_{it}')$ one should estimate s_{it}', using the functional relationship between speed and volume for roads of the improved type. Using these speeds, one then proceeds to estimate the average costs per vehicle-mile—c_i'— under the proposed changes in road characteristics. And using the prospective volumes of traffic V_{it}' one estimates the projected road maintenance costs M_t'. With these modifications in methodology, formula (1) remains valid as a measure of the present value of a large part of total direct benefits, but omits one component thereof—the gain in consumer surplus to the newly generated traffic.

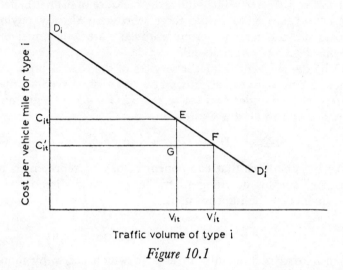

Figure 10.1

This is illustrated in the Figure 10.1. Here $D_i D_i'$ represents the demand function for the use of the road by vehicles of type i. On the vertical axis is measured the price which each successive unit of traffic would be willing to pay, per vehicle-mile, for traveling over the road. This price should be interpreted as the maximum total cost per vehicle-mile which that unit of traffic would be willing to bear, in order to travel on the road. With the unimproved road, the cost per vehicle-mile is c_{it}, and the traffic level becomes V_{it}—including all those traffic units willing to bear costs of c_{it} or more. Under the improvement, costs will fall to c_{it}' and traffic volume will now expand to V_{it}'. The gross benefits received by the incremental traffic are measured by $V_{it}EFV_{it}'$, but the costs they perceive are $V_{it}GFV_{it}'$. Therefore the triangle *EFG* measures their net benefit for the year t. They do not receive as much net benefit as the existing traffic because some of the reduction in costs per vehicle-mile is of no relevance for them. If c_{it} is 10 cents and

c'_{it} is $.07, a potential traveler willing to pay no more than 8 cents to use the road obtains no benefit from a reduction in cost from $.10 to $.08; at that point he may use the road, but he will be on the margin of indifference between using it and not using it. If the use of the road is now made available to him at a cost of $.07 per vehicle-mile, the measure of his net benefit is $.01 (= $.08 – $.07), while those who were already paying $.10 to use the road in its unimproved state will perceive a benefit of $.03 per vehicle-mile.

If the demand curve for the services of the road is linear, or if not, taking a linear approximation to that curve, we may express the triangle *EFG* as $\frac{1}{2}(c_{it} - c'_{it})(V'_{it} - V_{it})$. We must therefore add to (1) the expression

$$\frac{1}{2} \sum_t (1 + r)^{-t} \sum_i (c_{it} - c'_{it})(V'_{it} - V_{it}), \qquad (2)$$

in order to capture that component of benefit represented by consumer surplus accruing to traffic generated directly as a consequence of the improvement.

III. THE CASE OF PENETRATION ROADS

When a road is built into an area to which access by motor vehicles was previously impossible, the analysis of section II remains in principle unchanged, but in practice significant modifications in approach may be required. The difficulties here stem from the fact that V_t is zero, hence the component of benefits represented by $C_{it}EGC'_{it}$ in Figure 1.01 simply does not exist. All traffic is newly generated by the presence of the road, and all direct benefits to users therefore are in principle of the type represented by the triangle *EFG*. Figure 10.2 represents such a case.

Here the annual net benefit to users of type i is given by the triangle $D_iHC'_{it}$, which corresponds exactly to *EFG* in Figure 10.2. The special problems presented by the present case arise because (a) whereas for improvement of existing roads the increment in volume caused by the improvement $(V'_t - V_t)$ is likely to be relatively small in relation to V_t, this increment represents the entire volume of traffic in the case of a penetration road, and (b) whereas, in the case of road improvements, the costs per vehicle-mile c_{it} and c'_{it} of a given amount of traffic

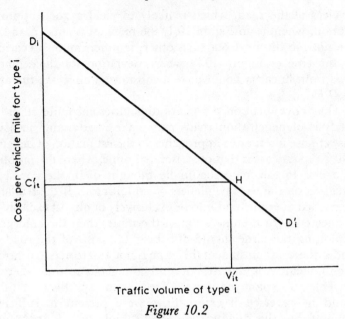

Figure 10.2

in the existing and improved roads can be rather precisely estimated, thus giving us a good estimate of the height of the triangle *EFG*, we do not have any correspondingly precise estimate of the height of the triangle $D_i HC'_{it}$ in the case of a penetration road. A problem is raised by (a) because the increment of traffic caused by an improvement is obviously subject to greater estimation error than the traffic based on the normal expansion of what we observe today; for a road improvement this error applies to a relatively small part of the total direct annual benefit, while for a penetration road the error applies to more than the whole (more, because from the triangle $D_i HC'_{it}$ we must deduct the annual maintenance costs of the road, M_t). A problem is raised by (b) because the existing cost of moving goods and people into an area to be newly penetrated by a road is likely to be high (if not, as, for example, in the case of easy transport by water, the analysis becomes quite similar to that of a road improvement). This cost does not provide a useful estimate of the location of point D_i. Moreover, the assumption of linearity of the demand curve for the services of the road, which is likely to yield a good approximation, when, as in Figure 10.1, the relevant points (E and F) are not too distant from each other, is much more precarious in the case of Figure 10.2, where deviations of the segment D_iH from linearity could have a substantial effect on the area of $D_iHC'_{it}$.

The above-mentioned types of difficulties encountered in the analysis of penetration roads can make it advisable in some cases to use alternative approaches to the estimation of benefits. The simplest case is that of an isolated mine, where the problem of access to the mine should be thought of in the course of deciding on the worthwhileness of exploiting it. If the traffic to be carried over the road is to be exclusively or almost exclusively connected with the operation of the mine, then the enterprise exploiting the mine should also bear the costs of the road. If under these circumstances the mine is not an attractive venture, the implication is that it is not advantageous to the society as a whole to exploit the mine. (Needless to say, this conclusion could be reversed if externalities were present in sufficient amount, but this qualification would apply to any apparently unprofitable investment whatever.)

A more complex case is that of a road which is opening up a new area to agricultural exploitation. Here the essence of the problem can best be seen by assuming that the area to be opened up consists entirely of public lands that have no value at present, owing to their remoteness. The benefits attributable to the road project would then be the total estimated yield which the government could get from the sale of the lands once the road was built, assuming that the market for land would be functioning well. If the land already had a value in its existing state, the benefit attributable to the road would be the excess of the prospective sale value of the land over its present market price.

Institutional arrangements and market imperfections, however, can make land-value comparisons fall wide of the mark as estimates of the benefits of penetration roads. To mention the most obvious case, the land (here assumed to be privately held) may have no true economic productivity in the absence of a road, but it may have a positive market price today because its owners anticipate that the government some day will build a road into the area. In this case, the prospective sale value of the land, once the road is built, and not the difference between this and today's market value of the land, is the relevant measure of the road's benefits. A second problem concerns possible improvements of the land. In all uses of land-value comparisons to assess the benefits of a road, the costs of any improvements in the land (clearing, leveling, irrigating, and so forth) which do not already exist today should be deducted from its prospective future value before attributing any benefit to the road.

Where direct use of land value comparisons is found to be unwarranted or excessively risky, one may attempt to assess the benefits of a road opening up a new area to agriculture on the basis of prospective agricultural production. Here, once again, care must be taken to deduct from the value of prospective farm output all the relevant associated costs, including those of clearing and improving the land (capital costs) as well as such current costs as labor, fertilizer, and transporting the inputs and outputs of agriculture over the road itself. And to the extent that complementary social investments such as the provision of electricity or drinking water are entailed in opening up the area to agriculture, their costs, too, must be deducted from the value of prospective farm output, before arriving at the benefit due to the road itself. Or, what amounts to essentially the same thing, the entire set of investments entailed in opening up the area can be evaluated as a 'package,' weighing the discounted value of expected flows of agricultural output against the discounted sum of all costs—capital and current, public and private—entailed in bringing forth that output.

It is of utmost importance to recognize that the use of changes in land values, the use of the present value of changes in agricultural output less costs and the estimation of the present value of annual triangles $D_i HC'_{it}$ in Figure 10.2 are three *alternative* ways of getting at essentially the same thing. If initially land prices contain no speculative component anticipating that a road would be built, the rise in land values induced by the road is simply the capitalized value of benefits obtained but not paid for by road users. It may not capture all of $D_i HC'_{it}$, for some users of the road other than farmers may be capturing part of it, and some road benefits perceived by farmers may not be capitalized into land values. But in any case the rise in land values is not additional to the present value of the demand triangles. Similarly, we can represent today's non-speculative value of land as the present value of expected future net output in the absence of the road, and relate it to a corresponding value in the presence of the road. This means that the change in land value will be the present value of the increase in output due to the road less the present value of the additional capital and current costs of achieving that output. Failure to recognize these three approaches as alternative ways of measuring the same thing has often led to double-counting of benefits and even in some cases to triple-counting!

IV. EXTERNALITIES CONNECTED WITH ROAD PROJECTS

It is appropriate, in the analysis of any project from the point of view of society as a whole, to take into account external or indirect benefits and costs. These can conveniently be summarized in the formula $\sum_t D_{it}(X'_{it} - X^o_{it})$, where D_{it} is the excess of benefits over costs associated with a unit change of the level of activity X_i at time t, X'_{it} is that level in the presence of the project in question, and X^o_{it} is that level in the absence of the project. Thus, for example, X_{1t} might be the number of unskilled laborers employed in a particular textile plant, and D_{1t} might be the excess of the wage paid to them over opportunity cost of their labor in alternative employments. Similarly, X_{2t} might be the output of a tire factory, and D_{2t} might be the excise tax collected per tire, representing the excess of the social benefit (here measured by the market price people pay for tires) over the resource cost of producing them. If, owing to the existence of a road project, more or less unskilled labor were to be employed in the textile plant, or more or less tires were to be produced in the tire factory, indirect benefits or costs, as given by the formula presented above, would have to be attributed to the project.

There is nothing in the cases cited above that is unique to road investment projects. If we were considering an electricity project or an irrigation project, we would want to ask how the level of employment of unskilled workers in the textile plant and how the output of the tire factory would change, if at all, as a consequence of the project, just as we would do in the case of a road project. In principle, the authorities in charge of project evaluation ought to identify all activities X_i for which marginal social benefit differs perceptibly from marginal social cost, and to provide project evaluators with estimates of the extent of the corresponding distortions, D_i. The project evaluators would then estimate the changes in the relevant activity levels caused by each particular project, to obtain $\sum_i D_{it}(X'_{it} - X^0_{it})$ for each year of the project's expected life, as a summary measure of the project's indirect benefits or costs.

Externalities Involving Traffic on Other Roads

Although, then, the general procedure for dealing with externalities contains nothing peculiar to road projects, there are nonetheless two types of distortions which are of special interest where road projects are concerned. These are (a) the likely excess of marginal social cost over marginal social benefit for traffic on roads, and (b) the likely excess of marginal social benefit over marginal social cost for traffic on railroads. Some readers may be surprised by the assertion that an excess of marginal cost over marginal benefit is likely in the case of road traffic, but a little reflection is sufficient to establish the point. All the studies that have been done of the relationship between average speed and volume of traffic on particular roads have shown that the higher the traffic volume, the lower the average speed. This negative relationship applies even at relatively low traffic volumes, long before anything that one might call congestion sets in. The consequence is that an increment of traffic on a road has the effect of slowing up the preexisting traffic, increasing its cost per vehicle-mile in terms of the time spent by the occupants and possibly in terms of other costs as well.

Let the function relating speed to volume be

$$S = a - bV, \tag{3}$$

and let the value of the occupants' time be H per vehicle-hour. The time-cost perceived by the occupants of a typical vehicle will be H/S per vehicle-mile; this is also the marginal private time-cost as seen by the typical driver. The total time cost of all users of the road will be VH/S, and the marginal social time-cost will be

$$\partial(VH/S)/\partial V = H\left[S - V\frac{\partial S}{\partial V}\right]/S^2 = H[a - bV + bV]/V^2 = \frac{aH}{S^2}.$$

(4)

Thus marginal social cost exceeds marginal private cost by the percentage:

$$\frac{MSC - MPC}{MPC} = \frac{\dfrac{aH}{S^2} - \dfrac{H}{S}}{(H/S)} = \frac{a - S}{S}.$$

(5)

This expression can be easily interpreted as the 'percentage speed deficit'. If, on the type of road in question, the average speed of travel (a) at very low traffic volumes is 60 miles per hour, and if at the actual traffic volume average speed is 40 miles per hour, then marginal social time-cost exceeds marginal private time-cost by 50 percent $[= (60 - 40)/40]$.

The presence of this externality suggests the possibility of collecting a tax which would face travelers with a marginal private cost equal to the marginal social cost entailed in their trips. Unfortunately, the design and administration of such a tax would be too complicated to be feasible even in developed countries with modern and efficient tax authorities. For the less developed countries it can therefore surely be ruled out as impossible. Nonetheless, we can recognize that the gasoline tax operates in a rough way to help offset the discrepancy between marginal private and marginal social cost of travel. But it is at most a very imperfect offset, as the discrepancy between social and private costs varies greatly with the volume of traffic, while the amount of gasoline consumed per mile is almost constant. Table 10.1 shows how the optimum tax (one designed just to offset the discrepancy between marginal social and marginal private costs) would vary for different speeds and different values of the percentage speed deficit, assuming the vehicle-hour to be valued at $1. It is seen there that where average speeds are as low as 20 miles per hour (as is often the case on earth and gravel roads), the optimum tax is likely to be in excess of $.01 per vehicle-mile. And even at a speed of 40 miles per hour, an optimum tax of 1 cent per mile would not be rare—this would require a speed deficit of 40 percent, meaning a situation in which the average speed of unimpeded traffic would be 56 mph as compared with an actual average speed of 40 mph. It is unlikely, therefore, that gasoline taxes compensate for more than a part of the typical discrepancy between

TABLE 10.1

Excess of Marginal Social Cost over Marginal Private Cost per Vehicle-Mile

(Based on assumed value of time of $1 per vehicle-hour and gasoline tax of zero)

| $\dfrac{a-S}{S}$ | miles per hour$_1$ | | | |
	20	30	40	50
.10	$.005	$.0033	$.0025	$.002
.20	.010	.0067	.005	.004
.30	.015	.0100	.0075	
.40	.020	.0133	.010	
.50	.025	.0167		

social and private costs—particularly when one realizes that the heaviest volumes of traffic occur at the times when the speed deficit is greatest, the latter being a direct function of traffic volume. We proceed, then, under the assumption that, in general, marginal social costs of travel on roads exceeds marginal private cost, even when the offsetting effects of gasoline taxes are taken into account.

We now distinguish two cases in which adjustment is warranted for externalities of the type we have been discussing, the first being a case in which the road improvement in question is a substitute for existing roads, and the second in which the relationship is one of complementarity. Broadly speaking, one can identify substitutability with urban complexes, in which there normally exist many alternative routes to get from one place to another, and complementarity with rural roads where there is normally only one relevant route between two places.

In the case of substitutability, a part of the newly generated traffic on the improved road will have been diverted from other roads. An external benefit appears here, for there is now less traffic on the substitute roads, and such traffic as remains will move faster, implying a saving of time-costs for the occupants of those vehicles. In the case of complementarity, traffic volumes will increase on the roads feeding into and out of the improved segment; travel on these roads will therefore be slower, implying an increase in the cost of travel for using them.

These effects are illustrated in Figure 10.3, which depicts the situation on a road, B, either competitive or complementary

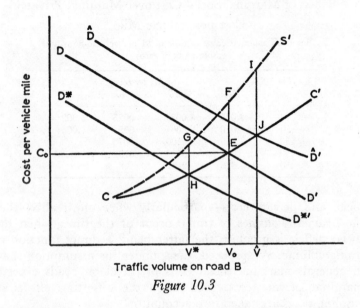

Figure 10.3

with the one (road A) on which the improvement is to be made. For simplicity, the traffic on this road is assumed to be all of one type, so that the costs facing each unit of that traffic will be the same for all vehicles. Let DD' be the demand curve for travel on road B, and let CC' be the curve relating private costs of travel per vehicle mile to the volume of traffic on that road. CS', the curve marginal to CC', represents the marginal social cost of travel on road B. The initial equilibrium, before road A is improved, will be at the traffic volume V_0, where the private cost curve intersects the demand curve.

If road B is competitive with road A, the improvement of A will cause the demand curve for travel on B to shift to the left, taking the position, say, $D^*D^{*\prime}$, and producing a new equilibrium level of traffic of V^*. The external benefit caused by the diversion of $(V_0 - V^*)$ units of traffic from road B will be measured by the area *EFGH*.

If road B is complementary with road A, the improvement of A will cause the demand curve for travel on B to shift to the right to the position, say, $\hat{D}\hat{D}'$, and yielding the equilibrium traffic volume $\hat{V}$. The external cost associated with the increase in traffic volume on B will in this case be measured by the area *EFIJ*.

Unless the change in traffic volume is large in relation to its initial level, the area *EFGH* or *EFIJ* can be closely approximated by the formula $C_0 f \Delta V (a - s_0)/s_0$. Here C_0 is the initial cost per vehicle-mile on road B, f is the fraction of C_0 represented by time-costs, ΔV is the change in traffic volume on road B induced by the improvement of A, a is the average speed of unimpeded traffic on roads of the same type as B, and s_0 is the initial average speed of traffic on road B. Here C_0 is equal to the height $V_0 E$; $C_0 f$ is that part of $V_0 E$ represented by time-costs; and $(a - s_0)/s_0$ is the fraction of $C_0 f$ that represents the excess of social over private costs in the initial situation. Thus, $C_0 f (a - s_0)/s_0$ is equal to the height *EF*. The approximation involved in the formula therefore entails assuming that the vertical distance between CC' and CS' remains constant at *EF* over the range of the change in traffic volume, rather than increasing to *IJ* in the case of growing traffic volume or declining to *GH* in the case of reduced traffic volume.

When traffic on a number of different roads is likely to be affected by the improvement of road A, the technique outlined above should be applied to each of them. This leads to an expression for the external effects of the improvement of A which is equal to $\sum_j C_{0j} f_j \Delta V_j (a_j - s_{0j})/s_{0j}$, where the symbols have the meanings defined above, and the index j varies over the number of other roads on which traffic volume is affected by the improvement of road A. At times it may be necessary to distinguish, for a given road, between periods with different initial traffic volumes. In this event, we may define several traffic volume intervals V_{jk} on road j; associated with each such interval will be a level of private costs, C_{0jk}, a fraction f_{jk} of such costs that is represented by time-costs, and an average speed of traffic s_{0jk}. The measure of the external effects of the improvement of road A then becomes

$$E = \sum_j \sum_k C_{0jk} f_{jk} \Delta V_{jk} (a_j - s_{0jk})/s_{0jk}.$$

This expression should be estimated for each year of the expected life of project A, and the value $\sum_i (1+r)^{-t} E_t$ should then be subtracted from the estimated present value of direct benefits of A. Note that E will be negative if substitute roads predominate in the set j, so that in this case net benefits will be algebraically larger after making the adjustment for these external effects.[4]

Externalities Involving Railroad Traffic

The problems involved in the relationships between road and rail transport can be complex, owing to the difficulty of isolating the relevant costs of rail transport. The marginal costs of carrying additional passengers or freight on trains which are in any event running are very low indeed; the marginal costs of running additional trains on runs where the track and station facilities will in any event be kept in working condition are at an intermediate level; and the marginal costs of providing rail service on a stretch of track as against the alternative of abandoning that stretch are higher still.

In what follows, we shall assume that the basic relationship between road and rail transport is one of substitutability, that is, that a project of road construction or improvement will tend to reduce the volume of rail traffic, if it has any effect at all on it. Consider now a road from B to C, which parallels a railroad that runs from A to D. Assume also that the stretch from B to C is but a small fraction of the total distance from A to D, and that all trains on the railroad ply the full distance from A to D, at least some of them stopping at B and C.

Under the above assumptions, it is likely that the improvement of the BC road will divert some traffic that otherwise would move by rail between these points. It is not likely, however, to affect the volume of rail traffic moving between A and B, between C and D, or between A and D. In this case the diversion of traffic from rail to road will probably not cause a reduction in the number and size of trains moving between A and D; they will just have more excess capacity than before over the stretch from B to C.[5] When traffic is thus diverted from rail to road, we measure the direct gross benefits of the diverted traffic as the area under the demand curve for travel on the road, and the direct costs as the average costs per vehicle-mile in the new situation, multiplied by the number of vehicle-miles of traffic diverted from the railroad. What have we neglected here? First, the diverted traffic ceases to benefit from the use of the railroad; we measure these forgone benefits by the passenger fares and freight rates that this diverted traffic would have paid to the railroad in the absence of the improvement. Second, the railroad no longer has to bear the marginal cost of carrying the diverted traffic. These are likely to be very low in relation to fares and freight rates in the case we are now examining. The net external effect will therefore almost certainly be negative, and will be measured by $\sum_i (F_i - R_i)\Delta X_i$,

where F_i is the fare or freight rate for the ith type of rail traffic, R_i is the marginal cost associated with carrying that traffic, and ΔX_i is the change in the volume, induced by the road improvement, of the ith type of traffic on the railroad. In some cases of this type, the relevant marginal costs of rail transport may be so low that one can safely neglect them, in which event the measure of the net external effect produced by the road improvement becomes $\sum_i F_i \Delta X_i$, which is equal to the loss of revenue to the railroad which the road project has occasioned.

The intermediate case occurs when the diversion of traffic to the road permits the railroad to reduce the number and/or size of trains. This can occur on a stretch like BC, if that stretch previously carried the heaviest traffic volumes on the railroad and hence determined the size and number of trains. However, it is more likely to occur where the road project connects one of the principal terminals of the railroad with some intermediate point—for example, if the road project is between C and D. In this event, some trains which previously went from A to D could now be turned around at C, reducing thereby the amount of equipment that the railroad had to operate and maintain, and the outlays of the railroad for operating and maintenance personnel. The savings of these costs must accordingly be added to $\sum_i (F_i - R_i)\Delta X_i$ before arriving at our estimate of the net external effect associated with diversion of traffic from the railroad. In practice, however, the added saving is unlikely to be sufficiently large to convert a net diseconomy into a net external benefit.

The final case occurs when the road project permits the abandonment of a segment of track. For this to occur the road project must almost necessarily connect a terminal point with an intermediate point along the road. The savings here include not only the direct marginal costs of haulage, the costs of equipment and maintenance which are saved by reduced rail traffic levels, but also the costs of track maintenance and repair, station operation, and so forth, over the stretch of track to be abandoned. Usually, moreover, the railroad right-of-way and its station and yard properties on the abandoned stretch will have some alternative economic use; the value of these properties in their alternative uses should therefore be counted as an indirect benefit of the road improvement project.

An additional cost is entailed in abandonment, however, which we have not yet discussed. This cost arises from the fact that, so long as the stretch of railroad is not abandoned, any diversion of traffic that takes place from rail to road is voluntary, while when abandonment occurs, some traffic for which the railroad would have been the preferred mode even in the presence of the road improvement must nonetheless cease to use the rails. The situation is depicted in Figures 10.4 and 10.5.

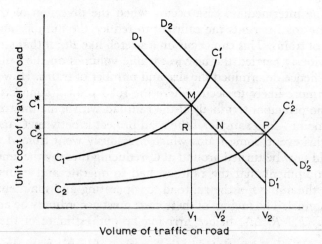

Figure 10.4

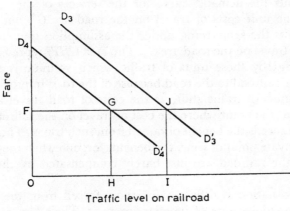

Figure 10.5

Figure 10.4 shows the situation on the road before and after improvement. C_1C_1' represents the private unit costs of travel on the road before the improvement; C_2C_2' after the improvement. D_1D_1' is the demand curve for the services of the road on the assumption that the railroad is operating and charging the fare level OF (from Figure 10.5); D_2D_2' is the demand curve for the services of the road assuming the railroad has been abandoned. C_1^* and V_1 are the initial levels of unit costs and traffic volume on the road; C_2^* and V_2 are the equilibrium levels after the road has been improved and the railroad abandoned. In this case the measure of direct benefits is the area $C_1^*MNC_2^*$ in Figure 10.4. The rectangle $C_1^*MRC_2^*$ represents the benefit perceived by traffic that would have used the unimproved road in any event; the triangle MNR represents the net benefit perceived by those who would not have used the road at a unit cost of C_1^*, but who would have used it at a unit cost of C_2^* even if the railroad were still operating. MNR includes the benefits obtained by those who would voluntarily have shifted their traffic from the railroad to the road at a road cost of C_2^*. The area NPV_2V_2' represents the costs incurred in travel on the road by traffic that has been involuntarily shifted to the road from the railroad because of the abandonment of service on the latter. No net benefit can be attributed to this traffic because of the involuntary nature of its transfer; indeed, a net cost is involved here. This is shown in Figure 10.5, where D_3D_3'

represents the demand curve for the services of the railroad when the unit costs of travel on the road are C_1^*, and D_4D_4' represents the same thing under the assumption that the unit costs of travel on the road are C_2^*. The area $GHIJ$ represents the fares paid by those units of traffic which voluntarily shifted from the railroad to the road because of the road improvement. These units of traffic shift, as the costs of road travel are reduced, at the point where the cost of travel on the railroad just barely exceeds the benefit obtained from such travel. Thus from their private point of view, the benefits forgone when they cease to use the railroad are just barely compensated by the fares saved.

The situation is different for those forced from the use of the railroad because of its abandonment. Their benefits from using the railroad are measured by the area OD_4GH, while their costs are measured by $OFGH$. From their private point of view, therefore, a loss of the triangle D_4GF is involved in the railroad's abandonment.

To summarize, then, the net benefit and cost situation of a road improvement project entailing the abandonment of service on a competing segment of railroad would be:

(a) the present value of cost savings to the users of the road (represented by $C_1^*MNC_2^*$),

less (b) the present value of those private net costs associated with abandonment of the railroad (represented by D_4GH),

less (c) the present value of the excess of rail fares over the direct marginal costs of operation,

plus (d) the present value of the savings stemming from lower equipment, maintenance, station operation costs, and so forth, for the railroad,

plus (e) the current market value in alternative uses of the properties to be abandoned.

It is often true that the net benefits of a road improvement, taken together with the abandonment of a competing segment of a railroad line, are strongly positive. This usually occurs when the railroad's total cost of maintaining service on the segment (including (d) and (e), above) exceed the operating profit represented by (c). The heavy and persistent losses of, for example, the Argentine national railway system suggest that such cases are not at all infrequent, and that a judicious program of road improvement could prove to have net external benefits associated with rail line abandonment. Where rail abandonment is not involved, however, there is a strong presumption that the external effects associated with diversion of traffic from rail to road will be negative.

V. SOME IMPLICATIONS AND GENERALIZATIONS

Up to now, we have set forth the basic principles and procedures to be applied in the analysis of costs and benefits of road projects. In this section we attempt to present some more general conclusions which are suggested or implied by the preceding analysis. We shall discuss, in turn, (a) critical traffic levels, (b) stage construction, (c) the problem of timing, (d) the problem of segment construction, and (e) the road-rail problem.

Critical Traffic Levels

It was shown in section II that the principal direct benefit of a road improvement was the reduction in road user costs for the traffic that would in any event have traveled on the unimproved road. The higher the traffic volume, therefore, the greater will be the presumed benefit. This is true not only because the benefits accrue to more traffic, but also because the cost-savings per vehicle, associated with a given improvement, are likely themselves to be greater at higher than at lower traffic volumes. This effect stems from the facts that costs per vehicle increase at an increasing rate with volume of traffic, and that their rate of increase at any given traffic volume is higher on poorer roads than on better roads.

Since benefits are so closely related to traffic volume, it is possible, for any given road, to estimate the critical level of traffic at which it would be worthwhile to upgrade the road, say, from gravel to macadam. Moreover, given that the cost situation is basically determined by the type of road and the price and wage structure of the country in question, it should be possible for the highway authorities of a country to develop analyses showing at what critical level of traffic it will normally be worthwhile to upgrade a road from earth to gravel, from gravel to paved, from two-lane paved to four-lane paved, for example. Such analyses could usefully go into more detail, specifying critical traffic levels for a given type of improvement according to gradient, drainage requirements, nature of sub-soil, and so forth.

In any event, critical traffic levels should be used as general guides to policy, not as a substitute for the detailed analysis of benefits and costs on each road. Properly employed, they serve the function of alerting the highway authorities as to which stretches of road should be considered as likely candidates for improvement, thus enabling them to employ their project evaluation personnel to better advantage.

One noteworthy aspect of critical traffic levels is that they are likely to vary considerably from country to country. Not only do costs of construction exhibit significant variation across countries, but also the benefits associated with a given improve-ment at given traffic levels are widely different in different countries—in large measure owing to the extreme differences that exist in the value of time. It is highly likely, therefore, that the critical level of traffic which would justify paving a road would be much higher in India, where the time-saving element of benefits is negligible, than in the United States, where time-saving is likely to be the biggest component of total benefits. One must accordingly be extremely wary of 'exporting' to other countries critical traffic levels derived on the basis of the situation prevailing in a particular country.

Stage Construction

In the light of the foregoing analysis, a strategy of stage con-struction of roads has a high degree of appeal. Such a strategy would entail upgrading a road from earth to gravel when the traffic level was sufficient to warrant that move, paving the road when traffic had so increased as to justify that move, and adding additional lines when that investment in turn was called for in the light of the traffic level.

Operating against the stage construction strategy is the argu-ment that it is likely to be more costly to go through a series of upgrading investments than to build, once-and-for-all, a higher quality road than may be merited by present levels of traffic. The problem of timing will be discussed directly in the next section; we therefore here concentrate on the question of the differential cost of stage versus unitary construction.

A recent World Bank study reappraising a road project in Iran gives estimated costs of two-stage construction of a road —first gravel then paved. The costs of a 5-meter-wide gravel road are estimated at 2·77 million rials per kilometer; the incremental costs of paving and widening to 6 meters are 2·0 million rials per kilometer. The total costs of single-stage construction of a 6-meter-wide paved road are 4·5 million rials per kilometer. The excess costs of stage construction are therefore estimated to be in the order of 5 percent. Similar estimates for stage construction of a 6-meter-wide gravel road, later widened to 7 meters and paved, are 3·46 million rials per kilometer for the first stage and 2·60 million rials for the second stage, as compared with 5·77 million rials per kilometer for single-stage construction of a 7-meter-wide paved road.[6]

Obviously the excess costs of stage construction should be analyzed in each particular case, and compared with the extra benefits that a higher-quality road will provide. Nonetheless, the Iranian data suggest that stage construction is highly likely to be worthwhile. In the first example, the excess cost of stage construction was ·27 million rials per kilometer. At a discount rate of 10 percent (certainly not excessive for a less developed country), the interest savings on postponement would be sufficient to offset this excess cost even if the postponement of the second stage were to be as brief as 1·1 years. For the second set of data the excess cost of ·29 million rials per kilometer could once again be offset by the interest saving entailed in the postponement of the second stage for as little as 1·1 years.

Nor are the incremental benefits of single-stage construction likely to justify it unless traffic levels are well above those required to warrant first-stage construction. Let V_1 be the critical traffic level which would justify construction of a gravel road, and V_2 be that which would justify upgrading to a paved road. Suppose that traffic has just now reached the level V_1, and is expected to reach V_2 in t^* years. Let K_1 be the capital cost of constructing the gravel road and K_2 that of the concrete road, and let K_2^* be the cost of upgrading from gravel to concrete. The present value of cost saving involved in stage construction will then be $(K_2 - K_1) - K_2^*(1 + r)^{-t^*}$. The factor $(1 + r)^{-t^*}$ is equal to approximately ·6 for $r = ·10$ and $t^* = 5$ years, and to approximately $\cdot 36$ for $t^* = 10$ years. If, as suggested by the Iranian data, K_1 is equal to $\cdot 6K_2$, and K_2^* is equal to $\cdot 45K_2$, the present value of cost saving will be equal to $\cdot 13K_2$ when $t^* = 5$ years, and $\cdot 24K_2$ when $t^* = 10$ years. The cost of the gravel road itself being $\cdot 6K_2$, this means that the extra benefits of having a paved road instead of a gravel road during the first t^* years would have to be 22 percent of the total costs of the gravel road in order to warrant single-stage construction if traffic would grow to justify the second stage in five years, and would have to amount to approximately 40 percent of the total cost of the gravel road if t^* were equal to ten years. It should be emphasized that these extra benefits would be just those accruing during the period between construction of the gravel road and its prospective upgrading to a paved road, as subsequent to t^* the benefits of either single-stage or two-stage construction would be the same.

We conclude, therefore, that although each case should in principle be examined on its merits, there is a strong presumption that stage construction will prove to be the optimal strategy in most cases. Moreover, stage construction has the added advantage of permitting investment decisions to be based on the existing observed volumes of traffic, rather than on predictions of future traffic growth which could be subject to substantial error. In the example just presented, the fact that traffic on an existing earth road has reached the level V_1 would be sufficient to justify the investment in a gravel road, so long as traffic was not expected to be reduced in the future. The highway authority, under stage construction, could wait to see when traffic would grow to V_2 so as to justify paving the road. If the highway authority attempts to justify now the construction of a paved road, on the other hand, it must be on the basis of a prediction of how far in the future the traffic level V_2 will be reached. If the highway authority errs in this prediction on the side of underestimating the actual growth of traffic, it may in some cases decide on multi-stage construction when single-stage construction would in fact have been economically justified. The cost of this type of error is likely to be small, however, because of the small excess of multistage over single-stage construction costs. If, on the other hand, the highway authority errs in the direction of overstating the actual growth of traffic, the error can be very costly indeed—as traffic may not reach the point where the next stage of improvement would be warranted for 15 or 20 years, if indeed ever. The asymmetry of the costliness of errors of prediction of the two types should therefore bias the authority's choice in the direction of multi-stage construction.

The Timing Problem

In this section we discuss the problem of the timing of road investments, a problem which is made easy by the typical nature of the benefit streams generated by roads. With relatively minor qualifications, one can say that the traffic volume carried on a road, and hence the benefits of that road, will depend at any time on the quality of the road and not, to any significant degree, on when the road was raised to that level of quality. Moreover, in the great bulk of cases, the normal pattern is for the traffic on a road to grow through time.

These two characteristics—benefits dependent on calendar time but not on the age of the project, and a rising benefit stream through time—make the timing problem amenable to an exceedingly simple solution. Assume that we have a gravel road and are contemplating paving it. Let B_t represent the undiscounted flow of benefits (road user savings plus maintenance savings plus net external benefits that will flow from having a paved rather than a gravel road in year t). Let K be the cost of paving the road.

If, under these assumptions we face the problem of whether to pave the road in year 0 or year 1, we must recognize that regardless of which of these decisions we take, the benefits of having a paved road from year 2 onward will be obtained. The benefits lost by postponing paving for a year will be those of that year—say, B_1. The gains to be obtained by postponing will be the use of the amount of K of investible funds for one year; this we measure by rK, where r as before represents the rate of discount to be used in cost-benefit analysis, reflecting the productivity that investible resources could have in alternative marginal uses.

The answer to the problem is therefore simple: when $rK > B_1$, postpone; when $rK < B_1$, pave. This leads to the rule that construction should be done at the time when benefits in the first year following construction will first exceed the discount rate times the capital cost.

A slight complication is introduced when construction costs themselves are expected to change through time. If construction costs are rising, we gain by constructing at year 0 not only the benefit flow in year 1, but also the saving in construction costs $(K_1 - K_0)$ entailed in building now rather than later. The rule is therefore modified to read: when $rK_t > B_{t+1} + (K_{t+1} - K_t)$, postpone; when $rK_t < B_{t+1} + (K_{t+1} - K_t)$, invest in the project. This same rule applies when construction costs are expected to decline; here the expression $(K_{t+1} - K_t)$ is negative, increasing the likelihood that postponement will be indicated.

The assumption that B_t will increase through time guarantees that if $B_1 > rK$, the discounted value of all future benefits $\sum_t B_t (1 + r)^{-t}$ will be greater than K (here assumed constant through time). This is the only sense in which the characteristic of growing benefits is relevant. If the future stream of benefits is expected to rise for a period and subsequently decline (as competing roads are built, for example), the basic criterion of $B_1 > rK$ remains the valid one as far as timing is concerned. Once this question has been settled, one must then make the further check to assure oneself that $\sum_t B_t (1 + r)^{-t}$ is greater than K_0. If so, year zero is the optimal time to construct the project.

Similarly, when construction costs are expected to change the criterion of $B_{t+1} + (K_{t+1} - K_t)$ exceeding rK_t remains a necessary condition for construction at time t. But if expected benefits do not continue to rise indefinitely in the future the additional condition that the present value of expected future benefits exceed the capital cost of the project must also be fulfilled to warrant construction. If K is an increasing function of time, the above conditions are sufficient to justify construction; if K is a declining function of time a further test is necessary:

$$\sum_{t=0}^{t^*} B_t (1 + r)^{-t} \text{ must exceed } K_0 - K_{t^*}(1 + r)^{-t^*} \text{ for all } t^* > 0.[7]$$

In this section we have reached the conclusion that in most cases decisions regarding the timing of road improvements will be governed by the value of benefits in the first year of operation on the improved road. Since these benefits are closely linked to the existing volume of traffic on the unimproved road, the relevance of taking investment decisions largely on the basis of existing and immediately prospective traffic levels is established. Benefits in the farther future can be obtained in any event by building later; there is therefore no economic need to 'build ahead of demand' where road improvements are concerned.

The Problem of Segment Construction

The preceding analysis also suggests that road improvement ought to be carried to different levels on the different segments of a given road, depending on the volume of traffic they carry. There is no reason why the road from A to D should not contain a paved segment from A to B, a gravel segment from B to C, and an earth segment from C to D, if those are the qualities of road which traffic levels on the respective segments justify. One can be sure that large amounts of investible resources have been wasted (in the sense of yielding less-than-economic returns) as a result of the penchant of highway authorities to bring all segments of a road to a given quality level. Unlike the case of stage construction, where some small cost savings may be involved in single-stage construction, construction of a road in segments is likely to be no more costly than its construction as a single project, hence unitary construction of the whole is not justifiable by cost considerations. We must therefore look to the benefit side to justify bringing the whole length of a given road to the same level of quality. Certainly cases will exist in which this decision will be warranted; they will have the attribute that each of the distinct segments of the road is carrying approximately the same amount of traffic. But most roads of significant length do not possess this attribute; hence we must conclude that optimal road investment strategies are probably not being followed in most cases where roads are built to a single standard of quality over their entire length.

A minor qualification to the above judgment must be introduced, however, stemming from the external effects of road improvements. The paving of a stretch of road AB will cause traffic to increase on the unpaved stretch BC as this is the path of access to or egress from AB for some of its additional traffic. The fact that AB is paved, therefore, will increase the benefits to be obtained from paving BC.

Let *B* be the total present value of benefits (direct and

indirect) that would accrue from paving the entire road AC; let B_1 be the total present value of benefits of paving the stretch AB only, and B_2 the total benefit of paving the stretch BC only. Because of the complementarity between AB and BC alluded to above, we have the result that $B_1 + B_2 < B$. Let B_3 be the present value of benefits of paving the stretch BC, given that AB is already paved. $B_1 + B_3$ must equal B, since the two projects together amount to paving the entire road AC.

If K_1 represents the cost of paving AB, K_2 the cost of paving BC, and $K (= K_1 + K_2)$ the cost of paving the entire road AC, the possibility thus emerges that it would not pay to pave BC alone $(K_2 > B_2)$, but that if the stretch AB was to be paved, it would also pay to pave the stretch BC $(K_2 < B_3)$. It is even possible that it would not be worthwhile to pave either AB or BC alone $(K_1 > B_1$ and $K_2 > B_2)$, but that paving both together would be justified $(K = K_1 + K_2 < B = B_1 + B_3)$.

All of these possibilities are due to the complementarity relationship between adjacent stretches of the same road. How relevant they are likely to be depends on the difference between the traffic levels on the two stretches AB and BC. If the critical traffic level for paving either stretch alone is 1,000 vehicles per day, and if traffic has reached that level on AB but only stands at 500 vehicles per day on BC, there is no relevant justification for paving BC, once AB is paved. Paving AB is warranted, by assumption, even counting the diseconomy involved in increasing the traffic level on BC. But the increase in traffic on BC induced by paving AB will only be a part of the increase in traffic on AB; it may amount, plausibly, to 50 or 100 vehicles per day, but it would be absurd to assume that paving AB would bring traffic on BC from 500 to nearly 1,000 vehicles per day. (If 1,000 vehicles per day are required to justify paving BC alone, slightly less than 1,000 would be required to justify paving BC when AB is also paved, because the external diseconomies associated with paving BC will be slightly less in the latter case than in the former.) Thus we conclude that if traffic on BC is quite close to the level which would justify paving that stretch alone, paving it may indeed become worthwhile when AB is also to be paved. But if traffic on BC is significantly below the critical level, it is highly unlikely that paving it will be worthwhile regardless of whether the stretch AB is paved or not. Since in the real world there are great disparities among traffic levels on given roads, we must maintain, in spite of the above qualification, our general conclusion that normally it will be optimal to upgrade different stretches of a given road at widely separated times, and that at any given time the typical road should contain stretches of distinctly disparate qualities.

The Road-Rail Problem

It was shown in section IV that whenever a road project would reduce rail traffic without causing abandonment of some portion of the rail line, the diversion of traffic away from the railroad would represent in all probability a negative external effect of the road project. The amount of the external diseconomy would be the fares and freight rates that the railroad ceased to collect minus any savings of costs which the railroad would have as a consequence of its reduced traffic volume. In such cases of nonabandonment, then, the only issue is to be sure to take the external diseconomy into account when evaluating the road project. If its benefits, thus adjusted, exceed its costs, the road project is justified in spite of its negative effect on rail traffic.

When abandonment of a segment of track is likely as a consequence of a road project, the cost savings to the railroad are certain to be greater than in the case of nonabandonment, and it is even possible that these savings will be sufficiently great to convert what would otherwise be an external diseconomy into an external economy of the road project. For this to happen, the present value of the cost savings to the railroad, including the value of its abandoned properties in alternative uses, must exceed the present value of the fares and freight charges that would have been paid by traffic on the abandoned line in the absence of the road project. In short, the abandoned stretch of track must have been unprofitable even in the absence of the road project, in order for abandonment to cause a net external benefit for the road investment. This case is relevant, because, for political and other reasons, many segments of track on which trains are run are kept in operation in spite of yielding net losses. A road project may therefore, by providing alternative communication facilities of adequate quality, so reduce the political opposition to rail abandonment as to make such a move possible.

Under the circumstances, then, of (a) abandonment of track and (b) unprofitability of the abandoned stretch in the absence of the road project there may be a positive external effect of the road project on the operations of a competing rail line. Whether the effect will be positive or not depends on whether the loss of consumer surplus on that traffic that is involuntarily driven from using the railroad by the abandonment decision exceeds the net benefit enjoyed by the railroad on account of abandonment.

We have not discussed the case of complementarity between a road project and an existing railroad because of its relative unimportance in the modern world. In most countries, the rail facilities were built many decades ago, and the road networks early gave adequate access to the rail terminals. Thus while in principle the improvement of road access to the railroad could stimulate the use of the latter, generating a probable external benefit for the road project in question, in practice the number of such cases and the magnitude of the effects is likely to be very small. We therefore do not enter into a detailed analysis of such cases here; their proper treatment can be inferred from that described in the text for road projects that compete with railways, recognizing that increments in rail traffic where fares and freight rates exceed the relevant marginal costs of haulage will generate net external benefits to a complementary road project.

Notes

[1] Jan de Weille, *Quantification of Road User Savings* Washington, D.C.: IBRD, 1966.

[2] Note that the average vehicle carries more than one passenger; De Weille's data suggest averages of 1·8 passengers per automobile and of 1·2 passengers per truck. The saving of $·01 per vehicle mile would therefore be reached at a value of time of about $·37 per hour for occupants of passenger vehicles and of about $·56 per hour for the occupants of trucks.

[3] Richard M. Soberman, 'Economic Analysis of Highway Design in Developing Countries,' Highway research Board, *Highway Research Record*, No. 115 (publication 1337), 1966.

[4] A similar adjustment of the analysis to take account of differing traffic volumes at different times may also be advisable in the analysis of the direct benefits of a road improvement, which was outlined in section II. The first term in expression (1) would then become $\sum_t (1 + r)^{-t} \sum_i \sum_k (c_{itk} - c'_{itk}) V_{itk}$, and expression (2) would

become $\frac{1}{2}\Sigma_t(1+r)^{-t}\Sigma_i\Sigma_k(c_{itk}-c'_{itk})(V'_{itk}-V_{itk})$. This adjustment allows us to take account of the fact that the benefits of a road improvement are likely to be greater, per vehicle-mile, in periods of high traffic density than in periods of very low volume with essentially unimpeded flow.

[5] Some reduction in the size of trains may be occasioned by the road improvement if, before the improvement, the heaviest traffic volumes on the railroad were between B and C. In this case, the demand for rail movement between B and C would be the determining factor governing the size and/or number of trains, and a reduction in that demand would permit shorter and/or fewer trains. In the text, we assume that the BC stretch does not have this characteristic.

[6] Herman G. van der Tak and Jan de Weille, *An Economic Reappraisal of a Road Project*, IBRD Report No. EC-147, p. 48.

[7] All criteria derived in this section can be deduced from the basic proposition that the proper time to construct a project is that construction time for which the net present value of the project is highest, when net present value is discounted to the same point in time for all construction times being compared. The net present value of the project constructed at time zero is

$$\sum_{t=1}^{\infty} B_t(1+r)^{-t} - K_0 \quad \text{(a)};$$

the net present value, as of time zero, of the project constructed at time t^* is

$\sum_{t=t^*+1}^{\infty} B_t(1+r)^{-t} - K_{t^*}(1+r)^{-t^*}$ (b). The last condition in the text simply states that in order for construction at time zero to be optimal, (a) must exceed (b) for all t^*. A good general discussion of the timing problem, in which these issues are treated, can be found in Stephen A. Marglin, *Approaches to Dynamic Investment Planning*, Amsterdam: North-Holland Publishing Co., 1963, chapter 2.

CHAPTER ELEVEN

COSTS AND BENEFITS OF THE ULLUM DAM PROJECT: AN ANALYTICAL FRAMEWORK AND AN EMPIRICAL EXPLORATION

I. INTRODUCTION

In this study we present the results of a brief but extremely intensive examination of the potential costs and benefits of the projected irrigation and power dam at Ullum, in the province of San Juan, Argentina. Our investigation has led us to conclude that a methodology based on the market value of water rights is likely to provide the most accurate way of assessing the irrigation benefits of the project in question. This paper will concentrate on developing this methodology, and on providing its underlying rationale. We shall also present the results of assessing the costs and benefits of the project under a variety of alternative assumptions concerning the key variables involved. The alternatives chosen provide in each case a range which, in our judgment and on the basis of the information available to us, spans the plausible values of the variable in question. However, we should note at the outset that constraints of time and resources have not permitted us to carry our empirical investigations as far as we would like. It is possible, therefore, that further work will indicate that, in the cases of one or more variables, the range that we have chosen should be extended, narrowed, or otherwise modified. It is partly for this reason that we shall present a detailed exposition of the

This Report was prepared in collaboration with Lucio G. Reca and Juan A. Zapata for Edison Consult, S.A., Buenos Aires, Argentina, October, 1969.

underlying methodology, so that changes based on additional information may readily be introduced.

II. A BRIEF DESCRIPTION OF THE REGION AND THE PROJECT

The proposed dam would be located in the San Juan river to the northwest of the city of San Juan, at a place called Ullum canyon. Various alternative heights of the dam have been discussed, but the one which appears at present to be the most advantageous would be of 65 meters. This would create a lake of some 4,000 hectares of surface, and with a water volume, when the dam is full, of some 440 Hm³. The area that would be inundated by this lake is largely rocky riverbed, but it also contains some 1,000 hectares of cultivated land, with their corresponding buildings, vineyards, orchards, fences, roads, etc. It is estimated that the probable market value of the property that would have to be expropriated for a dam of 440 Hm³ capacity would be approximately m$n 1,000 million or $3 million (U.S.).

The southern edge of the lake would be along some heights overlooking the lowland district of Zonda. Two elements should be noted here in relation to Zonda. The first is that in order to hold 440 Hm³ of water, a retaining wall of up to 10 meters in height and some 2,000 meters in length would have to be built so as to prevent the lake from spilling over into the valley of Zonda. The second element is that when the lake is formed there will be a substantial filtration of water through porous and pebbly layers into the subsoil underlying the plain of Zonda. If pumping in the Zonda district does not increase, this filtration will be essentially a once-and-for-all phenomenon, and will not impede the operation of the dam. On the other hand, if pumping in Zonda were to increase substantially a not inconsequential share (perhaps as much as 10 percent) of the water that would normally be distributed by the dam through its canal system would be diverted to the Zonda area.

The actual area to be served by the dam consists of some 128,000 hectares. Of these about 92,000 have permanent irrigation rights, while the rest have rights of other kinds—either so-called accidental rights (which in theory can be exercised only in years of abnormally-high river flow) or rights to water coming from certain slopes (vertientes) and arroyos that originally carried substantial quantities of water but that by now have largely dried up. Although a strict interpretation of the irrigation law would restrict deliveries to the owners of the approximately 92,000 hectares with permanent rights, except in years of abnormally high riverflow, in fact water is regularly delivered to perhaps 28,000 additional hectares even though they do not possess permanent rights.

Water rights in theory consist of some 10,000 m³/ha/year, but the riverflow is not capable of producing this much water, save in exceptional years. During the main irrigation season, which we have taken to be from 15 September to 15 March, the average amount of water available for irrigation in the region to be served by the proposed dam was 734 Hm³ during the seasons from 1945–46 to 1968–69. This would provide only 7,340 m³ per hectare if distributed among 100,000 has. and only about 6,200 m³ if distributed among 120,000 has., even forgetting about canal losses, which affect the distribution to nearly all hectares, and in many cases substantially. The median amount of water available during the main irrigation season was only 649·4 Hm³ during the same period.

The 10,000 m³/ha/year figure, which might be called the 'theoretical' water right, happens to be the approximate amount of water judged to be optimal in the cultivation of vineyards, which are by far the dominant mode of agricultural land use in the area. (Other crops of some significance are olives, apricots, onions, and garlic; but these are all of minor importance compared to grapes.) The consequence of this fact is that of the 100,000–120,000 hectares that in principle receive water each year, only some 60,000 are in fact irrigated. A farmer with water rights for 50 hectares is likely in fact to irrigate only about half of them.

The fact that the number of hectares with water rights substantially exceeds the number of hectares actually irrigated has given rise to a not inconsequential number of transactions in which unimproved land with water rights has been sold to buyers who have no intention of cultivating the land in question. Their motive is to get additional water for the land they already own. We have what we believe to be reliable information from dealers in farm real estate (martilleros), officials of the Dirección de Hidraulica, and a considerable number of experienced farmers (most of them with several properties) that in such transactions the excess of the selling price of land over and above what its value would be without water rights lies between 200,000 and 250,000 pesos per hectare.[1] This datum on the value of water rights will play a key role in the procedure that we will develop for the estimation of benefits.

The drilling of wells to exploit potential sources of ground water began in a serious way in the late 1950's. By the early 1960s there were over 3,000 wells in the area, and at present there are over 6,000. The use of ground water reached an estimated maximum of 200 Hm^3 in 1968–69. This was an unprecedentedly dry season as far as riverflow was concerned, and during this year the use of ground water for irrigation may have exceeded that of surface water during the main irrigation season.

Irrigation conditions vary very substantially in different parts of the area to be served by the projected dam at Ullum. In an area of 33,000 hectares to the west and south of the city of San Juan, the subsoil is highly porous, and the subterranean waters drift freely and without pressure. Here it is necessary to pump water all the way from the aquifer to the surface. Because of the slope of the surface, the required pumping height ranges from as little as 0·50 meters to as much as 95 meters in this region of free-flowing underground water.

In much of the remaining area served by the proposed dam, underground water can be found under pressure in confined aquifers. The area overlying the aquifers (not just the cultivated area) is of about 281,000 hectares. In the early days of drilling, it was not uncommon to find artesian wells (surgentes), in which the underground pressure was so great that the well water reached ground level without pumping. As more and more wells have been drilled and as the water levels in the confined aquifers has been lowered, artesian wells have become less and less common. Yet it is quite normal today to find, in the area of confined aquifers, wells drilled to depths of 100 or 200 meters that will produce water which is driven by underground pressure to between 20 and 30 meters from the surface.

These wells thus require only 20–30 meters of pumping, in spite of their depth.

The depth of wells drawing on confined aquifers varies greatly over the region. The deepest drilling to date has been done in the Sarmiento area, some 70 kilometers to the south of the city of San Juan, where depths of as much as 480 meters have been reached, with the water rising as a result of underground pressure to within 10 to 20 meters of the surface. At the other extreme, in the Rawson area, wells reach confined aquifers with good water at depths of only around 15 meters, with the water rising under pressure to within 1 meter of the surface. Between these extremes, informed judgment places the 'typical' depth of wells in confined aquifers at 100 to 200 meters, with a pumping depth of some 20 meters.

There are three related characteristics of the area of confined aquifers that deserve special mention. The first is the variability in the quality of water found; the second is the frequent presence of multiple aquifers; and the third is the problem, in some districts, of increasing salinization of water near the surface. Variable water quality is largely due to the fact that some aquifers carry water that is highly saline or otherwise ill-suited for irrigation. Where this feature is present in an area with multiple aquifers, the tubewells must be sealed to prevent them from absorbing water from 'bad' aquifers while at the same time being left porous at those depths where 'good' aquifers are found. Where salinization is a problem near the surface, because irrigation water is captured in underground pools defined by impermeable layers, the only genuine solution is improved drainage. The need for better drainage facilities in some parts of the area is quite imperative, and in others it is clearly increasing as underground contaminated pools rise closer to the surface. It is likely that investment in major drainage projects will be worthwhile (and indeed virtually necessary) regardless of whether the proposed Ullum dam project is or is not approved.

The abundance of wells in the region and their rapid rate of growth, attests to the fact that on the average such wells have proved to be profitable investments. Drilling continues at a rapid rate today, despite the financial pressures caused by two consecutive years of drought, and despite a steady increase in the required depths of both drilling and pumping. Drilling costs, adjusted for the risks of finding water of poor quality, or even worse of finding none at all, can accordingly serve as an important indicator of the prices that farmers willingly pay for water, and hence of the value that additional water provided by the Ullum dam project is likely to have. Care must be taken here, however, on two counts. First, the water from a successful well can be obtained when and as it is desired by the farmer, the flow being limited only by pumping capacity and the size and depth of the well itself. By contrast, surface irrigation water comes to the farmer in quantities and at times which are governed by the current riverflow on the one hand and by the allocation rules of the irrigation authorities on the other. Secondly, farmers may find it worth their while to pay a relatively high price for well-water with which to supplement their surface-water rights, even though they might not find it worthwhile to drill wells for the purpose of brining into cultivation land without surface-water rights.[2] For both these reasons, the value of a given amount of additional surface irrigation water is likely to be less than the cost that farmers willingly incur to obtain an equal amount of pump irrigation water of similar quality. This fact will be used to guard against any possible gross overstatement of the value of surface water.

III. THE BASIC METHODOLOGY

The basic approach to measuring the value of incremental irrigation water is simple. Let v be the value [in our case assumed to be between 200,000 and 250,000 pesos] that the market places on the water rights attaching to a hectare of unimproved land. It is the price that farmers willingly pay for such rights, and since the great majority of farmers are leaving good land idle, there is every reason to suppose that the price that the market attaches to water rights is a competitive price.

The annual value of the water covered by a hectare's rights will be rv, where r is the rate of discount (in real terms) reflected in the private market for agricultural land.

Let u be the number of units of water (per irrigation season) that are contained in a typical hectare's water rights (more will be said on this later). Then (rv/u) is the value per unit of incremental surface-water rights.

Let N be the number of units of additional water that will be provided during the irrigation season, by the proposed dam. Then (Nrv/u) is the value attributable to the incremental water that will flow from the dam during the irrigation season, assuming that the outflows of water within the season are approximately as random and unregulated as the natural flow of the river itself.[3] That is to say, (Nrv/u) is the value that the amount N of incremental irrigation-season water would have if it came simply in the form of a generally enlarged natural streamflow, with the same relative variability as before as among the months of the season.

However, it is clear that the dam will permit significant improvement of the within-season distribution of irrigation water, both by smoothing out erratic variations in riverflow and by distributing the limited quantities available in water-short years in such a fashion as to minimize the costs entailed in the shortage. Let f be the factor by which the existence of the dam will enhance the efficiency of use of water, and let Q be the number of units of water expected to be available, in the average season, in the presence of the dam. Then $(fQrv/u)$ is the expected increase in the value of the annual irrigation-season availability of water owing to the possibility of regulating the within-season flow. (We will assume alternative values of the efficiency factor, f, of 0, 5 percent and 10 percent.)

Annual benefits stemming from the increased water availability and the increased efficiency of its use, taken together, are thus equal to $(rv/u)(N + fQ)$. To obtain the present value of these benefits we discount by the factor $(\rho + \delta)$, where ρ is the social rate of discount to be applied in evaluating the project, and δ is the rate of depreciation of the dam.[4] The present value of the two classes of benefits, therefore, is $(rv/u)(N + fQ)(1/[\rho + \delta])$. This present value actualizes benefits to the year before the benefit stream begins—that is, to the last year of construction of the project. Accordingly, in comparing benefits and costs, we shall accumulate capital costs and discount operating costs to this same year.

IV. ON THE UNIT OF MEASUREMENT OF IRRIGATION WATER FOR DEALING WITH THE PROBLEM OF THIS STUDY

Up to this point, we believe, the reader will have encountered no difficulty in following what is in all its essentials a very straightforward procedure. Now, however, we must take into account certain complications and introduce certain concepts which may prove somewhat elusive to readers who are not themselves professional economists. These complications emerge from the apparently-simple question 'What does a farmer buy when he acquires a piece of unimproved land in order to transfer its water rights to his present farm?' Unfortunately, the simple answer of a certain number of cubic meters of water per year is not truly correct. What the farmer buys is the right to a certain fraction of the streamflow of the river. This varies substantially both from month to month and from year to year. In a sense, upon acquiring water rights, a farmer becomes a participant in a sort of lottery, in which his annual or monthly 'prize' is subject to a great many random movements.

These random movements have many dimensions—it is not only how much water, but when it comes that matters, in addition to how acurately the flow was predicted before the season started. But we shall concentrate here on how much water arrives during the irrigation season, as variation in this has probably been the most important source of risk facing farmers. Figure 11.1 represents the probability distribution of total streamflow during the main irrigation season (taken in this study to run from 15 September to 15 March).

Several points are marked off on the horizontal axis. D_1 represents that total-season streamflow which is exceeded 90 percent of the time—such a point is called the first decile of the distribution. C_1 represents that streamflow which is exceeded 75 percent of the time—it is called the first quartile of the distribution. M represents the median of the distribution—the streamflow which is exceeded 50 percent of the time, and C_2 represents the third quartile, the streamflow which is exceeded only 25 percent of the time. P is the mean or conventional average of the distribution, in this case the average streamflow over a period of many years.

A comparison of Figures 11.1 and 11.2 will illustrate the point at issue. The two distributions have the same average streamflow (P), but that of Figure 11.2 reflects much less variability

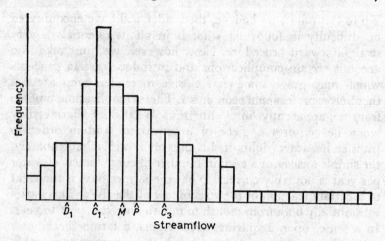

Figure 11.1. Hypothetical Streamflow Distribution

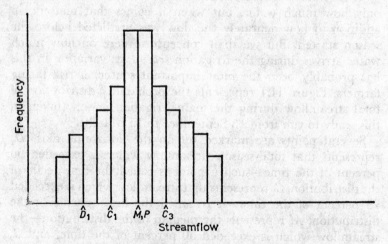

Figure 11.2. Hypothetical Streamflow Distribution

of streamflow. If a farmer could bid for irrigation rights in either the river described by Figure 11.1 or that described by

Figure 11.2, he would surely (assuming the average reaching his farm to be the same) be willing to pay more for the rights from the second river. Whether he is worried about how much water he can more or less count on having in at least 90 per cent of the years (D_1) or how much will be exceeded in 75 percent of the years (C_1) or how much will be exceeded in half the years (M), the figure is in each case higher for the distribution of Figure 11.2 than for that of Figure 11.1.

One convenient way of reflecting the preference for the second distribution over the first is to use as a measure of the volume of water not the mean but a weighted average of D_1, C_1, M, and C_3. This is what we have done in the present paper, using two alternative weighting patterns. The first, which we call index 1 is $I_1 = \cdot 4D_1 + \cdot 3C_1 + \cdot 2M + \cdot 1C_3$, and the second, which we call index 2, is $I_2 = \cdot 33D_1 + \cdot 27C_1 + \cdot 23M + \cdot 17C_3$. The first weighting pattern places a considerably higher premium on steadiness of waterflow than the second, but even the second places a substantial premium on steadiness as compared with the conventional average P. In essence these weighting patterns implicitly place a higher value on '90 percent-sure' water than on '50 percent-sure' water, and so on. In doing so they reflect the way farmers themselves view the risks caused by streamflow variations (as shown by the relatively substantial pumping costs that farmers are willing to bear to reduce those risks, as well as by other evidence).

V. ESTIMATING IRRIGATION-SEASON WATER VOLUMES

The farmers who transact in the market for water by buying and selling essentially unimproved land with water rights must implicitly have a view of the probability distribution of irrigation water. For some of them, this view is based upon careful study of the hydrological statistics of the region, while for others it is probably based principally upon their own experience. For this reason, in this analysis based on farmers' behavior in the marketplace, we have employed streamflow data for the period from 1945–46 through 1968–69, considering that much earlier data would be beyond the memory of most current participants in the land market.[5] In Table 11.1, column 1, we show the calculated distribution of water volumes expected to be available for irrigation during the main irrigation season. While the distribution is based on historical data, our use of it is to get an idea of what farmers are likely to expect when they buy water via irrigation rights. This is reflected in the fact that we have reduced seasonal steamflow by 24 Hm³ for each observation to allow for an expected domestic and industrial use of 4 Hm³ per month. This is a forward-looking estimate, for the most recent estimates of domestic and industrial use are 2·7 Hm³ per month, and for earlier years the amounts going to these uses were even lower. The figure in column 1 of Table 11.1 for any season should therefore not be interpreted as what was actually available for irrigation during that season, but rather as what, on the average, is likely to be available if that season's streamflow were to recur in a typical future year within the horizon relevant to farmers' decisions on the purchase or sale of land.

The expected domestic and industrial use of water is thus one source of difference between the figures of column 1 and the actual streamflows of the corresponding historical seasons. The second source of difference stems from the capacity of the canal system itself, which is about 100 m^3/sec. Whenever the historical data on streamflow showed an average figure in excess of 100 m^3/sec. for a month, the amount available for irrigation was set at 100 m^3/sec. because of the canal capacity limitation.

Column 2 of Table 11.1 presents estimates of the potential carryover of water from the preceding winter period into each of the seasons.

To obtain column 2, we reduced the actual streamflow from March 15 to September 15 by amounts which were estimated by the team from Harza Engineering Co. (Chicago and Buenos Aires) that is studying the Ullum dam project as the water requirements during these months on the assumption that 60,000 hectares are in fact irrigated.[6] The remaining off-season streamflow (given in column 2) was assumed to be stored in the dam.

Column 3 of Table 11.1 gives the amount of excess flow from the preceding irrigation season. This excess flow is simply the excess over an average of 100 m^3/sec., for whatever months of

TABLE 11.1
Irrigation Water Availabilities with and Without Dam
(15 September–15 March)

	Without Dam River-flow Available for Irrigation 15 September–14 March[a] Hm³ (1)	Potential Carryover from Previous Winter[b] Hm³ (2)	Potential Carryover from Previous Summer Hm³ (3)	Total ≤440 = (2) + (3) but ≤440 Hm³ (4)	Irrigation Season Water Availability with Dam 15 September–15 March (1) + (4) Hm³ (5)
1945–46	601·2	579·8		440	1041·2
1946–47	557·6	341·9		341·9	899·5
1947–48	649·4	226·8		226·8	876·2
1948–49	1038·2	254·6		254·6	1292·8
1949–50	542·1	307·4	78·3	385·7	927·8
1950–51	649·4	268·1		268·1	917·5
1951–52	523·4	264·4		264·4	787·8
1952–53	816·0	290·9		290·9	1106·9
1953–54	1305·7	379·2		379·2	1684·9
1954–55	1028·9	693·3	1183·0	440·0	1468·9
1955–56	766·0	502·0		440·0	1206·0
1956–57	434·9	270·3		270·3	705·2
1957–58	1070·9	256·4		256·4	1327·3
1958–59	546·8	279·7	61·7	341·4	888·2
1959–60	641·6	226·8		226·8	868·4
1960–61	714·7	245·4		245·4	960·1
1961–62	980·7	261·0		261·0	1241·7
1962–63	551·4	267·2	3·1	270·3	821·7
1963–64	1035·1	220·6		220·6	1255·7
1964–65	439·4	442·9	208·0	440·0	879·4
1965–66	1271·5	289·3		289·3	1560·8
1966–67	789·4	592·5		440·0	1229·4
1967–68	423·9	282·8		282·8	706·7
1968–69	238·8	172·3		172·3	411·1
Total	17617·0	7865·6		7448·2	25065·2
Average	734·0	327·7		310·3	1044·4

[a] Average streamflow during the six-month season, but where streamflow was greater than 100 m^3/sec. (the capacity of the canal system), the latter figure was used. The excess above canal capacity was considered as potential for storage, and entered in col. (3). In arriving at irrigation potential, streamflow was reduced by 4 Hm³ per month (24 Hm³ for the season) in concept of prospective residential and industrial use.

[b] Excess of winter streamflow over Harza estimates of off-season requirements for irrigation plus domestic and industrial use.

the preceding season the 100 m³/sec. figure was exceeded. This is water that would have been lost to the river in the absence of the dam; in the presence of the dam it is assumed to be stored and held for the next season.[7]

Column 4 of Table 11.1 is in most cases the total of columns 2 and 3, representing the total of stored water carried into the irrigation season in question. However, when that total exceeds 440 Hm³, the latter figure was substituted instead, reflecting the assumed capacity of the dam.

Column 5 of Table 11.1 gives the total amount of irrigation water that would have been available in each season in the presence of a dam operated under the assumed strategy. A comparison of the distribution of the figures in this column with that of those in column 1 will indicate the benefits that the dam would make possible through increased availability of irrigation water during the main season. Such a comparison is made in Figure 11.3.

Without dam (actual)

First decile (D₁) 428·3
First quartile (C₁) 544·5
Median (M) 649·4
Third quartile (C₃) 1004·8

Arithmetic mean   (P)   734·0
Quantity index I_1 [·4, ·3, ·2, ·1] 565·0
Quantity index I_2 [·33, ·27, ·23, ·17] 608·5

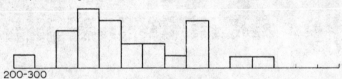

200-300

With dam of 440 Hm³ capacity (estimated)

First decile (D₁) 705·7
First quartile (C₁) 872·3
Median   (M) 944·0
Third quartile (C₃) 1248·7

Arithmetic mean   (P)   1044·4
Quantity index I_1 [4, ·3, ·2, ·1] 857·6
Quantity index I_2 [33, ·27, ·23, ·17] 897·8

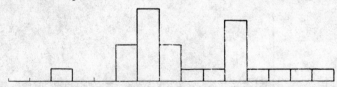

Figure 11.3. Water Available for Irrigation, 15 September to 15 March 1945–46 to 1968–69 (in Cubic Hectometers)

In spite of the rudimentary strategy of dam operation that is incorporated in our calculations, there are clearly substantial benefits that result from its presence. The mean amount of water in the irrigation season increases by 33 percent, from 734·0 Hm³ to 1,044·4 Hm³. But more important is the relative change in the distribution. While the relatively insecure water represented by the third quartile rises by only 24 percent, the median rises by 45 percent, and the very secure water represented by the first quartile and first decile rises by 60 and 65 percent respectively. Our two indexes of water quantity adjusted for degree of security rise by 48 percent for I_2 (with weights of ·33, ·27, ·23, ·17) and by 52 percent for I_1 (with weights of ·4, ·3, ·2, ·1). This is even without taking into account the still greater improvement in security of water supplies that could be generated by a more sophisticated strategy of dam management.

VI. ON PROJECT COSTS

We have not ourselves looked deeply into the question of project costs, and accordingly are basing our calculations on the best available estimates. In round numbers, these are that the capital cost of the project will be the equivalent of about $24,000,000 (U.S.) and that the value of the lands to be inundated is the equivalent of about $3,000,000 (U.S.). Ing. Pronsato, of Edison Consult, S.A. (Buenos Aires) estimates that the period of construction will be three and one-half years with the following distribution of costs:

Year	Percentage of Total Costs	Amount (in equivalents of U.S. dollars)
1 (last half)	7	$1,680,000
2	49	11,760,000
3	27	6,480,000
4	17	4,080,000
Total	100	$24,000,000

As our procedure for estimating benefits produces estimates which are discounted to the year before the project enters into operation (in this case year 4) these capital costs must be accumulated to that same year in order to be comparable. This is done in Table 11.2 for the two discount rates—10 percent and 15 percent per annum that we are applying in this study.

TABLE 11.2

Accumulated Capital Costs
(in equivalents of U.S. dollars)

Year Costs Incurred	Accumulated Costs	Social Discount Rate (ρ)	
		10 percent	15 percent
1	$1.680.000\ (1+\rho)^{2\frac{1}{2}}$	$2,134,400	$2,388,400
2	$11.760.000\ (1+\rho)^{2}$	14,229,600	15,552,600
3	$6.480.000\ (1+\rho)$	7,128,000	7,452,000
4	$4.080.000$	4,080,000	4,080,000
		$27,572,000	$29,473,000

The above figures do not include any costs of expropriation or any other allowance for the economic costs entailed in connection with the inundated lands. We believe that the relevant cost is the economic cost involved in the loss of these lands together with their associated buildings, fences, roads, vineyards and orchards, once flooding occurs, plus the value of the net product of these resources that may be forgone during the period of construction of the dam. We estimate the value of the resources that will be lost at the equivalent of $3,000,000 (U.S.), and the annual net product of those resources at the private rate of discount (r) times this figure. Since we are taking present values as of year 4, and since beginning with year 5 the resources in question will really be under water, we lose the full value of their net productivity from year 5 onwards. Their annual net productivity divided by the social rate of discount represents the present value, as of year 4, of the loss of productivity from year 5 onwards. Their annual net productivity divided by the private rate of discount should yield the market price of the resources in question, so long as the expected future stream of net yields would have been constant through time. On this assumption, the social cost of the lost productivity from year 5 onwards will be $3,000,000 \times (r/\rho)$, with discounting done to year 4.

Ing. Pronsato estimates that approximately 30 per cent of the total area to be expropriated will have to be acquired prior to the start of work. The production of this area will be lost from years 1 through 4, in addition to the period from year 5 onwards. We assume that, even though no further expropriations take place, there will be a gradual reduction in production on the remaining lands between years 2 and 4. Overall we shall assume that 30 percent of the normal net production is lost in year 1, 40 percent in year 2, 55 percent in year 3, and 70 percent in year 4. Normal net production, as before, is taken to be the private rate of discount (r) times the value of the properties in question.

Table 11.3 summarizes the calculation of the social costs due to the flooding of lands. The estimates range widely (from \$2.7 to 5.5 million [U.S.]) when the social and private rates are different, but are quite close together when the two rates are the same—being \$3.7 million (U.S.) when the rates are both 10 percent and \$4.0 million (U.S.) when the two rates are both 15 percent per annum.

The final component of the cost figure is the present value of the operating costs of the dam. These are in large measure wage and salary costs of a resident engineer and operating personnel, but they also include the materials to maintain the equipment in operating condition. Ing. Pronsato estimates these costs to be, at current levels of real wages, \$30,000 per year, and we project them to rise in real terms at the rate of $2\frac{1}{2}$ percent per year. Once again taking present values by approximating the projected flows with a perpetuity, we have for the present value of operating costs, the expression \$30,000/$(\rho - .025)$. This is \$400,000 when the social discount rate is 10 percent and \$240,000 when the social discount rate is 15 percent.

Table 11.4 summarizes our estimates of the present value of costs under the alternative assumptions we are using regarding ρ and r. As can be seen, the present value of costs (actualized to year 4) is relatively insensitive to alternative assumptions regarding discount rates, ranging between \$31.6 million (U.S.) to \$33.8 million (U.S.) over four alternative combinations treated.

VII. THE ESTIMATES OF BENEFITS

Estimates of the present value of benefits are presented for our three different quantity measures, I_1, I_2, and P, in Tables 11.5, 11.6, and 11.7. In each table there are four subtables, each

TABLE 11.3
Present Value of Social Costs due to Inundation of Lands
(in equivalents of U.S. dollars, actualized to year 4)

	10%	10%	15%	15%
Social rate of Discount (ρ)				
Private rate of Discount (r)	10%	15%	10%	15%
Loss in productivity of inundated lands from year 5 onwards = \$3,000,000 × (r/ρ)	\$3,000,000	\$4,500,000	\$2,000,000	\$3,000,000
Loss in productivity during year 1 = US \$3,000,000 × $r(1+\rho)^3 \times 0\cdot3$	119,790	179,685	136,890	205,335
Loss in productivity during year 2 = US \$3,000,000 × $r(1+\rho)^2 \times 0\cdot4$	145,200	217,800	158,712	238,050
Loss in productivity during year 3 = US \$3,000,000 × $r(1+\rho) \times 0\cdot55$	181,500	272,250	189,750	284,625
Loss in productivity during year 4 = US \$3,000,000 × $r \times 0\cdot7$	210,000	315,000	210,000	315,000
Total	\$3,656,490	\$5,484,735	\$2,695,352	\$4,043,010

TABLE 11.4

Present Value of Estimated Costs of Ullum Dam

(in millions of equivalent U.S. dollars, actualized to year 4)

	10%	10%	15%	15%
Social Rate of Discount (ρ)				
Private Rate of Discount (r)	10%	15%	10%	15%
Capital Costs	$27,572,000	$27,572,000	$29,473,000	$29,473,000
Costs due to Inundation	3,656,490	5,484,735	2,695,352	4,043,010
Operating Costs	400,000	400,000	240,000	240,000
Total	$31,628,490	$33,456,735	$32,408,352	$33,756,010
Total (Rounded)	$31,630,000	$33,460,000	$32,410,000	$33,760,000

TABLE 11.5

Present Value of Benefits Based on Changes in Quantity Index I_1

(Weighting pattern [·4, ·3, ·2, ·1])

Private Discount Rate		Social Discount Rate					
		15%			10%		
v	H	$f=0$	$f=\cdot05$	$f=\cdot1$	$f=0$	$f=\cdot05$	$f=\cdot1$
15%							
250	120	38,021	43,594	49,182	53,229	61,034	68,838
250	100	31,717	36,367	41,028	44,405	50,915	57,426
200	120	30,430	34,891	39,363	42,603	48,849	55,095
200	100	25,364	29,082	32,810	35,510	40,716	45,923
			Cost = 33,760			Cost = 33,460	
10%							
250	120	25,314	29,025	32,745	35,440	40,636	45,832
250	100	21,100	24,194	27,295	29,541	33,872	38,203
200	120		23,216	26,191	28,347	32,503	36,659
200	100			23,665	27,135	30,605	
			Cost = 32,410			Cost = 31,630	

corresponding to a certain combination of social and private discount rates. Within each subtable the columns refer to different values of the efficiency factor, f, and the rows refer to different values of the value of water rights per hectare, v, and the number of hectares, H, on the basis of which water is in fact distributed. The value of u, the number of units per hectare, which appears in the formulas of section III, is either (I_1/H), (I_2/H), or (P/H), depending on which quantity measure is used.

To carry through an illustrative calculation, consider the estimate in the lower right-hand corner of the subtable at the upper left of Table 11.5. In that row, the value of water per hectare, v, is 200,000 pesos. The index I_1, in the absence of the dam, has a value of 565·0 million units, and the number of hectares on the basis of which water is distributed is 100,000. Thus the typical hectare gets, in a typical year, 5,650 units. The private discount rate being 15 percent, the annual value of the water rights attaching to a hectare is 30,000 pesos, and the value of a unit of water is therefore $30,000/5,650$, or 5·31 pesos. The quantity index increases, as a consequence of the dam, by 292·6 million units. Valued at 5·31 pesos, this amounts to 1,553·7 million pesos.

In addition, because the factor f is assumed to be 0·1 in the particular cell that we are analyzing, we have a benefit from the improved efficiency of water use equal to 10 percent of what would otherwise be the value of a season's water in the presence of the dam. This value is 857·6 million times 5·31 pesos, or 4,554 million pesos. Ten percent of this is 455·4 million pesos. The total annual benefit is therefore 2,009 million pesos. The present value of this at a 15 percent discount rate and $2\frac{1}{2}$ percent annual depreciation is $(2,009/\cdot175) = 11,480$ million pesos. This, converted to dollars at 350 pesos per dollar, is equal to $32,810,000 (U.S.), the figure that appears in the table. The other figures presented in Tables 11.5, 11.6, and 11.7 are derived in a similar fashion.

VIII. INTERPRETATION OF THE RESULTS
With Different Social and Private Discount Rates

Tables 11.8, 11.9, and 11.10 present the benefit-cost ratios corresponding to the various combinations of assumptions we

TABLE 11.6

Present Value of Benefits Based on Changes in Quantity Index I_2

(Weighting pattern [·33, ·27, ·23, ·17])

Private Discount Rate			Social Discount Rate					
			15%			10%		
v	H		$f=0$	$f=·05$	$f=·1$	$f=0$	$f=·05$	$f=·1$
15%								
250	120		34,947	40,371	45,795	48,926	56,520	64,113
250	100		29,094	33,611	38,127	40,733	47,055	53,377
200	120		27,954	32,293	36,632	39,137	45,210	51,284
200	100		23,275	26,888	30,501	32,587	37,644	42,702
10%				15%			10%	
250	120			26,946	30,566	32,656	37,762	42,792
250	100					27,171	31,388	35,605
200	120					26,037	30,078	34,119
200	100						25,132	28,508

TABLE 11.7

Present Value of Benefits Based on Changes in Mean Water Volume

(Weighting [Mean])

Private Discount Rate			Social Discount Rate					
			15%			10%		
v	H		$f=0$	$f=·05$	$f=·1$	$f=0$	$f=·05$	$f=·1$
15%								
250	120		31,057	36,281	41,504	43,481	50,793	58,105
250	100		25,896	30,251	34,606	36,255	42,352	48,449
200	120		24,832	29,008	33,184	34,765	40,611	46,458
200	100		20,717	24,201	27,685	29,004	33,881	38,759
10%				15%			10%	
250	120			24,139	27,614	28,929	33,794	38,659
250	100					24,186	28,254	32,321
200	120					23,118	27,006	30,894
200	100						25,784	

TABLE 11.8

Benefit-Cost Ratios Based on Changes in Index I_1

(Weighting pattern [·4, ·3, ·2, ·1])

Private Discount Rate		Social Discount Rate 15%			Social Discount Rate 10%		
v	H	f = 0	f = ·05	f = ·1	f = 0	f = ·05	f = ·1
15%							
250	120	1·126	1·291	1·457	1·591	1·824	2·057
250	100	·939	1·077	1·215	1·327	1·522	1.716
200	120	·901	1·033	1·166	1·273	1·460	1·646
200	100	·751	·861	·972	1·06†	1·217	1·372
10%			15%			10%	
250	120	·781	·895	1·041	1·120	1·284	1·449
250	100	·651	·746	·842	·934	1·071	1·208
200	120		·716	·808	·896	1·027	1·159
200	100				·748	·858	·967

TABLE 11.9

Benefit Cost Ratios Based on Changes in Index I_2

(Weighting pattern [·33, ·27, ·23, ·18])

Private Discount Rate		Social Discount Rate					
15%		15%			10%		
v	H	$f=0$	$f=·05$	$f=·1$	$f=0$	$f=·05$	$f=·1$
250	120	1·035	1·196	1·356	1·462	1·689	1·916
250	100	·862	·995	1·129	1·217	1·406	1·595
200	120	·828	·956	1·085	1·169	1·351	1·532
200	100	·689	·796	·903	·974	1·125	1·276
10%			15%			10%	
250	120		·831	·943	1·032	1·194	1·353
250	100				·859	·992	1·125
200	120				·823	·851	1·079
200	100					·794	·901

TABLE 11.10

Benefit-Cost Ratio Based on Changes in Index

(Weighting pattern [Mean])

Private Discount Rate		Social Discount Rate					
15%		15%			10%		
v	H	$f=0$	$f=·05$	$f=·1$	$f=0$	$f=·05$	$f=·1$
250	120	·920	1·075	1·229	1·299	1·518	1·736
250	100	·767	·896	1·025	1·083	1·266	1·448
200	120	·735	·859	·983	1·039	1·214	1·388
200	100	·614	·717	·820	·867	1·012	1·158
10%			15%			10%	
250	120		·745	·852	·914	1·068	1·222
250	100				·765	·893	1·022
200	120				·731	·854	·977
200	100						·815

have used. Perhaps the outstanding feature of the table is the tendency for the project to be accepted in virtually all cases when the private rate of discount is 15 percent and the social rate 10 percent, and for it to be rejected in virtually all cases when the private rate of discount is 10 percent and the social rate 15 percent. The reason for this is obvious. When the private rate is 15 percent, and water rights cost 200,000 pesos per hectare, the annual value of water per hectare is 30,000 pesos. Discounting this at a social rate of discount of 10 percent reveals that from the social point of view, under these assumptions, the present value of the water rights is really worth 300,000 pesos. This is the basic reason why the figures in the upper right-hand quadrant of each of Tables 11.8, 11.9, and 11.10 are so favorable to the project.

On the other hand, when the private rate of discount is 10 percent and the social rate 15, the opposite occurs. When water rights cost 10 percent, the annual value of water per hectare is $20,000. When this is discounted at a social rate of 15 percent, the resulting social present value of a hectare's water rights is 133,000 pesos. Small wonder, then, that the benefit-cost ratios tend to be very low in the lower left-hand quadrant of each of Tables 11.8, 11.9, and 11.10. (It will be noticed that within each quadrant of each of these tables, the entries have been arrayed so that the benefit-cost ratio rises as one moves from left to right and from bottom to top. The entries in the lower left-hand quadrants were left incomplete, once it was found that even the highest ratios were significantly less than one.)

While it is easy to explain why the given assumptions lead to high ratios when the social rate is lower than the private, and to low ratios in the opposite case, the question of what rates are really correct for the Argentine case is quite another matter. We shall not be able here to give a full treatment of this subject, but certain basic points should be made. In the first place, as regards the relationship between social and private rates of discount, it is convenient first to define the social rate. This is itself a complicated concept,[8] but in general it can be viewed as the average yield that would be lost if capital were extracted from the private sector. The social yield of investment is a gross-of-tax concept, hence those parts of the private sector that are most heavily taxed (in general the corporate sector) tend to have the highest social productivity of capital. In areas where the use of capital is subject to subsidies—either directly or through special treatment under the income tax—the social yield of capital tends to be lowest. Following along this line, if the present project were in the corporate sector, with no special subsidies involved, it is likely that it would be proper to use a social rate lower than the gross-of-tax yield on corporate investments. Correspondingly if the project were in the housing sector, it is likely that the corresponding private discount rate would be lower than the social discount rate (=social opportunity cost of capital).

Though we have not made a thorough analysis of the subject, we feel confident that the social rate of discount does not lie above the private rate for vineyard cultivation in San Juan. The 10 percent tax to which the output is subject may or may not be as heavy a burden on capital as the corporation income tax is in the corporate sector, but it surely, in our judgment, makes the gross-of-tax yield on capital in vineyard operations at least equal to and possibly somewhat above the broad average opportunity cost for the country as a whole. On the other hand, we doubt very much that any excess of the private discount rate for vineyards over the social discount rate could be as great as the difference shown in the upper right-hand quadrants of Tables 11.8, 11.9, and 11.10.

For these reasons we are inclined to discard the results in both the upper-right and lower-lefthand quadrants of the tables, while reserving the thought that it might prove appropriate on further analysis of the relative tax position of vineyard operations to use a private discount rate perhaps 2 percentage points or so above the social rate.

When the Social and Private Rates of Discount are the Same

As we turn to the upper lefthand and lower righthand quadrants the panorama appears somewhat different. In each of the tables, in these quadrants, the benefit-cost ratios range from considerably less than one to considerably greater than one. We are therefore called upon to refine the ranges that we have allowed for the key parameters, on the basis of the best information and judgment that we can bring to bear.

As our investigations have proceeded, even during the writing of this report, we have become convinced of four things:

(1) It is virtually certain that the distribution of water is in fact made on the basis of some 120,000 hectares, rather than solely on the basis of the 92,000 hectares with permanent rights in the area to be served by the proposed dam. On this basis we discard rows 2 and 4 in each quadrant;

(2) The value of 250,000 pesos per hectare for water rights appears to be somewhat on the high side. Although transactions have been reported to us at figures as high as 300,000 pesos per hectare, it now is apparent to us that 200,000 pesos is a more representative figure than 250,000 pesos, as far as the bulk of transactions are concerned where the main purpose of the transaction is the ultimate transfer by the new owner of water rights from the acquired property to other property he owns. On this basis we discard the first two rows of each quadrant;

(3) All our informants agree that the supposition that the operation of the dam will lead to no improvement in the efficiency of water use is absurd. Indeed, our only purpose in introducing it was to provide a basis of comparison with what we felt were the far more plausible (and probably still very conservative) assumptions of $f = \cdot05$ and $f = \cdot10$. We therefore discard the first column of each of the tables; and

(4) Our informants also agree that a system which makes no allowance for the different relative values of '90 percent sure water', '50 percent sure water', '25 percent sure water', etc. is also absurd. We feel the same, and on this basis we discarded Table 11.10 in its entirety. It too, of course, can still serve as a basis of comparison.

These observations distill out of Tables 11.8, 11.9, and 11.10 the information presented in Table 11.11. It is seen there that the benefit-cost ratios in the eight cases are all near one, and exceed unity for six of the eight possibilities. It is also clear that with only a slight rise of the private discount rate above the social rate, the benefit-cost ratio for the combination of the quantity index I_1 with $f = \cdot05$ would also rise above unity. In any case, however, it is our opinion and that of our informants that the increase in efficiency of water use as a consequence of the proposed dam should probably be 10 percent or more.

TABLE 11.11

Benefit-Cost Ratios Under Preferred Assumptions

	Index I_1 (·4, ·3, ·2, ·1) *Social and Private Discount Rate*			*Quantity Index* I_2 (·33, ·27, ·23, ·17) *Social and Private Discount Rate*	
	15%	*10%*		*15%*	*10%*
$f = ·05$	1·033	1·027	$f = ·05$	·956	·951
$f = ·10$	1·166	1·159	$f = ·10$	1·085	1·079

One notable feature of Table 11.11 is the lack of sensitivity of the benefit-cost ratios to the rate of discount used. This stems from the procedure of basing our estimates on the value of water rights, so long as the private and social rates are the same. If the private discount rate is high this means that a 200,000 peso value of water rights per hectare means a high annual benefit from an additional hectare's quota of water. But if the social discount rate is equally high, the present value of that high annual benefit will be reduced, on discounting, back to 200,000 pesos. One can be quite confident that, performing the same exercise with discount rates ranging anywhere from, say, 5 percent to 20 percent, the results would not be significantly different from those reflected in Table 11.11. In this sense, one can say that the benefit-cost ratios of Table 11.11 are approximately valid, under the assumptions of this analysis, for a very wide range of discount rates. They are robust figures in the sense of being insensitive to discount-rate changes, so long as the private and social rates remain equal to one another.

On Discount Rates, Water Values, and Pumping Costs

Even though, for equal private and social discount rates, our results are very insensitive to changes in the rate, this does not mean that one can state with equal validity that the project would pass the test at a 20 percent discount rate as at a 10 percent discount rate. The reason is that, for a given market value of a hectare of water rights, the implied value of a cubic meter of water varies directly with the discount rate. On the assumptions of a 200,000 pesos-per-hectare value of water rights and of distribution on the basis of 120,000 hectares, we calculate the value of an average cubic meter of surface-irrigation water at 3·26 pesos, using a 10 percent rate. If the discount rate is 15 percent, this becomes 4·90 pesos, and if the discount rate is 20 percent, the implied value of surface-irrigation water is 6·52 pesos per m^3.

In interpreting these values it should be noted (a) that they refer to water which is subject to monthly and yearly variation—it is not sure water, and (b) that they refer to volumes of water distributed into each of the main canal systems, not to the volumes that the farmer actually places on his land. To adjust for the variability of streamflow and for the effects of canal losses, the above water values per m^3 must be raised substantially.

These figures, adjusted upward as indicated, can be compared with pumping costs, because pumping costs reflect prices that farmers willingly pay to get additional water. In dealing with pumping costs one should realize that the relevant costs are not those of the farmers who are lucky enough to find a free-flowing aquifer with good water at, say, 5 meters below the surface. We are interested in those figures that relate to wells that are marginally successful, in the sense that they cover full cost including the normal rate of return on the capital invested in them. Since wells of between 100 and 200 meters have been drilled in abundance, and since drilling continues at these depths, it appears that in general such wells have proved profitable.

There follow some figures for a 10″ well of 140 meters depth, based on a study by Ing. Daniel Coria Jofré. It is assumed that the water rises in this well to a depth from the surface of 30 meters. For this well we have

Capital Cost of Well	2200,000 pesos
Capital Cost of Equipment	2300,000 pesos
Lubrication and Maintenance per hour of operation	550 pesos/hour
Labor (per hour of operation)	50 pesos/hour
Total Variable Costs	600 pesos/hour

Yield of well approximately 600 m^3/hour. Variable costs per m^3 = 1 peso.

Fixed costs per m^3 depend on intensity of use and on the discount rate used. We shall assume that the well is used 1,000 hours per year, and alternatively apply discount rates of 10, 15, and 20 percent. We shall also apply exponential depreciation at 10 percent to all capital costs. Under these assumptions annual capital costs come to 450,000 pesos at a 10 percent rate, 675,000 pesos at a 15 percent rate, and 900,000 pesos at a 20 percent rate. Total costs per m^3 are therefore 5·5, 7·75 and 10·0 pesos at 1,000 hours of operation per year, depending on the discount rate used.

If the well is used for 2,000 hours a year (a high amount indeed), the total costs per m^3 are reduced to 3·25, 4·38, and 5·5 pesos under our three alternative discount-rate assumptions. Before comparing these figures with the implicit values of surface water, derived earlier, one must note several key points. First, these values assume that the farmer was successful in finding good water, on his first attempt at drilling. We know on the other hand that there are significant risks of failure in drilling—either in the sense of finding no water or, more importantly in San Juan, of finding bad water. Second, there are risks that even though good water is found, it will become contaminated later on. Finally, for farms with only one pump, there are risks of equipment failure at critical points in the season.

All of the above points mean, in effect, that farmers are paying more for their well water than we have calculated on the basis of Ing. Coria's data. But we believe it sufficient to note that pump-irrigation costs, as estimated, clearly exceed our implied values of surface-irrigation water when the well is used 1,000 hours a year, for all three discount rates. Where the well is used, 2,000 hours per year, the costs per m^3 of ground water and surface water are about equal for a 10 percent rate of discount, while ground-water costs are about 10 percent lower than surface-water costs when a 15 percent rate is used, and about 20 percent lower when a 20 percent rate is used.

We do not take these findings to show decisively that additional surface water would not be valuable enough to warrant the construction of the Ullum dam if the private and social rates of discount were 15 percent or 20 percent respectively.

But they do suggest that as the discount rate is raised, the relative balance becomes less favorable to the Ullum project, in the sense that the implied costs of irrigation water per m^3 increases faster than the cost actually borne by farmers for pumping (with both costs being evaluated using the same discount rate).

Finally, let us note that the rates of discount that correspond to this analysis (and to cost-benefit analyses quite generally) are conceptually real rates of interest. As long as benefits and costs are forecast on the basis of the present price level (that is, in terms of the 1969 general index and the 1969 value of the dollar) the interest rate used should be free of any factor of inflationary expectations. Allowance can and should be made, within this general framework, for changes in relative prices; as we have done in projecting the operating costs of the dam to rise at $2\frac{1}{2}$ percent per year, but unless the projection of benefits and costs includes a general inflation factor, the rate used for discounting must be what we have called a real rate. It is our judgment that the current structure of interest rates in Argentina reflects an anticipated inflation rate of some 5 or more percent. Thus our discount rate of 10 percent should be compared with market interest rates of 15 percent or more, and our discount rate of 15 percent should be compared with market interest rates of 20 percent or more. We judge that when this comparison is made, the interest rates used in this study cannot be judged to be too low. Our conclusion then, is that within the range of phenomena covered in the present study, the project at Ullum appears to have benefits in excess of costs at real discount rates of either 10 or 15 percent.

IX. SOME NEGLECTED ELEMENTS

In closing, we should like to note some issues that we simply have not been able to investigate:

(1) *The convenience of adding to the Ullum dam a hydroelectric facility.* We have regarded this as a separable component of the dam. Since our conclusion is that the dam is at least marginally acceptable at relatively high rates of discount, the only issue that arises is whether the benefits to be provided from the additional hydroelectric facilities will be sufficient so that their

present value covers the incremental costs of adding hydro-electric facilities to the Ullum project.

(2) *The possible effect of the dam and its use upon ground-water levels.* Here, the dam could affect ground-water levels in different ways in different areas, and the net effect could be either positive or negative.

(3) *The related issue of the probable seepage of dam water into the valley of Zonda.* It is clear that most of the water that filters through to the valley will be capable of being used for irrigation, and that much of it will probably return to the river at some downstream point. But the impact of this problem on the cost-benefit ratio of the project can be significant, particularly in view of the closeness to unity of the ratios obtained in Table 11.11.

Notes

[1] It should be noted that certain transfers of water are not possible. Water may be transferred within a given department and within a given canal system, but cannot be shifted from one department or from one canal system to another. Water may be transferred within a department on a permanent basis when the lands involved are the property of the same owner (this is the motivation for the kind of transaction of which we are speaking), but transfers between owners can be made only on a transitory basis, and with special permission from the water authority.

[2] A shortage of surface water may be so severe as to prevent a farmer from even assuring the survival of his full vineyard and/or orchard, as a certain amount of water is required simply to keep plants and trees alive. Even in less stringent circumstances, water shortages cause the roots of plants to grow deeper, making it more difficult and expensive to provide them adequate water in the future. For these reasons, farmers in times of crisis are likely to be willing to pay a high price for a critical minimum quantity of additional water. We were told of instances, during the recent drought, of farmers paying as much as 25, 50 and even more pesos per cubic meter of supplemental water from their neighbors. Obviously, however, such values are not to be attached to the incremental volume of irrigation water that would come from a project such as the Ullum dam.

[3] One might expect a fall in the value of a unit of water as a consequence of the substantial increase in the number of units that the dam would make possible in the irrigation season. A slight fall may indeed occur, as the lands newly brought into cultivation as a consequence of the increased availability of water during the irrigation season may be of somewhat lower quality than the average hectares actually cultivated. However, the share of available land that remains uncultivated due to lack of water, and its immediate proximity to cultivated land, suggests that the quality difference is slight and probably negligible.

[4] This treatment assumes that the depreciation of the dam (i.e. the reduction in the value of its annual benefits through silting, etc.) occurs exponentially. It also implicitly assumes an infinite physical life of the project. Neither assumption has

serious consequences. For example, a function declining exponentially at the rate of two per cent per year is closely approximated by a straight line for a substantial period. Straightline depreciation, at 2 per cent per annum, for example, would reduce an initial value of 100 to 80 in 10 years and to 70 in 15. Exponential depreciation at the same rate would reduce 100 to 81·6 in 10 years and to 73·7 in 15. Beyond 15 years or so discounting at the rates of 10 and 15 per cent which we shall use reduces the importance of any discrepancy that may emerge. By the same token the fraction of present value which is derived by this procedure from assumed benefits beyond the 50th year of life is less than one per cent of the total when rates of 10 or 15 per cent are used.

[5] There is also some indication in the statistics of a downward trend in stream-flow. Whether this reflects a true trend which should be extrapolated, or whether it is the result of random factors, we do not know. Basing an extrapolation of future streamflows on the data of the relatively recent past is an intermediate position between basing them on the data for the past 50 years (which would lead to higher predictions) and basing them on an extrapolation of the observed trend (which would lead to lower predictions).

[6] The Harza estimates of requirements (including domestic and industrial needs) for the months in question are as follows. March—60·5 Hm^3; April—20·8 Hm^3; May—14·8 Hm^3; June—11·9 Hm^3; July—12·4 Hm^3; August—57·8 Hm^3; September—84·2 Hm^3. We interpolated the data for March and September, assigning 40·5 Hm^3 to the first half and 20·0 Hm^3 to the second half of March, and assigning 38·8 Hm^3 to the first half and 45·4 Hm^3 to the second half of September.

[7] This means that the strategy of dam use that our exercise implies is not exactly to distribute as much water as possible during the irrigation season. More precisely, it is to distribute all carryover from the past, and all current streamflow, except the excess of streamflow over 100 m^3/sec. for whatever months streamflow averages more than 100 m^3/sec. This excess is the only source of inter-year storage under the assumed strategy.

[8] See Chapter 4.

CHAPTER TWELVE

ISSUES CONCERNING CAPITAL ASSISTANCE TO LESS-DEVELOPED COUNTRIES

I begin this brief report with a judgment based on close observation of various facets of the U.S. Foreign Aid program over the past thirteen years. This judgment is that the amount of progress that can be generated by a dollar of foreign aid has been greatly exaggerated by the proponents of aid. Perhaps the exaggeration was due to the phenomenal apparent success of the Marshall Plan, under which massive grants from the United States provided the capital equipment and other resources to stimulate the rapid economic recovery of a Western Europe already possessed of an advanced economic organization, high levels of professionalism and management, skilled cadres of labor, and relatively efficient, honest, and experienced governmental bureaucracies. In the Marshall Plan case the problem was one of restoring or replacing physical plant and equipment which, to the extent not actually destroyed during the war, was badly in need of renovation, repair, or replacement. We cannot know exactly how much of Europe's early postwar progress was directly attributable to the Marshall Plan, but there is no doubt that that share was substantial. The Marshall Plan's great success, in my judgment, was due to the fact that the U.S. was able to provide the principal missing factor (physical resources) in an economic environment which in nearly every other respect contained the elements necessary to generate its own recovery and stimulate its further growth. There can be no doubt that if the same transfer of resources as took place under the Marshall Plan were to occur today, it would have only a small fraction of the impact upon Western Europe output that the Marshall Plan generated.

In the less-developed countries there is no such simple path to progress as that which faced Western Europe in the years of the Marshall Plan. While simple theoretical models have been developed in which the bottleneck to progress turns out to be, depending on the circumstances, either a shortage of domestic resources (a 'savings gap') or a shortage of imported goods (a 'foreign exchange gap') there are at most only a few countries and periods to which such models can be applied in practice. In general, and as is well-known, the modernization of backward economies is an enormously complex, difficult, and time-consuming process. Barriers to growth abound: social and political elites unreceptive to change, gross deficiencies of the technical skills and capacities required by modernization, markets that are poorly organized and whose proper functioning is further impaired by ill-conceived public policies, systems of fiscal and also of foreign-trade policy that in their present state are if anything impediments to rather than promoters of modernization—these constitute only a partial listing. Without belaboring the point, I would suggest that most serious participants in and observers of our history of foreign aid would agree that we have not found to date, and cannot reasonably expect to find in the future, the same kind of touchstone to promoting the growth of the less-developed countries as was represented by the provision of physical resources to Western Europe under the Marshall Plan.

The above does not in the slightest degree imply that our foreign aid programs have not been worthwhile, and will not continue to be so. It does suggest that many people probably have been expecting too much of foreign aid. To put the problem in perspective, let me begin with an example of ordinary private investment by a family or a business concern. Investing an extra $1,000 at 6 percent causes a rise in annual family income of $60; investing an additional $1 million at a 12 percent yield causes a rise in a business's annual income of $120,000. By the same token, if what economists call the 'social rate of yield' of a public-sector investment of $10 million is 10 percent, we should expect on that account that the investment will bring a benefit to the nation equivalent to $1,000,000 per year.[1]

What sorts of social rates of yield do we expect of our own Federal investments within the United States? Senate Document 97, published in May, 1962, established for the evaluation of water-resource and related land-resource projects the use of 'the average rate of interest payable by the Treasury (that is, the *coupon rate*) on interest-bearing marketable securities of the United States outstanding at the end of the fiscal year preceding such computation which, upon original issue, had terms to maturity of 15 years or more'. For some time after the publication of Senate Document 97, the minimum acceptable rate of yield computed according to its formula was less than 3 per cent. It was 3¼ percent at the time of President Johnson's budget message of 1968, which proposed a rate of 4⅝ percent for the remainder of the fiscal year 1969. This example is taken from only one area, but it illustrates the point I wish to make: U.S. public investment decisions are judged in terms of discount rates well below those applying to private decisions in this economy, and in any case well below ten percent.

Ten percent is not a magic number, but it has gained substantial currency because it has been for many years the minimum rate of social yield which the World Bank required (save in exceptional cases) of the projects that it financed. The World Bank's requiring such a rate reflected its judgment concerning the scarcity of capital in the less-developed countries. Given that scarcity, investment projects and programs with social rates of yield below 10 percent should be rejected (even though the interest rate collected by the Bank might be lower), because it is to be presumed that many others can be found in the less-developed world that have social rates of yield above this level.

The World Bank's 10 percent criterion is accordingly substantially more stringent than those applied to public investment projects within the United States. I believe that it is a realistic minimum goal to set for the productivity that foreign aid funds will have. In the following section we shall attribute a 10 percent yield to the total accumulated U.S. aid to the principal aid recipients, to see how much higher their income might now be, as against what it would have been in the absence of U.S. foreign aid. That is to say, the following calculations assume that U.S. foreign-aid projects and programs have in fact generated benefits at the 10 percent rate that the World Bank normally expects of its projects.

We shall concentrate here upon total net U.S. loans and grants—that is: total loans and grants less repayments and interest. The sums in question are accumulated over the period 1946–68, as this is the form in which the data are given in the report *U.S. Overseas Loans and Grants*, prepared by AID for the House Foreign Affairs Committee (dated May 29, 1969). The figures cover AID loans and grants, Food for Freedom loans and grants, long-term loans of the Export-Import Bank, U.S. contributions to International Lending Organizations, and miscellaneous other U.S. programs. In short, the figures represent the comprehensive net U.S. contribution to the country in question, through the whole gamut of economic (not military) programs.

The conclusion that emerges from Table 12.1 is that the impact of U.S. aid on the real income per head of most recipient countries has probably been small—both in absolute magnitude and relative to existing levels of per capita income. Even the estimated contribution of $15.40 per head of accumulated U.S. aid is relatively small when compared with Korea's national income per head of some $400 in 1968. The estimated $29.10 contribution to Israel, in turn, is dwarfed by her 1968 per capita income of over $1,000; that to Chile ($12.80) seems small in relation to her per capita income of over $500. The only countries where our foreign aid may have caused a substantial percentage increase in national income are those where political and military moves were dominant—Taiwan, Vietnam, Laos, Jordan, Liberia, Libya, for example. *And we come to this judgment by attributing to aid dollars a rate of social yield more than twice that which is commonly applied in the evaluation of our own Federal projects and programs.* Given the standards we apply to ourselves, we should be more than pleased with the estimated results appearing in column 4 of Table 12.1. On the other hand, given the exaggerated expectations they have regarding the productivity of foreign aid, many will regard these results as a demonstration of its futility.

My own conclusions from the above are (a) that we must

TABLE 12.1

U.S. Net Economic Aid (Loans, Grants, Food for Freedom, etc.) 1946–68

	Millions of $		Millions	$ per head
	(1) Total Aid 1946–48	(2) Estimated Impact on 1968 National Income (1) × 10%	(3) Estimated Population, 1968	(4) Estimated Impact of Aid on Income per head, 1968 (2) ÷ (3)
India	6972	697·2	500	$1·40
Korea	4614	461·4	30	15·40
Vietnam	4001	400·1	17	23·50
Pakistan	3404	340·4	112	3·00
Brazil	2327	232·7	90	2·60
Turkey	2231	223·1	34	6·60
Republic of China (Taiwan)	2154	215·4	13	16·60
Yugoslavia	1884	188·4	21	9·00
Greece	1672	167·2	9	18·60
Spain	1281	128·1	34	3·80
Philippines	1247	124·7	35	3·60
Chile	1152	115·2	9	12·80
United Arab Republic	901	90·1	32	2·80
Israel	785	78·5	2·7	29·10
Iran	770	77·0	25	3·10
Colombia	719	71·9	19	3·80
Indonesia	602	60·2	170	0·35
Laos	591	59·1	3·2	18·50
Morocco	588	58·8	14	4·20
Jordan	575	57·5	2·2	26·10
Mexico	545	54·5	45·	1·20
Tunisia	545	54·5	5	10·90
Thailand	510	51·0	32	1·60
Congo (Kinshasa)	405	40·5	16	2·50
Dominican Republic	402	40·2	4	10·00
Ryukyu Islands	376	37·6	0·8	47·00
Afghanistan	345	34·5	16	2·20
Peru	325	32·5	13	2·50
Venezuela	293	29·3	9	3·30
Cambodia	254	25·4	6·5	3·90
Ghana	226	22·6	8	2·80
Nigeria	224	22·4	60	3·70
Guatemala	222	22·2	5	4·40
Liberia	208	20·8	1·2	17·30
Libya	202	20·2	1·7	11·90
Panama	201	20·1	1·4	14·40
Ethiopia	201	20·1	24	0·85
Total Covered	43,954			
Other LDCs	12,161			
Total LDCs	56,115			

lower our sights regarding the potential productivity of aid to realistic levels, and (b) that we must seek those *limited but plausible* ways in which aid funds may perhaps be given more leverage than is implied by the calculations of Table 12.1.

It is true that the World Bank's 10 percent criterion represents the *minimum* social rate of yield that it normally demands on its projects. This suggests that the *average* rate of yield in the projects financed by the Bank should be higher than 10 percent. From the World Bank project reports that I have seen, I believe this to be the case. Yet this does not mean that World Bank funds have a higher true impact than that represented by a 10 percent yield. For, as we all know, countries bring forward to the World Bank mainly their best and most 'bankable' projects. Many if not all of these projects would undoubtedly be undertaken even in the absence of World Bank financing. 'Funds are fungible', as they say in the trade, and because of this fact the net effect of project lending by the World Bank, by AID, and by other aid-giving agencies is to enable a longer list of projects to be actually undertaken by the recipient country. The power dam financed by a $10 million loan (which might have a social rate of yield of 15 percent per year) might well have been undertaken anyway, and the additional spending which the receipt of the $10 million loan occasions might well have a social rate of yield of five percent per annum or less. I shall return to the problems created by the 'fungibility of funds' below; for the moment suffice it to say that the mere fact that 10 percent per annum is normally applied as a minimum standard for World Bank projects does not mean that the effective social yield of World Bank funds (as distinct from the specific projects nominally financed by such funds) is greater than ten percent.

The U.S., at least insofar as project lending is concerned, has no sound basis to expect better results than those that have in fact been achieved by the World Bank. By and large, the World Bank has more consistently based its judgments on technical, economic criteria than has AID, and in addition countries have tended to go to the IBRD with their most readily 'bankable' projects, and to turn to AID for the financing of other projects. Under these circumstances, I believe that a ten percent per annum social yield on the projects it finances represents a reasonable, even perhaps a challenging goal for AID's project lending operations.

If the above is accepted, is there any way in which AID can expect to generate, for recipient countries, more benefit than the desired ten percent per annum yield on projects? I believe that some additional gain can be had, but to obtain it requires a great deal of conscious and sustained effort, as well as delicate diplomacy, on the part of AID. It is all too easy to delude ourselves into thinking that a $10 or $50 million dollar loan by the U.S. government was critical in preventing economic and political chaos in the recipient country. We must be constantly aware that both parties to the aid negotiation have an interest in so deluding themselves—the recipient government because this is the most convincing way to obtain the funds it desires, and the AID organization itself because of the high self-esteem that it can have when it believes itself to be playing such a critical and catalytic role. It is clear that loans or grants from AID make life easier for the recipient governments. But the realistic alternative to the loan or grant is rarely chaos. It is more likely some kinds of belt-tightening measures like higher taxes, lower spending, a tighter monetary policy, perhaps the displacement of some nonessential imports, etc. Many countries have survived many crises without foreign aid, and the planning and organization of an aid program can only be hampered and confused by a blind belief that aid is 'vital,' 'essential,' 'indispensable,' and so forth. Foreign aid is indeed productive in most cases, but it is not indispensable. AID's task is to maximize the contribution that its resources can make to the welfare of the recipient countries; the accomplishment of this task is only hindered by exaggerated visions of that potential contribution.

I believe, for a variety of reasons, that U.S. foreign aid should be largely concentrated on project loans, with program and sector loans playing a substantially smaller role than they have in recent years. Program and sector loans inevitably entail a significant degree of U.S. involvement with policy issues that would normally be internal decisions of the recipient country.

It is true that there have been occasions when this U.S. involvement has been highly productive and has caused a minimum degree of resentment or opposition on the part of key

local political groups. The characteristic of these 'most successful' program loans is, in my view, a careful and technical diagnosis of the problem to be attacked—a diagnosis which is
shared, not just superficially but in depth, by the experts of
AID and of the host government.

But more often than not, I fear, AID's and the recipient
government's experts have had rather substantially different
views of the functions and purposes of program and sector
loans. As a consequence, periodic reviews of performance have
often been a source of recurrent friction between the participant
governments. In my view, such friction is a natural concomitant
of program and sector loans, save in the exceptional cases
already alluded to. The more deeply AID becomes involved in
what the recipient countries consider to be their internal affairs,
the greater is this friction likely to be.

Differences between AID and the host government on the
nature and purpose of program or sector loans have the further,
perhaps unexpected effect of tending to prolong the period of
such aid, except where those differences are (as in the case of
the Goulart government in Brazil) extremely severe. Where the
purposes and functions of program aid are clearly seen and
agreed upon by both parties, such aid is likely to have a natural
and mutually-recognized termination point. Where there are
frictions and differences in these matters, and where the governments involved want to avoid an open breach, the path of least
resistance is likely to be one of continued reluctant accommo-
dation, with each government yielding more than it thinks it
ought to, with each feeling less than content about the outcome,
and with continued postponement of the termination of program
or sector aid because of the breach it would appear to signify.

A final weakness of program and sector loans is the absence
of any objective criterion for determining the distribution of
aid funds among the recipient countries. It is simplistic in the
extreme to think that we can estimate the amount of aid
'required' to generate a given level of national income or a
given rate of growth, yet even if we could do this we would still
not be far along the path to deciding which countries get how
much. Perhaps the closest one can come to rough guidelines
for the distribution of program and sector aid, is to suggest that
more aid per capita should be given to poorer countries than

to richer countries, and that more should be given to those making strong as against weak or negligible self-help efforts. It is a sad commentary that the distribution of per capita program and sector aid in the past has probably been negatively correlated both with the levels of the recipient countries' per capita incomes and with any reasonable index of the recipient's self-help efforts.

My conclusion from this analysis is that program and sector loans should be reserved for truly exceptional circumstances. In particular, they should be avoided unless close agreement can be obtained with the recipient government upon a set of limited and well-defined objectives which recognize and define the exceptional circumstances giving rise to the aid in question, and which explicitly contemplate its ultimate termination.

Project loans have the advantages over program or sector loans of being more decentralized, more subject to technical economic criteria, and less involved with what are generally regarded as being the internal policy decisions of the recipient governments. Their potential weakness lies, as already indicated, in the 'fungibility of funds'. How can lending agencies assure themselves that the additional projects or other expenditures that are effectively undertaken as a consequence of their loans will indeed meet high standards of prospective social yield? In my view, the best assurance to this effect must come from the massive and rapid improvement of the procedures by which the LDCs evaluate *their own* projects—that is, those in which international lending agencies are not involved. This calls for the dissemination of modern techniques of project evaluation and for the direct training of local cadres on a scale far greater than has hitherto been attempted. I say this in full awareness of the training and information-spreading efforts that have been mounted in the past by AID, by the World Bank (largely through the Economic Development Institute), by the OECD, by the Inter-American Development Bank and by other agencies, and of the financing of pre-feasibility and feasibility studies on projects by the above agencies plus the United Nations Development Program. The efforts of these agencies have been laudable, but they have not gone anywhere near far enough in relation to the overall task. For example, it is doubtful whether any of the LDCs have as many as one-twentieth or one-tenth of the trained project evaluators that they could profitably use.

The first order of business is therefore for the major international lending agencies to face up to the challenge of providing the necessary training for the LDCs own project evaluation cadres. The demand for such training on the part of the LDCs is and has been high; so far at least, the bottleneck has been the amount of resources devoted by the international agencies to the job, rather than any lack of demand.

The second order of business is to provide some mechanism to certify whether or not a country is making reasonable progress in improving its methods of project evaluation. This certification would serve as a check against the risks involved in the 'fungibility of funds'. It is a delicate task, and one which the U.S. government might prefer to be handled by an international agency such as the IBRD rather than by AID itself. The certification process, in particular, cannot hew to standards of perfection (no donor country's procedures would meet that test!). It should rather be guided by the goals of increasing over time the technical competence and the degree of professionalism of each country's project evaluation cadres, of assessing whether the technical skills available within a country are being adequately used, and of assuring that the country is taking reasonable advantage of the information and training facilities made available by the aid-giving agencies, and is making reasonable use of foreign consultants where local expertise is lacking.

Such a certification procedure can, I believe, be defended against charges of interfering in the internal affairs of the recipient countries. It would be professional and technical rather than political in orientation, and its scope would be limited to providing some assurance against the eventual dissipation of aid moneys through the 'fungibility of funds' route. Whether it is advisable that all major lending agencies reach an accord as to the requirements of certification is an issue on which I have not reached a final judgment. My present feeling is that such an accord would be desirable as such, but not necessary for the adequate functioning of the certification mechanism. For adequate functioning, I believe that an agreement between AID and the World Bank, with the latter serving as the certifying agency, would certainly suffice. It is quite possible, though more risky, that AID might 'go it alone' without the collaboration of any other lending agency.

In contemplating a major shift of emphasis away from program and sector loans and toward project loans, I am aware that certain functions of the former categories of loans might be jeopardized. In particular, the 'balance-of-payments support' provided by a number of program loans served the function of facilitating the importation of certain raw materials and component parts that were necessary for the operation of already-installed capital equipment. If project loans under the suggested program were confined to covering solely the foreign-currency capital costs of projects, there would be no direct replacement for the materials-import-facilitating function of some program loans. My own strong recommendation is that project aid not be simply confined to foreign-currency capital costs. AID project financing should, in my opinion, run the gamut of types of public-sector projects in the recipient country, and technical criteria should be applied in accepting or rejecting any particular project. Such criteria should not in principle include the fraction of project costs accruing in foreign currency. As a general rule, it is to be expected that external loans will cover more than the direct foreign-exchange costs of most projects, and as a consequence these loans will aid the recipients' balances of payments both directly and indirectly. AID should not, in my opinion, make explicit balance-of-payments loans, save in the most exceptional of circumstances (such as a major crop failure), when the rigid conditions outlined above for program lending are met.

I believe than an aid program based largely on project lending should recognize that no true aid is involved in loans to the recipient governments on the commercial terms that would in any case be available to those governments in the private capital markets of the world. Grants are totally aid, and the aid component of loans becomes greater as the terms of the loans become more 'concessional.' It seems reasonable, therefore, that aid should be granted to different countries on different terms, depending principally on how poor the recipient countries are. For simplicity, I would suggest the creation of three or four categories of countries, with progressively less-concessional terms applying to loans to higher-income-category recipients. The standards of social rate of yield demanded on aid-financed projects should in general be the same for all aid-eligible countries. These standards would provide an objective basis for the distribution of available loan funds. They would also mean that within any aid category the most aid would go to the countries making the greatest self-help efforts—in the sense of generating (relative to their incomes) the highest amount of projects meeting aid standards. Meanwhile, the distinction among categories would ensure that—for countries making a given effort in the sense implied above—more aid would be received by those in greatest poverty. The broad criteria of poverty and self-help—which were suggested earlier as being relevant for judging program loans (but *not* met by our actual program lending experience)—could thus be easily embodied in the project-lending framework here suggested.

It should be noted that an AID program based on the above recommendations would be exceedingly amenable to implementation through multilateral agencies, if that were desired. Such agencies have substantial experience and expertise in project lending, and could well be given the responsibility for distributing the bulk of AID's project funds. (The above is stated as a possibility, not an outright recommendation.)

It would also perhaps be possible to multilateralize some or all of whatever program lending would remain under the schema suggested above. Given the fact that we are suggesting that program loans should be explicitly exceptional, for specifically stated purposes, and in general with an agreed pattern of termination, the analogy with the IMF's standby agreements is attractive. Yet I personally find it very difficult to draw up a set of rules comparable to those embodied in the charter and the practices of the IMF that could reliably guide an international agency in program lending. The wide array of special circumstances that could give rise to a request for a program loan, and the need, emphasized above, for an explicit understanding between lender and recipient in all cases, both argue that it would be enormously more difficult to draft a charter to guide, say, the IBRD in program lending than it was to guide the IMF concerning standbys. Especially in the context of an aid policy, such as that suggested here, which contemplates a reduction in the relative importance of program loans, and emphasizes that they should be exceptional rather than routine, it strikes me as ill-advised to contemplate their institutionalization within a multilateral international agency. If U.S. foreign aid policy is to reduce the importance of sector and program loans and to increase that of project loans, it seems to me natural for the U.S. to seek the help of other organisms in the area of relative expansion (project loans) and to maintain its own control and seek its own counsel in the areas of relative contraction (program and sector loans).

Note

[1] This benefit may or may not be reflected in national income as it is ordinarily measured. Increased crop yields due to experiment-station research, added electrical generation due to new capacity, etc. will be so reflected. On the other hand, benefits from reductions in infant mortality on the one extreme, or from improved public recreational facilities on the other, will not (at least for a considerable time) show up in the national income measure. This does not mean that benefits are any less worthy when they are not reflected in national income. In what follows, I shall speak as if the measure of the benefit of investment was the increase in national income which it generates. This is solely for economy of language, and the benefits are meant also to include any true benefit which for whatever reason is not captured by our conventional methods of measuring national income.

INDEX